The heart of the battle . . .

for a new social contract

The heart of the battle...

for a new social contract

Edgar Faure

Translated from the French by
Gill Manning, M.A.

McGraw-Hill Book Company

New York   St. Louis   San Francisco   Sydney   London   Toronto
Singapore   Johannesburg

Library of Congress Cataloging in Publication Data

Faure, Edgar.
　The heart of the battle.

　Translation of L'âme du combat.
　Includes bibliographical references.
　1. Social contract.　2. Alienation (Social psychology)
　3. Consumption (Economics).　I. Title.
　JC336.F3513　　　　　320.9'44'083　　　　72–2091

ISBN 0–07–020108–0

Contents

v

For Laurie

Translator's preface

It has been my policy to keep 'Translator's notes' to a minimum. They will be found to be of two types. First, there are the 'linguistic' notes, necessary because a particular French word or phrase is untranslatable. Second, there are the 'informative' notes, designed to facilitate for the reader unfamiliar with French culture the reading of a text peppered with unexplained references to French literature and history.

I have taken the liberty of 'tidying up' the author's own rather chaotic footnotes by giving precise references to the editions of the texts mentioned in the footnotes. If a good English edition of a text, which the author refers to under its French title, is available, the reader will find the English title and appropriate reference in the footnotes.

Acknowledgements

I would like to thank Mrs Janet McNeill without whose unfailing patience and amazing ability to read my illegible handwriting the preparation of the typescript would have been impossible.

Thanks are also due to Mrs Hilary Footitt, to Mrs Marie-Pierrette Allum, and to Mr Eric Cahm for their generous cooperation on some difficult points.

Finally, grateful thanks to my husband whose willing cooperation and sustained interest made the completion of the task possible.

Gill Manning

Biographical introduction

The determining influence of social and family background

A.D.[1]—Although your book deals with political thought in general, you place a great deal of emphasis on your own personal political development. I feel, therefore, that it would be advantageous to start with a portrait of the thinker behind the work. I am not asking for precise biographical details or for anecdotes about your past life, but I should like to try, with your help, to determine those factors in your background, make-up and cultural development, which prepared you for a career in politics, and which prompted you, in the course of that career, to adopt certain attitudes and to develop the line of thought you are now at such pains to elucidate.

E.F.[1]—A sort of political cross-examination. I am quite willing to submit to it.

On my father's side I come from a line of peasants, who have their roots in the bleak plateau of Sault, near the Pyrenean borders of the Aude *département*. Nearly all Frenchmen are of peasant stock, and most of them derive from this a satisfaction which owes nothing to the rarity of the occurrence. However, there are several classes of peasants: landowners, who confer a certain status on their descendants, farmers, tenant-farmers, not to mention farmhands, and at least the first two of these categories could be further subdivided into three distinct classes. My Audois ancestors owned the land they worked and were comfortably off. My grandfather was the fourteenth and youngest child, as his middle name, Benjamin, suggests. Obviously, since the custom of equal partition of property among children did not exist in our province, there was no land for him to inherit, and so he decided to become a primary school teacher, a typical means of social advancement for someone of humble peasant or bourgeois stock. During the war, after his retirement from his post as headmaster of a school in Narbonne, I was on very close terms with him. He had a great influence on my early formative years. My most vivid memory is of the long walks we took together from our house along the Allées des Barques and the banks of the Robine Canal (for a long time afterwards any poetry about rivers evoked for me the awful, violent yellow of its slimy water) to the

[1] A.D.—Alain Duhamel, the head of the *En toute liberté* section of Fayard's, who published the French text. E.F.—Edgar Faure. (Translator's notes)

railway station, where he was responsible for accepting delivery of consignments of kerosene. The unmistakable smell of this commonplace petroleum derivative still brings back memories. My grandmother used to like telling me stories about the revolt of the wine-growers in the days of Marcellin Albert. The revolt had broken out in her street and marked the high-spot of her otherwise uneventful life. It is from my grandparents that I inherited a big country house, a vineyard planted with white grapes, a few fields, and a grave, all in the little parish[1] of Rouvenac in the Limoux district.

As was expected of them, my grandparents made 'sacrifices' to give their eldest son 'a start in life'. They bought him a lawyer's practice in the little town of Saint-Pons. Since it was a very small practice—one of those which, later, were to be alternately suppressed and reinstated: suppressed as a symbolic cut in public expenditure, reinstated, only to be suppressed again, when it was felt symbolic financial cuts would bring political advantage— he was allowed to appear in court, which suited him admirably. I was deeply impressed by his town house because of its garden and the plate bearing his professional title: *avoué avocat*[2]. A child's impressions are always exaggerated, and now I can see that the garden and the plate were really nothing out of the ordinary. To offset the considerable expense incurred in setting up the eldest son in this way, my father was asked either to choose a short course of study, or, if he preferred a long one, to undertake it in such a way as to minimize the strain on the family budget. He therefore decided to become an army-doctor, which is also a common method of social advancement (though less so in France than in Chekhov's Russia). After qualifying at the Lyons School of Medicine, he served in Algeria and in the outposts of the Sahara. On his return to France, he got married.

Although my mother's family lived in a village, they were well established members of the bourgeoisie. My grandfather was a doctor, as were his father and grandfather before him. It is even claimed that the family's connection with the medical profession stretched back in an unbroken chain to the *Ancien Régime*, where my ancestors were barber-surgeons. There was a harmless family tradition, handed down from generation to generation, to the effect that one of these barber-surgeons had been deprived of the nobiliary particle[3], which still persisted in another family of the same name, reputedly distant relations. My grandfather claimed that his uncompromisingly republican beliefs prevented him from looking up

[1] The French has *commune* here, which has no exact equivalent in English. A *commune* is a district under the administration of a mayor assisted by the local council. (Translator's note)

[2] *Avoué*—solicitor, attorney-at-law. *Avocat*—counsel, practicing barrister, US trial lawyer. (Translator's note)

[3] Nobiliary particle, the preposition *de*, indicating that a name derives from landed property. (Translator's note)

4

his family tree in the public records, although this would, at least, have put his mind at rest, even if there was no question of resuming this very minor title of nobility.

My doctor ancestors were less interested in the art of Aesculapius than in the cultivation of their vineyards. They were 'men of property', as we say in this region of the Midi, the phrase being understood in a professional sense. The dividing-up of my grandparents' estate gave rise to family quarrels worthy of Balzac. The outcome was one of those strange compromises which are often the result of a clash between the legal code and the business acumen of the provincial. My uncle, who was the village notary, inherited the house, the garden, the stocks of wine, and the winepress. My mother was left with the vines themselves, whose cultivation was supervised by my father from his barracks.

When I was born, my father was medical officer (with the rank of captain) to the first regiment of Hussars, stationed at Béziers. We lived on the street named after the famous engineer of the Midi canal, Paul Riquet, in a district where the street had been given the nickname, considered an appropriate one in my case, of the Poets' Plateau. All I can remember about the apartment, which was my first home, is that it had a balcony where they used to hold me up to witness a kind of ceremony, the return to barracks. The orderly officer would lead a spare horse by the bridle; my father, wearing his dress uniform of a black frogged jacket and red trousers, would mount the horse. I can still see him turning round to return my wave, his naturally severe face made even more severe by his beard and eyeglasses. . . . Then it was Verdun; the cavalrymen gave way to the artillery. I was growing up; I became acquainted with the orderly officer with the fine name, Duhautois, who used to carry me on his shoulders. For me Verdun meant the Porte Chaussée, a sweet-shop famous for its sugared almonds, and, above all, our house in the Rue Chevert. It was a real house with stairs, and in my mind's eye I see a great shining expanse of highly polished parquet floors. I remember, too, the social round of barrack life, memories of a few balls. . . . These images of town life still mingle in my memory with images of vineyards, holidays, the wine-harvest; but the focal point of my childhood memories is the annual period of waiting for the 'onion-seller', the Spaniard who recruited the itinerant workers in September. My parents would say repeatedly: 'Ernest is coming'. Both the man and his job, clouded in mystery, inspired me with fearful yet pleasurable anticipation. No doubt it was my first—and for a long time my only—contact with social problems. The fact that the extra hands were foreigners of rather exotic appearance prevented their employers, the 'men of property' from adopting a 'capitalist' attitude towards them, whereas the few home-based workers were considered almost as 'family retainers'.

I could not begin to recall my childhood memories, however briefly, without seeing in my mind's eye two object-totems: the piano and the metronome. My parents were enthusiastic music-lovers, and both my sister and myself were musically inclined. During our several moves, even if we were only going away on holiday, the presence of a piano, the buying or hiring of a piano, the possibility of practicing in some kind neighbor's house, the question of space: did we have room for a grand, a baby grand, or just an upright piano?, the choice or assessment of a music-teacher, the visit of the tuner, were constantly subjects of violent discussion. When Henriette went to study at the Conservatoire, she had to practice seven hours a day. I used to sit next to her piano to learn my lessons and do my homework without being inconvenienced in any way. That is why I can now put up with a great deal of extraneous noise. One day, I auditioned for Armand Ferté, my sister's music-teacher. I played Steibelt's *Storm Rondo*, and he said I had a promising future. But at that time I thought, God knows why, that musical virtuosity was an exclusively feminine calling. And so I rejected music as a career, although I had no idea what calling was destined to attract me in the dim future.

People from the Midi have a strong sense of belonging to a family, in spite of the occasional 'tiffs'. The great distance between our houses and the outbreak of war meant that the various branches of the family did not meet very often; but we wrote to each other to 'pass on the news', and a conversation with any one member of the family was an endless report on the goings-on of the others. My parents had some first cousins whom we called aunt and uncle, like they do in Brittany, while we called their children our first cousins, etc. Their careers followed the same pattern with almost mathematical precision. They all went to non-fee-paying schools; the men were officers; the women were teachers, and they married officers. There were some more distant relatives too, one a post-mistress and the other a parish priest. Their names, Mademoiselle Lignon and the Abbé Clerc, seem to have come straight out of a romantic novel. On my mother's side things were less predictable. The 'men of property' remained lost in their monotonous world of planting their American vines. Social advancement for them came from modernizing the wine-vaults and buying a car. Several of them were doctors (without patients) or lawyers (without briefs), for in this particular social milieu the young folk liked to prolong their studies, and with them their enjoyment of city life, waiting patiently for the day when their parents would hand over to them the running of the business, a step which their elders were in no hurry to take.

Marriages enlarged the family's horizons, though partners were never chosen too far outside the family milieu. When I was still in school my cousin, a qualified teacher[1], married a foot-soldier, who had inherited a

[1] The French has *agrégée* here for which there is no direct English equivalent. An *agrégé(e)* is a teacher who has passed the *agrégation*, a competitive examination conducted by the State for admission to posts on the teaching staff of the Lycées. (Translator's note)

6

fine name, and who was to prove worthy of it. My sister married an army-doctor, but his occupation was not a means of social advancement for him, for his grandfather had been a senator and one of his forefathers, Pagès de l'Ariège, was well known in Louis-Phillippe's time. It was Laurent Bordes Pagès who taught me the hitherto undiscovered value of a fervently Christian cultural experience. The risks attached to his job, which he carried out selflessly, all too soon put an end to this priceless budding friendship: 'Those who die young are the chosen ones of God'.

If we were to try now to interpret my family background sociologically, I would stress the following points:

Firstly, in spite of certain variations in professions and worldly success, it was a very consistent milieu. It was limited geographically to three adjacent *départments* of the same province: the Aude (my father's family) the Hérault (my mother's family) and the Ariège where my father, who left the Army after the Great War, had a practice at a spa. It was also limited socially and, in modern jargon, culturally in the broad sense of the word. All these men and women had the same coordinates. None of them felt out of place or embarrassed in the presence of the others. Everyone was on an equal footing.

What seems to me today the most remarkable factor is that this milieu —my own—was outside the compass of a capitalist economy. What we call the exploiter-exploited relationship was unheard of in this circle. Not one of the people I have described could be qualified as an exploiter, and none would ever have dreamed of considering himself exploited. Property was for us an instrument of work: we would not have considered renting out property, either the family house which, if it was not being lived in permanently, was our meeting place on high days and holidays, or the notary's office, for to us they represented the right to work and to be respected in that work.

Finally, I think I can put my finger on a state of mind common to all the members of my family: the acceptance by each one of his lot and a sort of contentment. The richer ones did not consider themselves as rich, and in fact were not really rich. The poor ones did not think of themselves as poor, and, in fact, they were not really poor either. That is not to say that self-interest and ambition counted for nothing in their lives. Their common attitude towards money must be understood. Money was considered important, as is clearly seen in the quarrels about inheritances, but not of prime importance. No one envisaged the possibility of a radical change in his circumstances by a great gain or loss of money. Their ambitions were modest, at least if we judge by what they achieved and by the manner in which social advancement was received. Out of all these soldiers, not one reached a higher rank than that of Lieutenant-Colonel, and some reached this position only just before retirement. I was never aware of the slightest hint of jealousy or bitterness in my immediate family circle. Perhaps you think that we had inherited happy dispositions. This may be so; but, it is also without doubt true that *moderate social advancement* brings with it a sense of fulfilment.

2

First political impressions
University life

A.D.—The description of your family background and the question of your career lead us to our subject: politics.

E.F.—Obviously, if social class and environment are anything to go by, you could not expect me to be a political extremist. No member of my family ever took an active part in politics, except my father who wanted to become an Aulus town-councillor. He succeeded, but only with great difficulty. However, his success gave me a chance to see how elections were organized in a rural municipality. I used to count the votes as they were read out, and I soon discovered the infallible rule that the candidate who leads at the beginning cannot be overtaken.

My father's aspirations to local office had nothing to do with the wider sphere of politics in general. He was inspired by a desire to have a say in local questions, such as the town's future as a spa, or the building of a road to join two valleys, the latter being his pet dream. Later in his life he was, in fact, in charge of the municipality's affairs, but this was during the liberation in his capacity as head of the locally organized Resistance. When elections were reinstated, his period of office came to an end. The road is still unbuilt, but the town's main street bears my father's name.

Apart from my father's example, I never heard of any near, or even distant, relative of mine being a candidate for political office. We had no party militants among us. What is more, I cannot ever remember an animated political discussion taking place among the members of my family. No one in our circle was, or ever could be, Right-wing, not even those who were connected to the landed gentry, like my uncle, the notary, and my cousin, the teacher[1]. The links that we had with the small land-owners, who worked their own land but whose attitude to the labor they employed was in no way feudal, the fact that, in the Midi, capitalism on a large scale is considered a product of the hostile North, finally, the presence in our family of a number of teachers, who taught students of all ages from the first forms in primary schools to teacher-training colleges, made us so firmly republican in our beliefs, that it was considered irrelevant

[1] See the footnote on page 6.

and even unseemly to talk about politics unnecessarily. If we had no Right-wingers among us, there were no Left-wingers either. As Tocqueville demonstrated so clearly, French Socialism put paid to its chances in the nineteenth century with its all-embracing attack on the property principle. Such an attack was bound to displease the immediate descendants of those farmers who had acquired confiscated land during the Revolution, as well as the tenants, whom the Revolution had freed from the control of their feudal lords and who could still remember their fears occasioned by the return of the king and the émigré nobility.

Although the situation had developed somewhat by the time I am talking about, our 'men of property' could not find it in their hearts to become Socialists, while our officers, although in no way 'sabre rattlers', could not look with favor on a party which refused to give budgetary support to the Armed Forces. Their choice, therefore, was limited to the various shades of moderate republicanism and to orthodox or independent radicalism, which, even so, represented a considerable gamut of opinions. Naturally, later on, socialism divorced from communism ceased to be regarded with horror by the wine-growers and the mountain people. My father voted Socialist, but for local reasons only, and he even got all the Communists to vote for him. But that was in the confusion of 1945 and was, in fact, the reason he lost the election.

A.D.—And so the influence of your family background made you steer clear of any kind of political extremism. But is it not true that your own personality inclines you to moderation?

E.F.—Yes, that is true, and for one very simple reason. I am not afraid to accept new ideas or reforms, but I abhor anarchy and violence. I can perfectly well imagine, and indeed hope for—this is my present position—a revolution in the true sense of the word. I would like to see a revolution which would in no way entail, would exclude rather, violence in all its forms.

A.D.—The 'quiet revolution'.

E.F.—Exactly. This is why I was able to claim that General de Gaulle was a revolutionary. Moreover, I can remember him saying something to that effect himself.

A.D.—Young people are commonly said to be attracted by extremes. Were you never tempted in this direction?

E.F.—Yes, of course. However, I would like to make it quite clear that I by no means accept as true Barrère's widely quoted striking phrase, 'If a man is not a socialist at twenty, he is devoid of feeling. If he is a socialist at forty, then he is devoid of intelligence'. At least I do not think this maxim can be applied to the contemporary situation. Barrère starts from the idea that a man at forty is no longer the same as he was at twenty; he also supposes that the world remains unchanged during the twenty years interval. Today, the man at forty is not the same as he was twenty years earlier, but the world in which the forty year old lives is very different from that of his youth. Far from being accustomed to a static situation, he is used to change. A man's *experience* of life combined with his intellectual capabilities may lead him to decide change is desirable, while another man, with less experience, would be led unthinkingly to the same conclusion by the turbulence of his own emotions. I think it is quite possible today that a man who was not a socialist at twenty might become one at forty, or even later. This is why men already advanced in years, who have had a hand in the shaping of events, who have been sorely tried, who have thought long and deeply about the situation, so often achieve a clear understanding of the confused longings of the young and can suggest viable solutions to their problems. You have only to look at the great twentieth-century revolutionaries, such as General de Gaulle; and why not include Herbert Marcuse too? Do you think his wide appeal is due only to an adolescent fad, to a conscious striving for eccentricity? His theories, which I neither wholly accept nor reject in their entirety, are the product of laborious research. They deal with fundamental human problems, as they are most poignantly experienced by our young people.

I would like now to return to your question and to tell you that, in fact, there were two so-called political extremes, of completely opposite tendencies, which did tempt me. The first, while I was still in school—I was fourteen at the time—was the Action Française[1]. I will be quite frank about it. I think it was chiefly my passion for history which roused in me, as it did in many others, a nostalgic longing for the glory of the past and for the return of the monarchy. Then again, Maurras's doctrine was the only one which made any attempt to present young men with an apparently coherent, precise and viable system for restructuring society, a political system of almost architectural stability. Last but not least, the Action Française was the only movement interested in young people. Its propaganda flourished in the schools. We took a childish delight in membership cards, pamphlets and badges, and were flattered by the interest taken in us.

However, I was not destined to become a Camelot du Roi[1], and, as soon as I became a student in the Latin Quarter, it did not take long for the strong-arm tactics of the group to disgust me irrevocably. At the same time, a little more information about the movement, combined with my making friends with students of the Center or the Left, opened my eyes to the defects of the 'doctrine'.

The second temptation to assail me came from the communist world, but it was more a question of curiosity and, this time, I acted prudently. I wanted more information about the great movements that were the driving

[1] Action Française, a royalist movement led by Charles Maurras. The movement took its name from the paper, *l'Action Française*, 1908–1944, which promulgated its anti-republican doctrine. The young men who sold the newspaper were called the Camelots du Roi. (Translator's note)

force behind a mysterious country which covered one seventh of the world's land surface. Brice Parain, who had been my temporary philosophy teacher for a term at the Lycée Voltaire, advised me to follow his example and learn Russian, so as to have a more thorough understanding of history in the making. When I was a second-year law student, I remembered his advice and enrolled at the School for Oriental Languages. The Soviet leaders had taken the major step of adopting the NEP[1], and most political commentators were prophesying that there would soon be an evolution towards a kind of bourgeois socialism. We know now that this was not the case. A few years later, after my marriage, I went to the USSR for the first time, accompanied by my wife, Lucie. Pierre Mendès-France was also one of the party. It was the time of the great famine when Russians begged for bread from tourists, when the *besprizorni* would glide along the trains and snatch luggage through the open windows, and the few scraps of information I could gather, thanks to my halting Russian, all painted the same dark picture. And yet, I did not think the whole system should be condemned out of hand: far from it. Some of the young party militants displayed an unbridled, constructive enthusiasm, which forced my admiration. I reserved judgment on the question whether communism was a necessary or even an admissible experience for Russia, but I concluded, after my voyage, that there was not the slightest justification for belonging to the French Communist Party.

Moreover, my intellectual interests had changed during my years of study. Although I had started my Russian studies out of a sense of curiosity about unknown political theories and the desire to understand a new society, I gradually found myself trapped in the shifting sands of eternal Russia. In our class, we hardly spoke about the Soviets. The Russian newspapers we used to read to practice our Russian were published in Paris by émigrés. One (*Renaissance*) was Right-wing and the other (*Les Dernières Nouvelles*) was the vehicle for Milioukov's semi-liberal opinions. Needless to say, I preferred the latter. But our studies were mainly concerned with grammar and linguistics. We used to expound our theories about passages taken from Tolstoy, which always seemed to be about peasants losing their cows, or about the plays of Ostrovsky and Griboyedov, which had as much relevance to the contemporary situation as those of Plautus. We even studied the poem in archaic Russian called *The tale of George the Brave*, of which I never knew the end. A whole culture was revealed to me. It was so different from our own, and yet so similar, because it dealt with the eternal problem of human relations. I learned Pushkin's poems by heart for my own pleasure. I thought Paul Boyer the most exciting teacher in Paris. His lessons were crammed full of ideas on all human problems. Although I was

[1] NEP—New Political Economy, from the Russian *Novaika Ekonomitcheskaia Politika*, a more liberal political economy inaugurated by Lenin after the Kronstadt Mutiny of 1921 and terminated in 1928. (Translator's note)

a great disappointment to him, because I did not seriously apply myself to his subject, he had a great influence on my education.

The most valuable thing for me in this initiation to Russian culture was undoubtedly—at least in the light of recent problems—the somewhat superficial study I made of the development of ideas in nineteenth century Russia. I saw how German ideology permeated Russian politics and how revolutionary feeling was born. The theme of the dissertation I wrote to obtain a diploma was borrowed from Turgenev's book, *Fathers and Sons*. I re-read this book during the May troubles and was struck by how anodyne it seems today. And yet, this is the book in which Bazarov (a character modelled on Pissarev, a contemporary) has this resounding line to say: 'Let us destroy everything first. We will see later how to rebuild'. It also contains a member of the 'old guard's' summing up of contemporary society. Before they were *Hegelians*, now they are *nihilists* (in Russian the two nouns form an assonance). So you can see I had studied and written about the transition from intoxication with philosophical ideas to nihilism, a trend which I find in our young demonstrators of today. However, Bazarov's words could serve as an epigraph to an interesting development in Marcuse's work. When he was asked a question similar to that put to Bazarov, Marcuse replied that everything was relative, and that if it was a question of replacing a prison with a house, it was advisable to destroy the prison first, and then construct the house later[1].

My infatuation with Russia was to have unforeseen effects on my professional life and choice of a career. I had been drawn quite naturally to seek the society of Russian students, and to frequent the émigré clubs. The Russians who were trying to establish themselves in business had many legal battles to fight. They consulted the legal experts among their exiled compatriots and willingly agreed, which was more than the vast majority of French people would have done, to entrust their cases to a very young lawyer, whose charges were moderate and whose enthusiasm was entirely at their disposition.

After my break with the Action Française, I was forced to admit that this organization was practically the only one which provided university students with a stimulus. It stood alone in providing a 'headquarters' for the exchange of ideas and information and was the only movement to suggest motives for action and agitation. I looked around for something to fill the void left by my withdrawal from politics, something which would not, however, involve violence. This is how I and a few friends came to found at the Law Faculty, a club whose aim was to seek information about and discuss politics. I went to the Dean of the Faculty, with whom I had

[1] Marcuse, H: *Five Lectures; Psychoanalysis, Politics and Utopia*. London, Allen Lane, the Penguin Press, 1970. p. 79.

a vague family connection, and the excellent fellow agreed immediately to place at our disposal a rather remote room, which had not been exclusively commandeered for another purpose and which, as it happened, was called the Russian Room. We chose two popular teachers, Achille Mestre and Giffard, the specialist in Romance studies, to start off our first meeting. After that we drifted along with no one in charge.

Political activity in the Latin Quarter was a cut-and-dried affair. If you were not for the Action Française you were against it, and, *ipso facto*, classed as belonging to a tacit coalition of the Center and the Left, which was not unlike the new majority beginning to form around Poincaré. The Leftist group was led by Pierre Mendès-France, with whom I became friends, and, in spite of upsets, our friendship has never wavered since that time.

The Center group was led by my friend, Charles Chavanet. We all agreed that he had a brilliant future in front of him, but he was killed soon afterwards in a climbing accident. He introduced me to Louis Jacquinot and Frédéric Dupont, two young 'leaders', a little older than I was, and already playing an active role in politics. It was they who took me to the dinners given by the Democratic Alliance, where I was captivated by Paul Reynaud's eloquence, but it was not just the presentation of his speeches which impressed me. Paul Reynaud was one of those politicians who have a deep understanding of the new social problems confronting the world. This is why he was more truly a man of the 'Left' than some so-called Left-wingers. I wrote a few articles on university politics for *L'Ère Nouvelle*, a paper with Radical tendencies. Alexandre, one of my teachers, had given me a subscription to *Libres Propos*, the revue directed by Alain, and I was extremely proud to see my articles printed there.

However, the Russian Room club (called the Club of the University of Paris, by inversion of the initials of the sporting PUC) became the nucleus of a broadly based republican and democratic alliance. The Action Française saw it as a threat, and when they failed to neutralize the club by flooding it with their own adherents, they resorted to violence. Royalist shock troops did battle with our hastily recruited strong-arm boys. It was a tame affair, and all that happened was that Mendès got a bloody nose. An economics teacher, completely lacking in tact, declared: 'We'll just have to put an end to the drivel they talk'. This opinion, delivered in a self-satisfied and sneering tone, by a narrow-minded fool, who knew nothing of the situation and who, with a supreme disregard for the academic principles drummed into us, refused to consider the facts, inspired me to write in a note-book, 'M.H. . . . the viewpoint of a brainwashed fool'. There will always be a mouthpiece for this kind of viewpoint, based on ignorance and on the stupid conviction that the idea put forward is in line with those of the majority. Naturally, as far as the Russian Room club was concerned, this brainwashed fool carried the day. More recently, I have had cause to observe that proponents of this kind of viewpoint are still to be found. They still find their targets with a certain measure of success. We were forced to move to a large room on the first floor of the Taverne du Panthéon to hold our meetings. It was not the same. It is on the campus, in an academic setting, that students must be allowed to meet to discuss social problems. Our sense of outrage at their daring to be so passionately interested in such problems is completely unjustified. Anyway, politics was only one of our evening activities. Something was due to the Arts. Like other generations before us we had our *cénacles*, our short-lived revues. One, a serious publication, called *Les Essais*, another *L'Ours en peluche*, devoted to the vein of humor so dear to Lefebvre. Our supreme achievement was *Le Cancrelat*, a title chosen by me (with an obvious reference to the Russian princess Tarakan), which we decided in advance would have only one number, the first (the others did not sell).

However, the group was already breaking up. Raymond Hubert went to work for the Agence Havas. Mendès-France was making preparations for his move to the Eure; my lawyer friends were swallowed up in attorney's practices, where they were introduced to legal procedures while at the same time earning just enough money to keep them in bus-tickets. One morning I went to work in an office on the Avenue de l'Opéra. My employer was Maître Leboucq, an excellent man who was acting for the Department of Finance. I was given a desk in a tiny office where I was entrusted with copying out by hand dossiers, i.e. the interminable succession of procedural points which precede legal decisions. At noon I picked up the volume of Proust, which I had laid aside as I entered the office, and decided that that was the end of my career as a solicitor's clerk.

I had been called to the Bar as soon as I got my degree, no other qualification being necessary. In those days, the CAPA[1] did not exist. Although I was still a minor and completely incapable of directing my own affairs, I suddenly found I had unlimited power to settle the affairs of other people, and I had the right to brave the majesty of the courts. Young men should be given responsibility whenever possible. With a sense of wonder I immersed myself in active life. There was the robing-room, fellow barristers, prisons, judges, policemen, the accused men, journalists, rubbernecks. It is a great mistake to allow students to pursue purely theoretical studies for years at a time. We should insist that they complete them by, or even sandwich them between, periods of professional, practical experience, which in no way hinder pure theoretical study, as I and many others can testify.

That same year I presented myself, on the off chance, for the examination of the Conference. I had done no preparation at all. I had not even been to court sessions. The first speech I ever heard was the one I made myself.

[1] Certificat d'aptitude à la profession d'avocat. Certificate of professional competence as a barrister. (Translator's note)

Guillaumin, the President of the Bar and who was also President of the Municipal Council of Paris, gave me a kind reception and predicted that I would become a teacher at the Law Faculty after being for a time secretary to the Conference. It was to be some time before this prophecy came true in its entirety.

Apparently, there was some doubt as to whether I should have first or second prize. Finally, I was awarded second prize, but even this was an undreamt-of success. I was placed between Jacques Millerand, the son of a President of the Republic, and Jacques Fourcade, the son of a President of the Bar who was also a Senator. This success opened up for me the gates of the highest Law Court, although I had not completed my studies and had no influential family connections.

3

The 'Thirties

The first effect of my marriage was to convince me that my choice of a career, which now enabled me to offer my wife a home, had been the right one. More important, I felt that my decision to try to build up a practice of my own was justified. Without going into details, I will simply say that I was as fortunate as I possibly could be, and quickly achieved my ambition.

My earliest clients had made me conversant with the motion picture and oil industries, these being fields in which Russians are active and legal battles not uncommon. I appeared for Edwige Feuillère and against Danielle Darrieux, for *La Femme du Bout du Monde* and against *Le Capitaine Craddock*. The law-suits arising from the mundane importation of oil with its attendant customs regulations were less glamorous, but often had a direct bearing on world problems. For example, when Cardenas, the Mexican President, decided to nationalize his country's oil deposits, which were worked by big foreign companies, the companies combined to try to prevent the sale on the free market of this oil tainted with socialism. Stocks of the oil were seized and all but the biggest operators were threatened with ruin. Marius Moutet and I were called upon to defend in court the right of each nation to make use of its national resources as it saw fit. We had to defend a nation's right to true independence; not just political independence, which might be a mere show, but economic independence as well.

It was at this time that a second social and family influence began to shape my character. I had a new set of 'co-ordinates' by which to fix my position. Lucie Meyer, my wife, belonged to a Jewish family of Alsatian origin. In order to remain French, her father had left the Haut-Rhin province when he came of age. In spite of their provincial origins, the family were typical of the Parisian bourgeoisie, having a high regard for culture. Lucie opened up for me the whole world of the arts, for up to that time music had been the only branch of the arts with which I was familiar. She taught me to look at monuments and museums, at France and Europe. In literature and philosophy she forced me to realize that the too rapid development of my thought, with always a precise object in view, had left great gaps in my knowledge. I could quote Turgenev's opinions on Hegel, but I had not read Hegel. I could argue for or against Marxism, but the length of *Capital* had always put me off. I had a great deal to catch up on. I had to learn to pursue intellectual researches, which might bring no immediate gain, with the same thoroughness that, in my professional life, I brought to legal matters.

In Julien Cain, who became my uncle by marriage and also an intimate friend, I was to have the privilege of knowing one of the cleverest and most idealistic men of the age. I still think of him as a twentieth century *Encyclopédiste*[1], a personification of the *Aufklärung*. He was already internationally famous. After heroic service as an infantryman during the First World War, he had been put in charge of the French national libraries, and, for some time, he was principal private secretary to the President of the Chamber. His knowledge of politics and politicians was boundless. I had met Lucienne Cain at Paul Boyer's classes. She was a translator and critic of the works of Berdyaev, and she now welcomed me affectionately but without laying aside her (almost) lethal irony. In their drawing-room I met several prominent people of widely differing talents who, I am sure, do not remember me, for, strange as it may seem, my role there was just that of a listener.

I was fully occupied defending my clients, fulfilling social engagements and also getting the final qualifications I needed. Thus, my only contribution to politics at this hectic time was that of an interested observer. Besides, I think that it is a mistake for politicians to enter politics too soon. They should first work hard to make a way for themselves in a challenging profession, especially one which will bring them into contact with people and concrete problems. The knowledge I gained at this time about the administration of French industry and international economic affairs was later to prove very useful to me in my ministerial career.

The riots of 6 February 1934 caused me to adopt a more positive commitment to the Left. I disapproved of the rather doubtful nature of the Leagues' activities, while my journeys in the provinces and holidays in the country had opened my eyes to the extent of the fear felt by a wide section of the French population because of these activities. At the same time, the policy of deflation, which the administration so foolishly pursued, caused great despondency and bitterness.

Just before the war, I submitted a law thesis on the policies controlling the oil business in France. It was published under the title: *Le pétrole dans la paix et dans la guerre*[2]. The subject naturally led me to conclude that the only way to ensure world peace was to bring about an alliance between the Western powers and Soviet Russia. Ever since then, arguments about the relative merits of the economic structure of the East and West, about the

---

[1] *Encyclopédiste*—one of Diderot's collaborators on the *Encyclopédie ou dictionnaire raisonné des sciences, des arts et des métiers* (published 1751–1780). (Translator's note)

[2] Faure, E., *Le pétrole dans la paix et dans la guerre*. Paris, Éditions de la Nouvelle Revue Critique, 1939.

validity of Marxism or liberalism have seemed to me irrelevant and of secondary importance.

But it was to take some time before history was to agree with my wise analysis!

I spent most of the war working in the censorship department of the press agency, then called the Agence Havas (now the Agence France-Presse). In spite of its decrepit appearance and lack of comforts, the office on the Place de la Bourse was, in my eyes at least, an isolated outpost of modernity, an enclave of futuristic devices. After the well regulated hours and the ceremonial of the legal world with its time-consuming procedures and non-mechanized methods, I found myself in the world of radio dispatches and teleprinters. It was a world of abbreviations, sudden happenings and fleeting impressions; a world which knew nothing of second thoughts, distance, and time zones. Day and night were as one, as we constantly made adjustments to allow for differences in time throughout the world. The fall of Warsaw, war in Finland, a speech by Hitler, the wanderings of the *Admiral Graf Spee,* stories which all the correspondents transmitted all over the world at the same time . . . with Louis Joxe and Maurice Schumann I experienced many a hectic hour. Not, however, during the invasion, because I was then at a school for trainee officers at Rennes, where I was conscientiously learning the correct proportions of horse-drawn and mechanized vehicles in a medical service convoy.

A.D.—When did you decide to leave for North Africa?

E.F.—I started to think about leaving France right at the beginning of the occupation, but my plans did not take shape until Russia declared war on Germany. I thought an Allied victory probable, but believed that the war would last for a long time and that the opposing sides would establish bases in other continents besides Europe. Inevitably, the Allies would occupy Africa, and I concluded that I should cross the Mediterranean at the right time. The arrest of Jean Dumaine, a friend of mine, in a train where I was supposed to join him, made me more determined than ever, and I spent the whole of the summer of 1942 making plans. I watched carefully for signs of the imminence of the Allied landings and was able to get a berth, along with my wife and my daughter, on the *Gouverneur Général Chanzy,* the last ferry to leave France for Tunis, where I had arranged professional cover for myself.

What I had not foreseen, however, was that the Maghreb would only be occupied piecemeal. We retreated to Hammamet with a few other French people, who were in a similar situation and who, like us, wanted to avoid compulsory repatriation. It was here that I picked up the rudiments of Arabic, with a member of the Tunisian National Party[1] for a teacher. He was the editor of a small revue and had decided to become friends with me.

[1] Le Destour in French. (Translator's note)

It was because of this Tunisian experience that I later achieved a clearer understanding of the necessity for a liberal colonial policy.

The arrival of the Allies allowed me to reach Algiers, where I met up again with Louis Joxe. He immediately invited me to join him on the Liberation Committee, of which he was Secretary General.

Preparations for a career in the legislative assembly

Aims and achievements

A.D.—In fact, the Algiers Liberation Committee can be seen as the starting point of your political career.

E.F.—Yes, I think so. During this crucial time it was exciting to live and work so close to General de Gaulle, even though he was only rarely to be seen. (In fact, he never addressed more than a few words to me.) I was part of a government team. I prepared and revised legislative texts (ordinances[1]). I met Mendès France, my old friend, who was now head of the Ministry of Finance, Couve de Murville, President Queuille, Paul Giacobbi. I had close links with Francis de Menthon and Paul Coste-Floret. I edited the new *Journal Officiel* and my wife, after having worked on the editorial staff of *L'Arche*, founded *La Nef*. Working committees were set up, usually at the instigation of André Philip, to draw up the institutional and social reforms, which were to come into force at the liberation. There is one aspect of this period of preparation and waiting that I must insist upon. Can you imagine the extent to which our interest, and mine in particular, was focused on the Soviet Union? Our eyes were fixed on Stalingrad as though our salvation depended on the outcome of this one epic struggle. My enthusiasm for things Russian, born at the time of my studies at the School for Oriental Languages, was reawakened, for it had been somewhat dampened by the volte-face of 1939. I read and translated the articles and books, which reached us from Moscow, while my wife founded the first Center for Slavonic Studies. I made the acquaintance of several Soviet diplomats. I thought we should try to prolong the cordial relations born of the necessities of war when peace returned. Influenced by the general current of ideas, I thought—moreover, I still think—it possible to effect a lasting conciliation between Soviet Marxism and the liberalism of the capitalist West (for war economies had watered down capitalism) and to work out a new form of humanism acceptable to both sides. Besides, I thought it likely that the

---

[1] The decrees issued by the provisional French Government (1940–1946) have in French the very precise title of *ordonnances*, here translated as 'ordinances'. (Translator's note)

industrial powers would have to evolve economic policies based on a compromise, combining the advantages of the two systems. In fact, Jean Monnet, whom I had just met for the first time, was already working on the blueprint for a planned economy.

My ideas gathered strength when General de Gaulle asked me to accompany Francis de Menthon to represent France at the Nüremberg trials. (In the meantime, I had followed Mendès France into the Ministry of National Economics, but had left it with him after the failure of a body which had represented a major attempt to achieve a lively, progressive economy.)

We believed passionately in the possibility of establishing a basis for international justice. We thought we could initiate an era when heads of state, whose actions had had catastrophic results for mankind, could be held personally responsible for their crimes. The flags of the four Great Powers flew over this unique Tribunal. The Russian flag had its place beside the others, and I saw this a symbol of lasting peace. I often met the Soviet attorneys, General Rudenko, Colonel Pokrovsky, and also writers, Constantin Fedine, for example. I thought their ideas were similar to ours, and no doubt they were.

I had decided to try to get elected to the Assembly. Already, before the war, I felt that my professional successes, although outstanding, were not enough to satisfy me completely. After the years I had spent devoted to questions affecting collective interests and which raised eternal human problems, I felt I could no longer limit my horizons to the ephemeral problems of the individual. I chose the Radical Party and the Rassemblement des Gauches, though not without reservations, for I had some very close friends—I'm thinking especially of Paul and Alfred Coste-Floret—in the new MRP[1], and they wanted me to join their team. However, my pre-war evolution had placed me in a Radical environment, although I had never joined the Party. I remembered Alain with his constant theme of resisting bureaucracy. I was, as you know, a close friend of Mendès France, President Queuille honored me with his confidence, and, at the very point in time when several people thought its days were numbered, the old Great Party managed to assemble a young team: Jacques Chaban-Delmas, Bourgès-Manoury, Félix Gaillard, etc. I was pleased to take my place among them, although I felt equal pleasure in finding René Pleven, François Mitterand, and Claudius Petit in the allied group, the UDSR[2]. It was Edouard Herriot who finally made my mind up for me. I admired his farsightedness in international affairs—had not he always recognized the Soviets and tried to safeguard American friendship during the absurd affair of the war debts?—while his ideas on arbitration and disarmament, as well as those on the necessity for an East-West *détente*, fitted in per-

[1] MRP Mouvement Républicain Populaire.
[2] UDSR Union Démocratique et Socialiste de la Résistance. (Translator's notes)

fectly with my own. I have often been teased about my waverings at this time. And yet now I can see how close my own Radical tendencies were to those of most of the leaders of the Christian-Democrats.

When I entered the Assembly as representative for the Jura, I had already decided upon the general aims which were to regulate my conduct:

on the one hand, to work towards a type of society somewhere between liberalism and socialism (a society which would allow advances to be made in social justice without slowing up the process of the creation of wealth);

on the other hand, to work towards the creation of a balance between the international powers capable of guaranteeing a lasting peace, relying upon agreed formulas for arbitration and the legal settling of disputes. This would imply, so far as it was in our power, an end to the cold war between East and West.

You will easily find concrete evidence of these preoccupations in the first two bills I brought before the Assembly. One dealt with employee investment in the company they worked for; the other advocated the creation of an international court for the rights of man.

From February 1949, I had ministerial responsibility. This is not the place to describe these developments. They belong, with more or less importance, to the annals of contemporary history. However, I am accountable for my sincerity, for the constancy of my views. And so I would like to enumerate, in a brief resumé, the principal steps in what I see as an unbroken line of development.

Economic and financial policy

Having acquired the technical background, which can only come from experience, by occupying successively the post of Secretary of State to the Treasury and that of Minister for the Budget, I was given the opportunity of controlling France's finances, first, for a few weeks in 1952, then, for a longer period from 1953 to early 1956. My constant preoccupation was to gear economic policies to social needs. I wanted to add to the classic criteria for financial and economic management, criteria which are all too often seen as the only ones possible (I am thinking of the notorious 'indexes') the criterion of social balance which, moral considerations apart, is just as meaningful and effective as the classic procedures. There is a persistent misconception, the offspring of out-of-date economic theories, to the effect that the interests of investors are diametrically opposed to those of wage-earners, whereas, in fact, the interests of these two groups are compatible. The first economic policy I put into effect was the establishment of the sliding scale, a measure which was very unpopular with some of the moderate elements who supported my administration and even with some of my own ministers. In the Assembly, I lost no time in asserting that this policy was a necessary step in my overall plan, and not just a tactical concession to the SFIO[1], as they pretended to believe. This was the measure which allowed me, on my return in 1953, to launch my eighteen months' plan and to effect a recovery of the economy by giving the workers a sense of security, thanks to the procedure of regular consultation, and by assuring a healthy consumer boom by an increase in purchasing power. A carefully calculated balance between investment and consumer spending is the key to any expansionist policy, while expansion is the key to a non-inflationary economy. I pursued a similar policy with regard to the farmers, guaranteeing them an outlet for their produce in a year of over-production. The results of these policies can be ascertained by consulting the Treasury Records. Thanks to them, and without a devaluation and a rise in prices, we were able to guarantee, over a period of two-and-a-half years, a considerable, steady, *comparable* increase in the indexes of production, exports, and purchasing power, while, at the same time, effecting an improvement in the gold and currency reserves.

It was this experience, coupled with consideration of later growth forecasts, which led me, in 1963 at the time of the miners' strike (yet another 'success' for orthodox economic policy) to outline a far-ranging interpretation of my policies with the theory of the New Social Contract.

International politics

In spite of the hopes of the immediate post-war years, the aberrations of Stalinism obviously made impossible the evolution of international politics along the lines I had wished.

I had no hesitation, therefore, in supporting NATO, since there was no more satisfactory way of guaranteeing our security. However, starting with the Lisbon Conference of February 1952, I insisted upon the importance of not limiting ourselves to purely military matters, and on the necessity of concentrating our efforts on the evolution of an economic and social strategy geared to help the popular masses and the countries of the Third World.

When I became head of government again in 1955, after the death of Stalin, I thought the moment had come to renew the policy of *détente*. Consequently, I took the initiative of calling the Geneva Summit Conference, the results of which, as we know, were beneficial for a time. At the risk of being charged with hopeless idealism, I laid before the Conference a plan for disarmament, linked to a common fund for mutual help, which would give the plan an added justification and an automatic guarantee. I still think that this type of international agreement, linking the contractual decrease in military budgets to an *organic* cooperation for development, is the best, and probably the only, means of getting the disarmament pro-

[1] SFIO Section Française de l'Internationale Ouvrière; French Section of the International Working Men's Association. (Translator's note)

blem out of the farcical impasse it is in and of galvanizing into action the powerful world-wide and hitherto untapped resources of popular opinion.

In a similar vein, I tried, as Minister of Agriculture, to encourage the big agricultural producers to accept a certain degree of joint cooperation and planning, so that any surpluses could be used to the benefit of the under-developed countries. At France's suggestion, the European Community has already adopted a precise resolution instituting this type of contribution and at the time the OECD[1] accepted the main gist of my proposals.

It is not possible here for me to mention, however briefly, the initiatives I took and the positions I adopted with regard to other matters, such as wrangles over established legal procedures, the rebuilding of Europe, the recognition of China, etc. However, I think I can claim that the different measures which I put through always complemented each other and were in line with my unwavering general resolve.

I remain convinced that, in their broad outlines, the objectives I had begun to formulate nearly twenty-five years ago and which I tried to put into practice are relevant to the present day.

However, great changes took place during this period. They oblige us to look at certain old problems differently and they confront us with new ones. Finally, I feel it necessary to unite the old and new problems in an overall scheme, which demands a system of thought where priorities are clearly defined. This is the goal to which my efforts are directed at this present time.

[1] OECD Organization for Economic Cooperation and Development. (Translator's note)

Part 1

Action and theory in politics

'It is not that we men have thoughts, but rather thoughts come to us, mortal men, for whom thought is the very cradle of being.'
Heidegger

5

A systematic analysis of my position in relation to Marxism

The author of these lines owes his celebrity to the role he has played in government. It will therefore seem natural for this book about politics to open with the important question of the relationship between theory and action, between doctrine and government.

Such is my object. And as this problem was broached by Marx at the beginning of the last century and has since then been systematically explored by his disciples, it will give me an opportunity to define my position in relation to this school of thought. The first point I would like to make is that, as far as basic political principles are concerned, the antagonism existing between Marxist and non-Marxist theorists is totally irrelevant.

If you look at orthodox Marxist texts, it is impossible not to be put off by their dogmatism, by the *ratio autoritatis* they claim for themselves, by their marked tendency to resort to quotation to help them over a contentious point, in the same way that celebrated Roman lawyers used to rely on texts taken from the great legal experts to settle contemporary court cases. Not once do these authors give the impression that they experienced the slightest doubt. Not once do you feel that they gave the 'bourgeois' theories, which they are supposed to be analyzing objectively, the slightest chance of convincing them: 'Let this little grass keep his chance!'[1] On the other hand, I do not think that non-Marxist writers attribute enough importance to a school of thought, which has made a vital contribution to political science, even if one rejects some or all of its conclusions, either on the grounds of their fundamental invalidity or because one considers them out-of-date. More than a political and economic system, Marxism is a philosophy. More than a collection of recommendations, forecasts, and experiences, it is a way of life. Just as one cannot look at the world after the advent of Christianity in the same way as before, so too, one cannot view it in the same way after the advent of Marxism. The general contempt for Marxism displayed by those authors who do not accept its doctrines is a fundamental mistake on their part.

---

[1] The phrase in inverted commas was in English in the original. (Translator's note)

Does one have to be a Christian to be interested in the soul, sin, and redemption? Does one have to be a Marxist to want more information about the uses made of analysis in the dialectic, whose similarity with the Christian Trinity has, moreover, often been commented upon?[1]

The most valuable contributions to the elaboration of a political system have been provided by certain Marxist writers of independent judgment, generally considered as dissidents, and whose opinions I shall quote on several occasions. However, they are Marxists, which I cannot claim to be, and as such are usually at pains to conserve everything from the original doctrine that has not been irrevocably proved wrong. My interest, on the other hand, is to take from the doctrine anything which might be relevant to the eternal or day to day problems which are my concern. Moreover, they are philosophers rather than political theorists, although they would maintain that there is no distinction between the two. Nevertheless, the language and the methods used are not identical, with the result that I find it difficult to understand some of their more obscure points. What is more, I have noticed that the more difficult passages in their theoretical works, apart from those which belong to the realm of pure metaphysics, are the result of a determined, and in my opinion a desperate, effort to breathe new life into certain doctrinal concepts whose useful life ended long ago.

The reader of modern texts, some written by orthodox or inventive Marxists the others by non-Marxists, cannot help but notice the existence of a gap in contemporary thought as expressed by its most authoritative and brilliant exponents. This impression is strengthened if, rather than listening to the pundits, one considers the attitudes of the current young prophets of revolution. Although their attention is concentrated on the same society, the same human reality taking shape before their eyes, they seem to belong to civilizations separated by thousands of years in time or by astral distances in space. The opposing sides employ an armory of words and concepts so alien to each other, that not only does it seem difficult for them to understand one another, but one simply cannot imagine how they could find a common ground for confrontation.

This point was fully brought home to me when I held office in the Rue de Grenelle. I tried to open a dialogue with the 'demonstrators', who rejected my offer on the grounds that I was, by definition and essence, the rejection of their demands personified. Invoking Latin clarity of thought and Cartesian method, several members of my entourage made fun of the young people's pretentious refusal to listen to anyone else's point of view, an attitude which my colleagues thought was the last word in absurdity. And yet, from the rebels' viewpoint, our supposed lucidity and

[1] To such an extent that, according to certain interpretations, the three terms of the Hegelian triad have a theological origin in the three persons of the Trinity. Cf. Bruaire, C. *Logique et religion dans la philosophie de Hegel.* Paris, Seuil, 1964.

method are only the means we employ to close our minds to outside ideas; to them, they represent a deliberate attempt to confuse the issue, an incomprehensible contempt for the real state of affairs.

It seems to me of paramount importance, even if the task is an ambitious one, to put an end to this dichotomy of who is 'right' in politics, for it gives rise to fundamental misunderstandings. It is imperative for those thinkers who do not class themselves as Marxists to define their position *in relation* to it, sympathetically, in the etymological sense of the word. In any case, their position should *in no way* be one of systematic rejection or of pure ignorance (these two attitudes being, moreover, perfectly compatible and often quite inseparable). It is not simply a question of using to good account any positive aspects of this vast system of interpretation, elucidation, and political direction which are still relevant to the contemporary situation, but also of learning a lesson from those parts of the doctrine which have been proved wrong and have had to be jettisoned:

'. . . But to give light implies
No less a sombre moiety of shade'[1].

[1] Valéry, P. *Le cimitière marin*, translated by C. Day Lewis as *The graveyard by the sea*. London, Martin Secker and Warburg, 1945. (Translator's note)

6

The Marxist conception of the unity of theory and practice

'It is by realizing its own aims that Marxism outlives its useful life. Its merit is to have discovered the questions which allow others to transcend its conclusions.'

L. Soubise

To transcend Marxism one must first admit its existence. But it is enough to admit it as an important development in philosophy, just as agnostics can and must admit the existence of Christianity, without necessarily being classed as believers or behaving like practicing Christians. It is in this spirit that I shall be led to put forward, as one of the conclusions of this work, the desirability of a third school of thought, which would seek, not precise formulas for a conciliation and synthesis of socialism and liberalism—which would imply compromise and a mutual weakening of the constituent forces—but a reconciliation which would involve a potential joining of forces and a transcendence of the original doctrines.

I would now like to return to the question in hand, but, to tell the truth, I do not think that I had moved appreciably away from it, for it provides a classical justification for the remarks I have just made. The theme of the unity of theory and practice is, in fact, one of the basic principles of Marxist ideology. But it is not the exclusive preserve of Marxism, for its source can be found in Hegel and even earlier. Moreover, even if one refuses to accept the Marxist interpretation of this point, or if one tries to reject the concept in itself, it forces itself on the mind as one of the fundamental problems of political science.

Now, where will you find present-day politicians, professing to be non-Marxists, to put forward, explain, explore, or discuss this problem? How can this grave omission be justified? Is it not important for public opinion to be informed about the attitude of its leaders and pundits on certain points? It is not just a question of intellectual curiosity, nor of providing amusement for sophists, but of a discussion which is of vital importance to the historical process and to the life of social organizations.

The eleventh 'essay on Feuerbach'

It is in the last of the essays on Feuerbach, an important work of a few pages, that Marx spelled out the famous maxim: 'Philosophers have done nothing except interpret the world in various ways; what matters is to transform it'.

This statement must be considered in the light of an idea, often expressed by Marx, to the effect that it would be a delusion to imagine that thought could be less restricted and could attain even loftier heights if it were detached from the commonplace problems of the world. This attempt to reach a higher plane of thought would simply be to wall up the mind. 'To rise above the world by pure meditation is, in reality, to remain a prisoner of meditation.'

The eleventh 'essay on Feuerbach' has recently been criticized by Brice Parrain who disputed, not its meaning, but its novelty. He points out, with some justification, that it is nothing new for philosophers to claim to influence the outside world. Doubtless, it has always been so. No doubt one can add to the number of rightly called philosophers, who were in Brice Parrain's thoughts, the great founders of religions such as Mohammed and Calvin. Nevertheless, Marx's statement does put forward a principle, it is based on systematic analysis and has a bearing on the march of history.

If, in this last essay, Marx has placed himself in the position of the philosopher attracted towards the real world, in other texts he adopted the opposite and contradictory hypothesis of reality seen as calling philosophy into question.

It is by his acts that a man must demonstrate the truth, that is to say the real nature, the power, the innermost depths of his thought. The controversy over the reality or the non-reality of thought, over thought divorced from action is pure scholasticism.

Here Marx is obviously inspired by Hegel:

One must not imagine that man thinks with one part of his being and wills with the other part. The idea that man keeps thought in one pocket and will in the other is totally meaningless[1].

Some time later Marx wrote in the *Contribution to the critique of Hegel's philosophy of right:* 'It is not enough that thought strive to actualize itself; actuality must itself strive toward thought'[2].

The theme of the unity of thought and action proposes a constant interaction, an enriching of thought by action as well as action by thought.

[1] Similarity pointed out by Korsch in *Karl Marx*. London, Chapman and Hall, 1938. p. 93.

[2] *Contribution to the critique of Hegel's philosophy of right*. Cambridge, The University Press, 1970. p. 138.

The very word unity or unification, which is sometimes substituted for it, leads to some confusion on this point. One must avoid the quite common and, moreover, very excusable misinterpretation to the effect that Marxist dogma claims to impose preconceived ideas on a hostile reality, which differs widely from the hypothetical reality posited and whose resistance must be overcome at any price. If this has too often been the case, it would be wrong to see it as a result of fidelity to the master's doctrine. It is rather due to a deformation of the doctrine. As it tends towards thought, action can shape and influence it. This process is better expressed by the word circularity, as used by the most recent commentators[1].

Having thus defined the general theme, I believe it could be examined from three points of view: that of common linguistic usage and 'practical politics', that of philosophy and, finally, that of the politics of revolution. The first has absolutely no connection with Hegel, Marx, or any other school of thought. The second is Hegelian in the true sense of the word. The third, while being influenced by Hegelianism, can be considered as being specifically linked to revolutionary Marxism and, naturally, to its offshoots, such as Leninism and Maoism.

(1) At the most basic level of natural common sense and without reference to any ideology in particular, we may assume that any activity gains from being inspired by a motivating doctrine, and that, conversely, action often leads to a reconsideration of the principles which inspired it. This is the meaning of the popular expressions: 'to be as good as one's word' (the expression of one's thought) and to 'learn from experience'. In more scientific terms we could say, as does P. Fougeyrollas, that here we have two problems, both older than Marxism and with an obvious link between them: 'The problem of the determination of the end result of a certain course of action, and that of finding the effective means to bring about a certain end'. (Marx did not claim to have invented these problems, but only to have brought them together, to have fused them.)

In the realm of politics, the normal channel for the transfer from theory to action is the choice and execution of a program. We know what usually happens. From this point of view, theory-action unity may seem a mere

[1] The word *intussusception* has been employed too, (intussusception and circularity being the two terms favored by L. Soubise, to whose important study, *Marxisme après Marx*, (Paris, Aubier Montaigne, 1967), pp. 154 and 175 I refer here). Intussusception has an even more precise meaning than circularity, but is unlikely to become common usage. *Praxis*, a no less pedantic word, but one which is less easy to understand, is, on the other hand, used all too often. It is a totally ambiguous word and merely adds another element of confusion to an already involved discussion. It is applied, according to the context, to one of the terms of the equation, namely action, but also, with various nuances of meaning, to the impregnation of the first term by the second (practical, conscious, critical, voluntary activity), or to the two terms combined.

Whatever words are used there is no easy answer to the problem of the unity of theory and practice. In fact, the perfect solution can never be reached. It is a goal towards which one strives. Some commentators believe it would only be reached at an impossible limit.

commonplace. It could just as easily be used as a justification for empiricism and political changes in direction. But a cursory glance at the past reveals how wrong it would be to accept a superficial, unacademic interpretation of this phenomenon, which just distorts the truth. How much disappointment and disillusionment with politics, especially among young people, has been the result of the gap between theory and practice, a *décalage* often due to the inadequate, static nature of the doctrine itself, to so many unrealistic proclamations and manifestoes, which are nothing but a show of words, and to the general contempt displayed by far too many politicians for the 'direct link' which should exist between political beliefs and policies. One can ridicule the ambitions of political philosophy with its specialized language; however, it is no mean achievement to goad us into taking seriously the search for a sincere and effective relationship between the two poles (intellectual and practical) of the activity of those who govern us, or have ambitions of doing so.

(2) From the philosophical standpoint, theory-action unity is a sideshoot of the Hegelian idea of creative action and of the creation of man by himself, a topic I shall cover more fully later.

(3) Finally, the idea of theory-action unity is evident in the eschatological concept of the proletariat as a chosen class, summoned by history to the extraordinary mission of realizing its destiny by destroying itself as an entity, along with all the other classes, and by annihilating the very concept of social class. If the time seemed ripe for philosophy to transform the world in 1845, it was because of the need for, and imminence of, the advent of revolution. As far as revolution is concerned, history has proved Marx's essays on Feuerbach wrong, but it has also given remarkable proof that he was right about some things.

Lenin, Stalin, Mao, and theory-action unity

If, in spite of his personal initiatives in 1848, Marx never had an opportunity to apply himself to practical politics in any significant way, his followers and disciples have assured him a triumphal revenge. To say that V. I. Lenin was a committed apostle of theory-action unity would be an understatement. He *was* this unity. He personified it. He was the incarnation of this circularity, which can be taken here in its most concrete and precise sense, that of the circulation of the blood. To those who have studied his life story, it seems that no part of his personal life was untouched by this unity. It seems that in writing the history of this man, one is not writing the history of a man; in writing the history of Leninism, one is not writing about a doctrine. In Lenin's case, one is dealing with a living doctrine and a 'theorized' man. It is as if the idea, borne along by arterial pressure to the capillary of the smallest action, returns, enriched by this contact with the everyday world, to bring a new urgency to the harmonious, life-giving rhythms of the common center where perception and decision are born.

Steeped in Marxism (and therefore in Hegelianism), not only in his social, economic, and political theories, but in the whole of his philosophical outlook to the point of forcing himself to acquire an erudition obviously at variance with his personal tastes and, according to the experts, with his ability, Lenin, we know, had no difficulty in passing from the realms of pure thought to direct action with a surprising grasp of strategic and tactical procedure. Just as he had been a staunch defender of the purity of the doctrine against the slightest hint of verbo-conceptual deviation, so he would adopt the practice of making good inadequacies in the doctrine by fusing it with data taken from contemporary experience. If the NEP[1] seems to us just another temporary compromise, an empirical choice, he was capable, too, of making decisions with lasting irrevocable effects; for example, the decision that it was necessary to abandon the permanent revolution, to accept the implementation of socialism in just one part of the world[2] (which allows contemporary Soviet leaders to claim they are following Lenin's advice in accepting peaceful coexistence). Finally, there was the decision to prepare to abandon the industrial proletariat as a motive force for revolutionary action and to substitute for it new movements, born of the longings of the peoples of far-flung, mysterious continents.

Stalin, like Lenin (however different our opinion of him may be), is an illustration of the theory-action syndrome, a theorist about action, a man who put his philosophy into practice. His theoretical works are of considerable volume, and are indissolubly linked with his political actions, which they help to explain. His are the writings which have provided, in a concentrated form, the clearest and most striking presentation of the three 'materialisms'. At the same time, it must be remembered that, in spite of his mistakes, and later his aberrations, his actions, seen as a whole, assured for Soviet Socialism a future that had long seemed doubtful.

Finally, Mao is very obviously a theorist as well as a man of action and combat. Just as in Lenin's case, theory and action are the warp and weave of his existence.

Our Western minds, unaccustomed to the dialectic, do not always see a distinction between, for example, pragmatic, empirical decisions, which have no doctrinal backing and which are the products of a cynical or resigned belief that life cannot be altered by doctrinal theory, and revolutionary behavior, which is quite different, in spite of the apparent similarity of certain external signs. Revolutionary action is based on an ardent, unchangeable set of beliefs, from which it is inseparable, even in a period of pause or revision. For the revolutionary, revision merely means the

1 The NEP see footnote on page 12. (Translator's note)
2 Which is not exactly the same as 'socialism in a single country'.

same end must be achieved by a different means, or that a temporary retreat is necessary in order to mount a more vigorous offensive later. It is rarely a question of a real retreat, but more often of a detour in an oblique direction. Thus, the movement of the Chinese revolution should be compared to a spiral rather than to an alternating linear movement[1]. The way in which Mao 'changes direction', as revealed in the alternation of the Chinese campaigns, seems to have reached its pitch of perfection in his reaction to the 'cultural revolution', especially if it is true, as seems likely, that it took him by surprise. Here we have something resembling what polo players call changing feet at the gallop. Be that as it may, the fact that a campaign for the 'correct use of terminology' has been added to the series of campaigns—begun at Yenan—aimed at ascertaining the 'correct style'[2] is ample proof of Mao's undisputed mastery of the concept of circularity and of his brilliant intuitive grasp of one of the chief problems of our age, namely alienation through language.

Are we to deduce from these examples that the unity of doctrine and action is a specifically Marxist phenomenon and can be applied only to revolutionary situations? I do not think so. Commonsense can be relied upon to provide a reassuring explanation. It is during periods of transition that there is a particular need for political action to be inspired and directed by a concerted plan, so that constant reference may be made to a scale of values, whose scope transcends that of political management alone. It is a world in turmoil which needs to be explained in terms of a far-reaching conception of what is human. What is true for revolution is true for a reform. 'There is no revolution without reformation', as Hegel so rightly said. There is no reason to distinguish here between a reform which brings about real changes and revolution which is essentially reforming in character. The only distinction lies in the choice of means. Now, it is possible to imagine an attempt at reformation which, while trying to adapt the general system of institutions and social organization to great changes in the human condition, such as those we see today, might achieve its ends by other than so-called revolutionary means or by the dictatorship of the proletariat. It can, therefore, safely be said that, in the modern world, no attempt to change the human condition can be made without bringing into play the unity of theory and action, which was expounded, but not invented, by Marx.

[1] Cf. Faure, E. *The Serpent and the Tortoise*, translated by Lovett F. Edwards. New York, Macmillan, 1958. 'Chine 1963', *Revue des Deux Mondes*.
2 He means 'style of work in the Party'. See works quoted above.

7

The inadequacy of the techno-structure

The need for a fundamental world-view.
A diagram of the political implications

The inadequacy of the techno-structure

The search for a philosophical justification for action should not, in my opinion, be confined to extraordinary crises in our history, nor should it be limited to an heroic conception of government. The truth is that we have embarked upon a period of time in which I would say 'crisis is the norm' and which we may suppose will continue to be *permanently extraordinary* for a very long time.

In a static world, or one which seems so because the rate of progress is so slow, in a stagnant economy, where expansion is imperceptible, in a society whose institutions are acceptable, with only minor adaptations, to many succeeding generations, the administration of the state can safely be left to the civil servants. All that is asked of the rulers is competence, integrity, and attention to detail, the qualities of the civil servant in fact. An absence of mistakes is preferred to an abundance of new ideas. When the sea is calm, the automatic pilot system works wonders. But who would believe that this description could apply to the age we live in?

The constant invasion of affairs of state by technical problems is not the only way in which our world differs from ancient empires with their endless periods of inactivity. Technicians are needed to deal with technical problems; but we live in a technical age, and so the necessary technicians are available, and when they leave or fall out of favor, they can be replaced. They are competent to deal with the paper work which accumulates; but that is not enough. It is as though each technological breakthrough gave rise to serious problems far beyond the scope of mere technology.

When experts are called upon to take decisions they are called technocrats. When government is confronted by a never-ending stream of technical problems, it quite naturally sees its task as finding the solutions for just these technical problems and taking the requisite decisions. When politicians behave like technocrats, technocrats behave like politicians, and it becomes difficult to tell them apart, especially as they usually come from the same background, products of a similar education, between whom democratic society raises no barriers of birth, favor, or class, barriers which, even in earlier ages (think how many ministers were chosen from among the ranks of the intendants) were never insurmountable.

The Fifth Republic has greatly encouraged, and this is not necessarily a bad thing, free movement between the professions of technocrat and politician. A prominent civil servant, an accountant, a managing director, especially if, before receiving the electoral blessing, he has been called to a ministerial post or to some para-governmental mission, can easily find a constituency. The electors, rightly impressed by his abilities and his influence, often prefer such a man to a rival, who has risen by a stormy career in local politics, unless, thanks to the marvellous institution of the appointment of proxies, ambition and know-how can be married in a single team, which will be the envy of neighboring constituencies . . . Which, in their turn . . .

If it is difficult to distinguish between the politicians and the technocrats at the 'highest level' of government, it is even more difficult for us, or for the man himself, to separate the qualities belonging to one or the other vocation when they occur in the same man. A governmental structure made up of politicized technocrats and politicians endowed with a solid technical background easily becomes, in the word used by Galbraith to describe big business, a techno-structure. This techno-structure, like others, tends to perpetuate itself, to identify the voting public with the conformist body of shareholders; and, in fact, the reactions of these two sections of society are similar. The techno-structure relies on its own competence to avoid crises and on the public's reluctance to bring down an administration whose merits it cannot dispute. And if a periodic craving for novelty has to be satisfied, that is no problem! The techno-structure can satisfy this desire without having recourse to the turbulent winds of earlier days, winds which certainly brought change in their wake, but devastation too. It is enough if someone leaves, if someone else is brought in, a slight reshuffle is all that is necessary; in other words the endless round of dismissal and reappointment continues.

The need for a fundamental world-view

This new type of society may produce government by competent individuals, but it also presents problems whose solution demands totally different qualities. It is of the essence of technical progress, in so far as it changes the human condition, to pose social questions far beyond the competence of the technical administrator to solve. On the other hand, government by experts, with its built-in and justifiable confidence in the scrupulous accuracy of its dossiers, in the perfect manipulation of files, in its ability to settle disputes according to a set system, carries within it the pernicious seeds of self-satisfaction. A clear conscience has no feeling for the confused stirrings of troubled consciousness around it. It is not enough to solve problems, one must foresee them, and even that can be done by statistics. It is not enough to foresee trouble, one must sense it. Dreaded storms burst forth from a cloudless sky. May 1968 is a warning to us.

A diagram of the political implications

It is for these reasons that I think a political decision, taken at the highest level, should always take into account its own underlying philosophical doctrine. If, as usually happens, the decision was originally inspired by considerations dictated by outside circumstances, the validity of these considerations must constantly be called into question, and their inadequacy must be a constant source of concern. Naturally, the first consideration of a minister called upon to take charge of an important department is for the guiding principles which dominate his own sphere of activity. Thus he can institute or improve a financial policy, a policy for the building industry or for public transport, for education and culture, etc. Such was my own experience. But it must never be forgotten that these policies must be inter-related; they must fit in to a total scheme dictated by a basic and general conception of the whole. To have recourse to a more modern metaphor, we could imagine the application to politics of what the scientists call a *tree* or *diagram* of implications, in which the several branches are in sequence and are coordinated according to the definition at the top of the chosen objective (in the case of politics, the desire to fit in with the overriding world-view).

Each man is indivisible, each society constitutes a whole. Any attempt to split them into constituent parts for the sake of convenience is completely artificial, a mere exercise in abstract thought. The artifice is even more apparent and dangerous when the *unity* of man and the *totality* of the social unit are placed in orbit, as it were, and are swept along their separate paths at ever-increasing speed. Modern man is in motion in a world in motion. In order to grasp the reality of the situation, we must cast both our knowledge and our will towards the future. I am thinking of the hunter who can calculate with great accuracy the position of his target before taking aim, but who has no power to dictate where that target should be. But for us it is different. The opinion we form of contemporary reality immediately becomes one of the elements in this ever-changing reality. When we later look at the world about us, it will be partly what we ourselves have made it.

Perhaps the men and the society of tomorrow will not be what we would wish them to be; but it is our will, or rather our lack of it, or our being weak-willed, which may be responsible for the failure of future generations to realize their optimum potential. If we choose the right path we are never sure of winning, but if we choose the wrong path, there is no doubt as to the outcome, we are sure to lose. In the modern world, an authentically humanist political system is perhaps not a realistic proposition and may not bear fruit. On the other hand, a policy which turns its back on either humanism or the modern world, or on both of them together, will surely graft itself on to reality and bear bitter fruit. However, we do have the satisfaction of knowing that in the modern world, with its spontaneous dissemination of information, ideas in themselves constitute actions and have a real power to influence the course of events.

We can almost go back to the ideas current in 1845 about the interpretation and the transformation of the world. The world was already engaged in an earth-shattering transformation. The most impressive revolution imaginable—the advent of the modern world—was in progress. No further impetus is necessary to unleash its grandiose advance, it can only be a question of guiding it, of 'educating' it in some way. Our most effective course of action is to interpret the march of events. To help the social being to a fuller understanding of what is happening to him is already to govern, in the best sense of the word, for he becomes aware of his true purpose in life and can apply to that end the considerable means placed at his disposal by the very progress which disconcerts him. Instead of having a confused feeling that he is the slave of progress, he will become aware that progress is his slave. Unlike Marx, I do not believe it necessary for philosophy to disappear altogether—and I see no sign of its decline; the opposite is rather the case—for politics to find its own source of inspiration in a basic analysis of the human problem. Modern man does not ask politics to bring about the improvement of his material condition, which can be guaranteed by technology. Basically, what he asks—or should ask—of politics is his justification as a social being, the key to harmonious relationships with other members of the species, with society, with the world of nature. If politics provide the answer to these questions and can assuage the anxiety, which often accompanies or masks them, if even it can only be seen that this is the aim of politics, then politics will cease to appear, as is all too often the case, like a foreign, mysterious, alien phenomenon. The all too prevalent dichotomy between man's civic responsibilities and his ordinary everyday preoccupations will be abolished. If political authority is no longer guaranteed by the priests or supported by religious ritual, and if it no longer seems likely, as was feared at one time, that a scientific oligarchy will usurp the role of the political rulers, this is not to say that political authority should be divorced from all kinds of inspiration, in the non-magical sense of the word. If the central political authority is able to present contemporary man with an image of the man of the following century, if it can be seen that a consistent basic philosophy influences its every action and that all its actions tend towards one overriding objective, the people will be sympathetic to its aims, its task will be made easier and the greatest sacrifices will be accepted. The choices to be made will appear clear-cut; confrontations will cease to appear obscure or pointless; the fights between the so-called political parties will cease to be a mere show cloaked in the rising mists of apathy, in which the opposing camps are alike condemned to an endless, ignominious, irrevocable defeat.

At the very time when each day gives us a greater degree of control over nature, is it not even more necessary to ensure and fully justify the power of man over man, that is to say the political expression of the social being, in each and every one?

One man close to me had understood this and, although an unhappy combination of circumstances coupled, no doubt, with a certain unwillingness to explain his actions have resulted in his ceasing to be understood, at least the way forward has been pointed out and it is up to us to see that the lesson is not lost.

8

Beyond the social contract

This preliminary analysis will lead to a clearer understanding of my intentions in writing this book, in which I have set myself the task of out-doing my earlier efforts to draw up a doctrine for political action.

Before, when I spoke of a 'new social contract', I had made no claim to present it as the basis for a general philosophical outlook on political and economic society in the modern world. For me it was no more than a theme for conjecture, a field for research. This is why I confined my earlier writings to one article and a report, which provided me with material for a second article. This became the focal point for several other short studies on allied themes.

Later, I tried to widen the scope of my political analyses. This was the aim of my book, *Prévoir le présent*[1]. Once again, I based my researches for this book on observations of a society with a growth economy, a 'profit-making' society, which provides the scope and the means for a social contract assuring far more than the absolute necessities of existence, a theme which I developed more fully than previously. However, at the same time I was working on, and undoubtedly was more interested in, a new line of thought: the overriding importance of foreign policy.

For me, these two themes have remained inextricably linked. In a modern society, which has reached a certain degree of technological and economic competence, it becomes possible to draw up plans for a new socialism on the home front, a socialism which I called a 'socialism of shared wealth'. At the same time, it becomes possible in the field of foreign affairs to put into operation a policy for which I thought the 'humanism of a middle power' would be a suitable name. It is true that, in the first place, the prospects for growth in an expanding economy, as illustrated by the spectacular rise in the standard of living over a period of twelve, fifteen, or eighteen years, should normally allow room for the necessary adjustments to reduce the disparities existing between the social classes in our country without there being any need to have recourse to the costly process of revolution. On this very point, the Sakharov report, which took the USA as its example, precisely demonstrated that the total consumer goods bought by the wealthy over a period of five years represent a lower

[1] Faure, E. *Prévoir le présent*. Paris, Gallimard, 1966.

percentage of the gross national product than would be represented by the cost of a five-year period of stagnation, the minimum cost of a social revolution. Then again, the prospect of future prosperity should allow us, for the same reasons, to iron out international problems and social conflicts. At the same time, the very scientific and technological progress, which makes the prosperity possible, also renders the threat of a catastrophic war even more terrifying than before. On this score, the section of the Sakharov report commenting on the 'cheapness' of nuclear war and the limited chances of survival offered by defense technology are but additional proofs of the need for agreement. Pope Paul VI found an admirable phrase to express the way in which economic expansion and foreign policy are interconnected, 'Development is the new name for peace'. No development is possible with the threat of world war hanging over us. Similarly, a lasting peace is unattainable unless possibilities for development are available to all nations.

These were the essential themes of my earlier works. There is nothing which I wish to retract. Perhaps I did overestimate the interest the French people have in foreign affairs and, consequently, I exaggerated the significance of the support they offered to the Gaullist conception of national independence as an active weapon in the service of peace. I will come back to this problem later. The most serious limitation I can see now is that my researches were by no means as exhaustive or as universally valid as I was tempted to believe. There was something lacking. To use, for the sake of convenience, the usual terminology current in political studies, I could now say that having seen the 'economic' and 'international' aspects of the problems I was dealing with, I had neglected the 'cultural' aspect, both in the role it plays in economic life as such and in its own right, i.e. as a universal value encompassing all those human activities which lie outside the sphere of the production cycle. Any theoretical doctrine, whose validity and coherence on these three planes was beyond dispute, could easily, by deduction, be applied to other analogous problems, especially those arising from those so-called internal affairs where the inductive method of reasoning is considered inappropriate.

And so my task was to add a final dimension to the doctrine and, in so doing, to transcend it. Is this to say that the element missing until then was more important than the others? It is difficult to establish a scale of importance. In the search for a solution to a problem, one always believes that the one avenue not yet explored is, for that very reason, the crucial one. I am afraid, too, that the profound impressions made upon me by my period of office, during parlous times, at the Rue de Grenelle caused me to yield to the quite common human temptation of believing my own preoccupations were more important than those of other people. However, I do believe that the dimension which I had called the 'cultural' dimension, to use the most convenient, because the most commonly used, terminology, allows us to get to the heart of the problem. For what is the cultural dimension if it is not the human dimension of the problems dealt with? The issue is a crucial one, for it calls into question the Marxist distinction between the infrastructure and the superstructure. I was very pleased to discover that my views on this last point coincided with those of Maurice Clavel[1].

The pages which follow will attempt to prove the validity of this proposition.

I propose to take as a starting point for this 'three-dimensional' research two widely used and consistently connected concepts: one, the consumer society, and the other, alienation. I have not chosen these two concepts simply to be fashionable or because they offer the most convenient starting point, but because these two concepts, for better or worse, sum up or evoke the essential problems of modern society as I see it. It seems to me, therefore, that this two-pronged study should constitute a necessary preliminary inquiry and perhaps, after all, a satisfactory run-up to the task of tackling, in the light of the new dimension, the relationship between man, the world and society. This is the great question of our days, which I would like, in this work, to study in depth in all its complexity, whereas before, in earlier works, I had only made tentative stabs at it.

[1] Clavel, M. 'Qui est aliené?' in *La Nef, La Société de Consommation*. No. 37. pp. 172 et seq.

Part 2

Alienation

9

The two alienations

A word very much in fashion for some years now, the term alienation possesses the amazing ability to offer shelter to the multiform evils of our age. Its range is so great that, today, the whole of literature, the whole of art must depict alienated life or cease to exist. Alienation is the name given to every kind of mental or spiritual uneasiness, of intellectual unsoundness, of social impotence. It no longer applies solely to violence and thefts perpetrated against colonized peoples, the proletariat, coloreds, or displaced persons. By a process of irresistible contamination it has reached the privileged classes, and has finally become the symbol of the disgust which rich societies feel for themselves.

Can this chameleon-like concept, born of Hegelian-Marxism but with an application far beyond the confines of this doctrine and endowed latterly with a questionable exuberance, still serve any useful purpose? In spite of distortions, and even complete travesties of meaning, I still believe that this word corresponds to an entirely genuine and meaningful concept: the desire to transcend the classical idea of liberty, to enrich it, to confer upon it new standards in line with changes taking place in society and in the world. Hitherto, the idea of liberty has tended to be limited to its purely legal definitions, which are no longer adequate, although millions of men, especially those deprived of civil liberties, still retain or are rediscovering a great interest in them.

By saying a man does not *want* to be or *must* not be alienated (for a man may often accept his alienation or be unaware of it), one is implying that his needs go beyond being permitted by society to change his address, to express his opinions, to vote, or even to earn his living. The modern trend is to see dis-alienation as the right to realize the individual's full potential: in so far as the adjective can be applied to ethics, dis-alienation is *arétique*[1], (from the Greek ἀρετη', rather inaccurately translated in English as virtue, which, when applied to individual character, really means 'the excellence of the complete personality').

[1] *Arétique*. This word means 'essential for moral excellence'. As the only English word derived from the same Greek root is *aretology*, defined by Dr Samuel Johnson as 'that part of moral philosophy which treats of virtue, its nature and the means of attaining it', it was decided to retain the French word *arétique* as this seemed the only way to make the point about its derivation from the Greek ἀρετη' meaningful. (Translator's note)

And so the concept of alienation, which is still considered to have an effective and standard meaning in spite of all its metamorphoses, merits our special attention; I think, therefore, it is imperative to agree upon its usage and meaning. My effort to establish its meaning here, although necessarily brief, should still, for all that, serve a useful purpose.

Usage and meaning of the word alienation

The German word is *Entfremdung*, which means, literally, the fact of *becoming* or of *being* other or estranged. We will note that in this case the term may be applied equally well to an action in the process of being accomplished, for example the fact of alienating oneself, of alienating something (in current French usage, a bill of sale, the transfer of an item of property) or to a state: the fact of having always been alienated or alienated for a long time. This second attribute does not apply in the case of French, for alienation (of an item of property) means the sale of this item at the moment of negotiation, and not the state of an item of property of which one has already disposed (which is the property of someone else). On the other hand, it does apply if we mean the state of metal alienation. Marx, too, points out two possible applications of the word and draws attention to yet another distinction. For the craftsman, the laborer, alienation is an action; he dispossesses himself (through the work contract, through the execution of his work). For those who do not work, on the other hand, alienation is a *state*. (I shall come back to this distinction later when I deal with the alienation of the exploiters.)

The translation of the German *Entfremdung* by the French *aliénation* is possible because of the original meaning of the Latin *alienus*, 'other', 'estranged', a meaning which has consequently been somewhat distorted. The French words *aliéné*, *aliénation*, are usually employed in two precise 'applied' fields of meaning: madness and the sale of property. With a wider but less common application they are used to express the idea of distancing, separation, usually when talking of the affections and feelings.

Literally, one of the accepted meanings of *alienatio* 'the transferring of oneself' can doubtless be applied to the 'fact of becoming estranged from oneself', but really this is a new concept, a product of Hegelian philosophy and of Marxism.

The subject is somewhat complicated by the existence of a second German word, *Entaüsserung*, whose meaning is almost identical to that of *Entfremdung* but seemingly with a suggestion of dispossession. Marx however uses the two words indiscriminately. Hyppolite and Raymond Aron translate *Entaüsserung* by *extraination*[1]. However, neither *Entfremdung* nor *Entaüsserung* correspond to the French meaning of alienation: i.e. disposal of, which is translated as *Veraüsserung*.

[1] *Extraination—renunciation.* (Translator's note)

50

Be that as it may, the word *alienation* is now well established. Besides, it is easy to discern the connection between its recent meaning and earlier more common meanings.

If the madman is, in fact, said to be alienated, it is because he has ceased to 'belong to himself'. He is, according to the primitive interpretation, 'possessed'. Surely this is the original prototype of our alienations: the alienation of sin in which evil power of the other holds sway over a man, ('If then I do that which I would not', writes St Paul[1], 'it is no more I that do it, but sin that dwelleth in me'), and which causes the permanent fragmentation and dislocation of the primitive, happy world.

On the other hand, if the word alienation in the sense of the disposal of property is usually applied to the sale of objects, the property can, in a society where slavery is tolerated, be men. It is even possible[2] for a free man to sell himself as a slave. He thus alienates himself, rendering his position similar to that of Marx's alienated proletariat, though the latter were not, legally speaking, slaves.

And so it is dispossession, in a legal, philosophical and psycho-pathological sense, which provides the unifying idea behind the many-faceted concept of alienation and which forms the basis for its usage. Colloquial usage readily confirms this. Take, for example, the expression, 'I can't call my soul my own' (too much work, too many worries) or 'I want to live my own life' (indicating that up to then the speaker was living a life that was not of his own choosing. In such cases, one is dealing with a sort of alienation of the whole life).

But these are extreme examples of the dispossession of the complete personality. It is possible to imagine situations in which this phenomenon would only be partially produced. This is the meaning most commonly understood in colloquial speech, and one can, therefore, understand that alienation is spoken of when it is a question of limitation, constraint, a failure to realize full potential. This is why this protean concept tends to be applied to all the negative situations of existence, to become inflated with all human deprivations, to become, as one says in ecclesiastical language, 'pneumatic'.

Since I am a politician and not a philosopher, I am naturally interested in political, social, and economic concepts, and have no desire to venture into the world of philosophy. However, these incursions cannot be avoided. For the political and socio-economic illustrations of alienation are closely, sometimes inextricably, linked to its ontological categories

[1] *Romans*, Chapter 6, V. 17–18. (Translator's note)
[2] The sale of oneself as a slave was, moreover, forbidden in Roman Law, which proves the practice did exist. There is evidence that, in later years, a similar procedure, *commendatio*, became perfectly legal and, at certain times, was quite commonly practiced. Under this procedure free men would place themselves entirely at the disposition of masters, chosen as such, in return for their material upkeep.

and in the works of the different authors they go hand in hand, sometimes with no distinction made between them.

Both my own reading and my readers, especially the more militant ones, forbid me to separate this topic from its philosophical basis. For the self-styled Left-wing revolutionaries, although well versed in Marxism and post-Marxism, are usually extremely ill-informed about the economic aspects of the doctrine, while their knowledge of the facts and the influence of other Marxist-inspired systems throughout the world is equally scanty. They have rarely read *Capital,* and even if they have, they have limited themselves to a purely philosophical viewpoint, as indeed they are invited to do so by the austere, esoteric 'reading', detached from all economic considerations and political applications, which L. Althusser recommends to them.

Besides, it is well known that at the point of origin of the May disturbances and behind the crisis, which is not yet over, one could detect a certain disproportion between the philosophical and sociological culture of a certain number of young students and intellectuals. Their complete lack of scientific or economic culture was equally apparent.

This point had to be made, just when my own study is going to lead me to try to distinguish between philosophical abstraction and concrete analysis, although I shall not play down their close connection in any way. Let me state from the outset that the concept of alienation contains two distinct and even contradictory ideas. In fact it would be better if the same word were not used for them both. The alienation which I have described as philosophical alienation would be better named objectification (*Vergegenständlichung*) which, in Hegelian language, is used to describe the same phenomenon with a very subtle shade of meaning. Objectification-alienation is a movement: an element in a process which leads to a positive, progressive result. It is a 'good alienation'. The other, on the contrary, reveals itself by the destruction, or at least a lasting restriction of the personality—which can only be reversed by a collective effort over a period of many years. It is a retrogressive alienation, a 'bad alienation'.

10

Objectification-alienation:
the debate between Hegel and Marx

Hegel gives a comprehensive, one could almost say intransigent, description of alienation. An ubiquitous alienation—in time and space, in action and thought, in the individual and the collective—pervades his whole system of thought of which only the principal features can be enumerated here.

Alienation arises as soon as there is awareness of an object. As soon as self-consciousness, identified in this case with abstract thought, becomes aware of an object, i.e. in the author's terminology *posits* an object, immediately there occurs dispossession and alienation of the consciousness which, projected out of itself in some way, becomes incorporated in that object. The object (posited by consciousness) is nothing other than consciousness (itself). It is objectified consciousness. To regain its own identity, consciousness must therefore *suppress* and *transcend* the object: this double idea of *suppression* and *transcendence* is contained in the German words: *aufheben, aufgehoben.* Here we touch upon in a precise, if not concrete, form the idea of *negation of negation.* The object was a denial of, an invalidation of, the existence of the consciousness, since the latter disappeared as a separate entity when it considered the object. From the moment when the object itself is abolished in its turn or, if you prefer, transcended, consciousness returns to itself and ceases to be alienated. According to Hegel, *objectivity* (conception of objects) is therefore an alienated relationship of man, for this relationship is not controlled by the essence of man. This is an indication of the extent of alienation. It is also an indication of its intensity.

Since Hegel sees an objectification, and therefore an alienation, in the very fact of thinking about an object, we must expect, with even more reason, to see the same process at work when it is no longer a question of thinking about an object but of *creating* one. And, no less naturally, the way passing via objectification and alienation leads to counter-alienation and transcendence. But, although the assertion that the very fact of apprehending the outside world is a source of alienation of consciousness may seem disconcerting, it is, on the other hand, difficult to resist the contagious assurance of the Hegelian system when its author abandons the realm of pure abstraction to consider the real world of man's activity, the world in which he works. Let us forget for the moment the variations in Hegel's use of the term and the customary confusion in the usage of the term work: work as an activity in a general sense, work as the production of commodities, work as the production of ideas and institutions and, finally, the general and historical concept of the work of the 'mind' which is, according to Marx, the Hegelian model of all work: 'The only work which Hegel knows and recognizes is the work of the mind'.

In spite of these difficulties, the process of alienation in the object, then of the transcendence of this object, becomes absolutely clear in the case where the object is not merely posited by consciousness, but positively created by the activity of man. In this case, in fact, the creation of the object by a man's work is in itself alienating, but by creating the object man affirms his own power over the world of objects and thus creates himself. Work is creative; not only of commodities, but of the personality. For it humanizes nature, and through work nature, until then hostile and mute, appears as a production: a human thing and no longer a mere object; capable of presenting man with a mirror in which he recognizes and comprehends his own being. It is therefore through work that man creates and perpetuates himself. This is the idea which will be expressed in a much simpler and more familiar way by the French philosopher who was to propose the catchphrase: 'Create and in creating, create yourself'.

Nevertheless, it falls to Hegel to provide the striking illustration of alienating-dis-alienating work in the dramatic analysis of the relationships which unite the master and slave. Master and slave are, as we know, brothers in desire, but, whereas the master possesses the things he desires and at the same time denies them to others (for enjoyment and negation amount to the same thing), the slave, who also desires these things but does not possess them, cannot succeed in destroying them. He can only work to fashion these objects. Work is, therefore, postponed and suppressed enjoyment. But in the hard fact of the slave's forced labor there lies the promise of a reversal of the relationships between master and slave: for the master, who can only enjoy objects produced by the slave, becomes dependent upon the producer: slave of the slave; while, on the other hand, the slave who dictates to his master, becomes the master of the master. Thus, paradoxically, the work of a slave leads to the final realization of the wishes of the slave, sometimes without his even being aware of it. Work, originally a means of escape from helplessness, becomes a means of escape from bondage. So that, although forced labor seemed to give the slave nothing more than the feeling of estrangement from the self, its end result is to cause the (servile) consciousness to rediscover its own identity.

This picture presents two essential themes which Marx was not to forget. Firstly, man cannot prove his quality as a super-natural being (in other words, his humanity) except by creating an artificial object; this is why it is the prerogative of the servile consciousness to incarnate the ideal self-consciousness. Secondly, work alone is capable of giving human existence its universality: for the master, who does not work, and whose role is limited to that of a consumer of the products another has produced, is condemned to a satisfaction which concerns no one but himself and, unlike the slave, could not be the object of another's gratitude.

The prominence given to the description of alienation-dis-alienation in the *Phenomenology of mind* must not, however, cause us to forget that this theme is overtaken, orchestrated, transcended, and idealized in a more grandiose vision: that of the alienation of the mind in the process of historical totalization. Indeed, we know that the whole course of history and the life of humanity are fused in the *absolutization of the mind*. While this process remains unfinished, while the mind is not absolute, it is the mind which is alienated by the varied creations of human knowledge (human essence being conceived of as knowledge), for example institutions, morality, laws, as well as the affluence produced by an economic system[1].

Marx rigorously simplified and stylized this abundant system where alienations are made and unmade in a never-ending succession of impulses. Of all the Hegelian themes the one which struck Marx most of all and which seemed to him to provide the answer to the riddle of the historic future of man was that the history of man does not belong to natural history; the production of the self by the self is not a fact of nature; it is work which provides the means for the perpetuation of man by himself. Marx is an enthusiastic and faithful disciple of Hegel on this point. He wrote: 'The greatness of Hegel's *Phenomenology* and of its final conclusions lies . . . in the fact that Hegel . . . seizes the essence of work and conceives of objective man, true because real, as the result of his own work'.

He is so enthusiastic that the monopolization of the vital force—work—by a machinery of objects—capital—will appear to him, not as one alienation among others, but as the prototypal alienation, without which the alienations of the mind and the emotions would not even exist: profane or sacred, the imaginary worlds of philosophy and religion are superimposed on reality like a mask or a coat of make-up, and yet they are born of reality: they are the ghostly creations ready to collapse like a house of cards on the day when man's labor is capable of attaining freedom.

[1] The institutions founded by man and the culture he creates engender laws which are peculiar to them and with which human freedom must comply; man is therefore transcended by the increasing wealth of his economic, social, and political milieu. Finally, he forgets that he himself and the realization of his full potential is the end to which his whole activity tends and he sacrifices himself to the social machine. Men are always at pains to perpetuate an established culture, thus perpetuating their own frustration. The history of humanity is therefore the history of the alienation of man's true interests, and, at the same time, the history of their realization. That man's true interest should be hidden in and by his social background is, for Hegel, an example of the *cunning of reason* and one of those negative elements without which there can be no progress towards a superior form of life. (Hegel, *The philosophy of history*, translated by J. Sibree, New York, Wiley Book Co., 1944. p. 74; Marcuse's commentary, *Reason and revolution*. London, Routledge and Kegan Paul, 1955. p. 28.)

This is the crucial point where Hegel and Marx differ on the subject of alienation; but, at the same time, it provides the key to the ideas they hold in common.

In Hegel's mystical system, work is *always* an alienation followed by a transcendence, and no attention is ever paid to the historical conditions. Better still: it is when man is alienated (in the social sense in which Marx understood it) that work appears as essentially liberating and *dis-alienating*; a paradox which is striking in the Master and Slave dialectic. Without a shadow of a doubt, the slave is essentially alienated as much in the social and legal sense as in the philosophical sense. Being the property of another, he cannot belong to himself. But it is the slave's work which dis-alienates him: it is by working that he achieves, in the language we are already familiar with, 'the first transcendence of alienated objectivity'.

Marx's analysis is quite different. For him work, in itself, cannot be held to be alienating; the objectification of which it is an example is not necessarily an alienation; it could even be a source of happiness; if this is not the case, it is because of the circumstances which deprive the worker of the commodities he produces and, at the same time, make his very labor a commodity. Let us go even further: objectification is nothing more than a mode of expression natural to every individual, and the individual can attain his autonomy only through his relationship with objects and other people. How can we refuse to see Marx as a disciple of Hegel after this? It is enough to think of that cultural object, language, which is always received from other people and yet without it no process of individualization is possible. The same could be said of the family, the geographical or technical environment. Marx asserts firmly, in opposition to Hegelian idealism, that the being who would deny and alienate himself by conceiving of an object could not exist. For him this is the definition of an impossible problem. 'A being who would never come into contact with real objects . . . is a non-objective being, i.e. a non-being', nothing at all.

Our two authors' fundamental disagreement in diagnosis leads them to recommend completely different courses of treatment for alienation. Hegel never makes alienation a symptom; for him it is a reality to be integrated and transcended. For Marx, on the other hand, alienation is never a reality, but the symptom of another reality, which it both reveals and hides at the same time. This is why Marx's only concern is to unravel alienation (to see the hidden faces of the cards) in order to suppress it more easily. To overcome human alienation cannot simply be a question of thinking about it. This would be to attribute too much importance to abstract ideas, and Marx knows full well that 'mere ideas can never provide an escape from the old state of affairs; they can only lead to a different way of thinking about the old state of ideas'[1].

Of course, Hegel has no difficulty in dispensing with the object; but only

[1] *The Holy Family*. Moscow, Foreign Languages Publishing House, 1956. p. 160.

56

by substituting, from the outset, the idea of the object for the object. This sleight of hand leaves hard reality intact, and this is the aspect of Hegelian philosophy which Marx sees as a great exercise in mystification: to believe that language is redemptive, that knowledge alone dis-alienates, that it is enough—since concept and history coincide from beginning to end—for the mind to retrace the steps which it is reputed to have already taken. Thus, Hegel never escapes from the repetitive justification of what is, or was. Far from being dis-alienating, his philosophy creates one more mythology, adds a speculative heaven to the religious heaven, and makes even more difficult the unravelling of alienation. Man must not entrust his hopes of a non-alienated life to knowledge but to praxis, i.e. to the attempt to change the world, not in name only, but in a real and concrete way.

The tragedy of alienation, which is the seed-bed of both these systems of thought, does not have the same meaning for the two philosophers, nor does it lead to the same result. Hegelian alienation, inextricably bound up with the negative process of all objectification is, even in a crisis of consciousness, a step forward, a source of progress, a 'good' alienation. Marxist alienation is much more stark and brutal: it is the result of a theft: an impoverishment much more than an enrichment. But, from another point of view, Hegelian alienation presents an insurmountable obstacle: absolute knowledge itself still contains within itself the contradictory trends of the moments it has transcended and the tension of alienation. Marxist alienation, on the other hand, is only a historical event, which can be overcome and destroyed by another historical event. The promise of a better future thus compensates for the harshness of the Marxist analysis.

11

Hegelian–Marxist humanism

'Man is the only being whose aspirations transcend that which he has been, is, will be, or becomes.'

P. Fougeyrollas

When one's feet remain planted firmly in the real world and one is searching for a political interpretation of contemporary society, the doctrinal antagonism existing between Hegel and Marx, though of considerable importance for the drawing up of ideologies and philosophical systems, seems a secondary consideration and has no value except as an interesting intellectual exercise. From the point of view of a political analysis, the differences between them are indeed less marked, and one is struck by the degree of agreement between these two systems of thought on the essential characteristics of what must be described as a common humanism.

These characteristics can be summarized as follows.

(a) Man must always be considered as a constituent part of the human race in its entirety. *Man is a generic being*[1]. No man can be detached from the species, and, consequently, there can be no division of the species into two (or several) categories of men, some of whom would be superior, and others inferior, beings. Hegelianism and Marxism are both hostile to any *élitist* or *segregative* concept of humanity. On this point, the two doctrines share common ground with both true Christian humanism (which had been long ignored during the preceding centuries), and with the true meaning of democracy (which had just emerged in the course of the French Revolution, but which was still a rather confused concept at the very time when the industrial revolution would expose it to new trials).

(b) This identification of man (unit) with the species (totality) is not simply put forward as a hypothesis, it is rigorously backed up by the picture of man, as a producer-laborer and creator, thereby distinguishing himself from all the other animal species, while at the same time identifying himself with all the other members of the human race.

This idea was already to be found in Feuerbach: 'Man is not a particular being like other animals, but an universal being'. This idea is greatly

---

[1] This idea is expressed in German by one particular word: *Gattungsmensch* (generic man).

58

embroidered upon (albeit rather obscurely) by Hegel and amplified by Marx: '*By the practical production of an objective world*—the elaboration of non-organic nature—*man proves he is a generic being*'.

(c) The following step, however, is even more decisive. Man is not only a producer (of commodities and objects) but of himself. He is not only a creator but a *self-creator*. 'Through work (being) attains its own identity' (Hegel). Marx emphasizes that Hegel 'seizes the very essence of work and conceives of objective man, true because real, as the result of his own work', whence the crucial phrases: 'The perpetuation of man by his own work' and 'Man produces man'.

The vital importance of such a process is obvious. To proclaim that all men are equal, that human dignity must be respected, even in the most insignificant individual, such statements appeal to noble-minded persons, but have no demonstrative value. To say that man differs from the animals by his creative ability, that is a first step. To emphasize that man is his own creator, a manufacturer of the human, that is the decisive, indisputable factor, which makes of each member of the species, of each individual, the co-author—and as such worthy of respect—of the sum total of the collective achievements. This brings us to the fourth point.

(d) The humanist interpretation of history. The sum of all men together produces the sum of what is human. The entire species is responsible and must be honored for its progress and achievements.

History is made by all men and not by a few isolated members of the species. It is the masses, not individuals who make history.

Such an interpretation is not necessarily the prerogative of the Marxists. It just so happens that contemporary non-Marxist philosophers of history almost all rather curiously adopted an aristocratic and élitist interpretation of history, which seriously detracted from the best elements of their work and made their followers suspect. This is true, not only in the case of Spengler, whose work is marked by racist overtones and somewhat devalued by the later exploitation of this particular aspect of his work (although we must be fair and point out that this aspect by no means represents the whole of his work[1]), but even more so in the case of A. Toynbee, apostle of the Anglo-Scandinavian type of democracy. However, Toynbee's philosophy of history contains a few elements taken from Hegel and Marx. Like Marx, he believes that the birth of civilization dates from the separation of the classes; he hopes for the union of *homo sapiens* and *homo faber* in *homo concors*; he also desires that all work, in so far as it is creative activity, should be considered of equal value and that physical and mental work should go hand in hand. However, he refuses to see man's progressive taming of nature as the motive force of history. He disputes the role of the masses in history, for he sees them as inert and non-creative.

[1] He has been seen as the spiritual son of Goethe but also as the father of Hitler, which is a rather surprising lineage.

Placing a great deal of emphasis on the decisive importance of territorial expansion and of manifestations of militarism (without paying sufficient attention to their underlying economic causes) he believes that only certain exceptional individuals, or possibly governing minorities, have the right to shape society.

Many are the 'bourgeois' historians and sociologists of lesser renown, who are motivated by similar prejudices. They are convinced of the validity of a cyclic theory, inspired by the belief that everything returns from whence it came—a belief dear to the ancients—and of the pessimism perfectly expressed in Paul Valéry's famous reflection on the transience of civilizations. But this point of view, which has in any case been justifiably disputed by P. Sorokin[1], has not been demonstrated historically, and, more important still, there is nothing to indicate that modern civilization, which has mastered nature on a global scale to an extent never achieved before, bears within itself the same signs of imminent collapse as did former civilizations.

I will continue this investigation no further. All I would like to do is to emphasize that the analysis of objectification-alienation, which seems to bring Hegel and Marx into conflict, really unites them as far as their essential conclusions are concerned, i.e. the formation of man by work, the perpetuation of man by man, the humanist and optimistic philosophy of the progress of history and of the collective advancement of humanity.

Far from becoming less relevant and forceful, these ideas, based on the concept of objectification-alienation, are given even more edge by the most recent researches and are relevant to our modern-day preoccupations. Thus, the idea of generic man strikes a chord in the revolutionary young, and on this point, even if we refused to accept the young people's conclusions, how could we fail to understand them?

How can one fail to be impressed and worried by this remark made by the famous Rudi Duschke:

> Those of us who have understood what the world has to offer, who have glimpsed the undreamed of possibilities for self-fulfilment, those of us who have seen the global victories that are within our grasp, we are the ones who have had a startling vision: a totally new world is hidden from us, refused us. This is why the individual must commit the act of total opposition, *not as a representative of any one class, but as a representative of the species*, against a scepticism which threatens to annihilate the species[2].

Thus, even modern political science provides a surprising justification for what might appear as a purely abstract concept, the concept of self-

[1] Sorokin, P. *Social and cultural dynamics.* London, George Allen and Unwin, 1937; *The crisis of our age.* London, Angus and Robertson, 1942.

[2] See Marcuse, *Five lectures,* p. 82. (Duschke's quote is not given in full in the English edition but just summarized briefly. (Translator's note))

creative man, and for the social mechanisms described in the *Phenomenology of mind* and the *Economic and philosophical manuscripts* of 1844. Works dealing with child psychology, psycho-analysis (such as those of Melanie Klein and Chasseguet-Sorgel) as well as those dealing with the theory of literature (especially those of Michel de M'huzen, E. Kris, L. Kubie) all illustrate, in different ways, man's ability to grasp the objective world while at the same time pondering upon the knowledge he thus gains, and so give Hegelian 'objectification' a hitherto unsuspected, and henceforth indisputable, relevance.

The triple affirmation of man as a generic being, an indomitable unit in a unified whole—a producer—creator—capable of mastering nature through his own work—finally, his own creator, the indefatigable agent of individual and collective progress, these concepts incline us, almost force us to adopt an optimistic view of history; they promote a heady confidence in the present-future by whose quickening movement we are borne along. Never such an interpretation, such optimism, such confidence have seemed, at one and the same time, more necessary, more probable or more threatened. It is a constant source of wonder that two systems of thought, each more than an hundred years old, should, by some inexplicable foresight, be so completely geared to the problems and anxieties of modern society. It is obviously the lot of our age, an age of mass production and consumption, to provide for the spectacular improvement of the position of each member *of* the mass *within* the mass, without interrupting the continuous march of history and without compromising, in the most precise meaning of the word, the solidarity (*solidum*) of the species as a whole.

And so the theories described in this part of my study cannot be seen as mere accidents of inspired thinking, as brilliant, but now outmoded developments in philosophical analysis. They take on substance and reality, warmth, and color. They provide the key to the present success of philosophical systems which one might have thought were now outmoded and which in some respects have been proved wrong. This is where Marxism reveals itself as a humanism, a point which Marx himself had deliberately emphasized, although the most recent commentators on his work take exception, in his name, to his own philosophy[1]. This is the aspect which has

---

[1] Marx himself used the expression, humanism: 'Real humanism'. 'We see here that consequent naturalism or humanism is different from both humanism and materialism and yet at the same time it is the element of truth which unites them'. *Economic and philosophical manuscripts*. Moscow, Foreign Languages Publishing House, 1959. p. 156. Cf. Marcuse, H. *Reason and revolution*. pp. 114–115.

L. Althusser believes that this humanism is to be found only in the early works and that Marx's thought developed in a completely different direction later; but this question, which I do not claim to settle here, makes no difference as far as I am concerned. Cf. L. Althusser, *For Marx*, translated by Ben Brewster, Allen Lane, The Penguin Press, 1969. For the opposite view see Sève, L. *Marxisme et la théorie de la personnalité*. Paris, Éditions sociales, 1969.

In fact, even if one assumed that L. Althusser was right on all counts, it would still be

allowed Marxism to retain, or more precisely to obtain, the power to attract followers which it would be stupid to underestimate and shameful to disdain. Our embarrassment at welcoming Marx's great contribution to this difficult problem should be minimized by the fact that it is difficult to isolate Marxist thought—thanks to the contradictions which merely serve to unite them—from that of Hegel or even that of Feuerbach, all three systems being drawn from a common background whose origins are distant and whose ramifications are many.

All thought about man belongs to man.

---

true that Marx's early works, which have recently come to prominence, thanks to the work of some brilliant commentators, have had at least as great if not greater influence on the young than the ideas contained in *Capital*, which is much more difficult to read and where whole sections, which are no longer relevant, tend to dampen the enthusiasm. Besides, the importance so rightly attributed by L. Althusser to the production-relations (an essential element in all later Marxist doctrine, especially 'the Stalinist creed') is by no means incompatible with the concept, found in the early works, of man the creator, the self-creator, a concept borrowed by Marx from Hegel. The very striking formula according to which man's higher activity fashions him as his own capital appears in the *Grundrisse* and not in the *Manuscripts* or the *German ideology*. It matters little, in this respect, that reference is made in the passage under consideration to an activity which takes place during the time not allotted to the production process. Finally, it seems to me that L. Althusser's assertion that in *Capital* Marx disclaims an earler 'anthropological' conception does not take into account the idea (which is one of the weakest points in the Marxist doctrine) that only the labor of men can produce a surplus-value, whereas the use of the most advanced machines would never produce anything over the equivalent of their cost. R. Luxembourg tried to explain away this anomaly by her conception of a tacit association between all the capitalist firms, but the abstract and somewhat symbolic nature of this explanation smacks of idealism.

All the same, whatever the problems of interpretation presented by Marxism in its various stages of development, it seems clear to me that the success of Marxism is due, basically, to the combination of a high conception of man's capabilities (humanism) with an attempt to apply rigorous scientific analysis to social problems, and, finally, to the close liaison established between the economic and social factors. This problem as a whole is comprehensively treated by Raymond Aron in *D'une Sainte Famille à l'autre*, Paris, Gallimard, 1969.

12

The concrete description of alienation in Hegel and Marx
Limitation–alienation

The second type of alienation (limitation) presents a striking contrast with the one we have just studied (objectification). Instead of being positive and stimulating, it is negative[1], enervating and frustrating. Instead of implying a relatively difficult attempt at abstraction, whose validity might always be challenged, it is supported by reasoned argument and is based on contemporary, everyday reality.

For Hegel, as for Marx, the worker's alienation is total in the widely accepted, popular meaning of the word: no longer belonging to oneself. This is the net result of a number of imposed circumstances:

(a) work is obligatory. The worker is not free to refuse to do the work demanded of him, nor may he change his work if what he does is distasteful to him. He cannot impose conditions;

(b) pay is wretched; the worker receives just enough to prevent death from starvation (if that!);

(c) work takes up the lion's share of the worker's time; in fact he is allowed no more than the minimum free time absolutely necessary to prevent death from exhaustion;

[1] Objectification-alienation, as I have just indicated, is a *movement*. This movement sets in motion the process which is immediately followed by transcendence. Limitation-alienation, on the other hand, is a *state*. The madman, the maniac, the slave and, in so far as he may be likened to them, the proletarian are set in their stations in life and may remain there indefinitely. Their alienation is not movement, but a period of waiting for the one movement which will extricate them from their situation, either individually or, better still, collectively: i.e. revolutionary action, which will dis-alienate the proletariat. The result is that, in the terminology of the dialectic, the first alienation is a *negation*, which is not true of the second. As far as this second alienation is concerned, it is the liberating, dis-alienating movement (in the theory of revolution) which will be *negation*. The negation of the negation will itself be the attainment of a new state of freedom. L. Soubise has an excellent description of this 'overlapping': 'Alienation is positive, praxis negative; dis-alienation is negation of the negation' (*Op. cit.* p. 20). Here the words are understood in a sense directly contrary to common usage, since objectification-alienation, which is a source of progress, is a negation, while limitation-alienation, which is an unhappy state, is not negation, but position. Thus, the good alienation in this case is negative, while the bad alienation is positive. Let us not forget that, generally speaking, in the logic of the dialectic it is negation which is the element of progress.

(d) because of the division of labor, work is totally devoid of interest, purely mechanical and repetitive; it allows no scope for the exercise of intellectual or mental faculties;

(e) as for the time spent not working, this can only be spent in purely animal occupations (eating, sleeping, and begetting), the reasons being the shortage of free time available, the fact that the worker is stupefied by his day's work and, finally, the dearth of resources at the worker's disposal which would allow him to make his life slightly more comfortable, or to acquire culture;

(f) Let us add that the worker has no chance of escaping from his condition, which can but deteriorate.

It is perfectly understandable that in these conditions a human being finds himself downgraded to the level of an animal; alienation is dehumanization. It must be said that more than adequate justification for this pessimistic view can be found in the wretched condition of the working class during the first stages of the development of an industrial society. This wretchedness was especially apparent in England (Engel's first field of study), but it existed in other countries too, notably Germany. We know that during the early years devoted to journalism, Karl Marx was particularly affected by the Silesian weavers' revolt: five thousand wretched people, whose wages had been reduced to a few worthless coins and whose uprising was brutally suppressed.

Hegel, and later Marx, taking a concrete situation as a starting point were sure to give it a philosophical interpretation, which is as follows:

The man who sells all his labor, all his activity, without keeping any part of them for his own use, sells far more than these objective things. He sells his very capacity for work, which has no existence beyond the sum of effective work which it accomplishes.

. . . The use made of my abilities is indistinguishable from my abilities themselves, and therefore from me, unless it is quantitatively limited. The sum total of the visible manifestations of ability is that ability itself, just as the sum total of accidents is the substance, and the sum total of particularities the universal.

Similarly, the man who sells his time is really selling his life, the proportion of life sold depending on the length of time sold. These two arguments are linked; they represent two sides of the same problem. The man sells both his work and his time, and, in so doing, his ability to work and his very life.

I can relinquish to others an isolated commodity created by my physical and mental capabilities and faculties or even the use of my capabilities for a limited time, because the limitation put upon them makes them exterior to my whole, universal being.

On the contrary)

By the externalization (the sale) of all my tangible time (made tangible by work) and of every commodity I produce, their substantial reality, that is to say my own activity and 'total' universal reality, my personality itself becomes the property of another.

We owe the basic analysis to Hegel, but Marx was responsible for coining the striking phrase, *one man during an hour* (one man's hour)[1].

I feel my study cannot continue any further without an analysis of the principal stages in Hegel and Marx's thinking on the subject of limitation-alienation.

In Hegel

(a) The concept would seem to appear for the first time in a rather imprecise form in the *Theologische Jugendschriften*.

In this instance, he is dealing with property to which he already displays the hostility which we will find systematized in Marx. According to Hegel, property presents the disadvantage of linking the living to the inanimate, to 'dead things', of creating a world alien to human life, a 'dead world', and he provides a really curious example of what he means taken from the situation of two people in love.

The lover who sees his beloved as the owner of property must feel this particularity as a serious obstacle to the sense of community he seeks to create between their two lives; for this particularity binds the one partner to *dead things*, which do not belong to the other, and, as such, remain necessarily outside their union.

How can one love a woman who owns property? (a mischievous spirit whispers in my ear that the holding of goods in common is part of the institution of marriage).

(b) In the so-called Jena works (manuscripts of a series of philosophy lectures, delivered between 1802 and 1806 and therefore much earlier than the *Philosophy of right* [1821] although published much later), we find the theme of the division of labor (owing to mechanization) reasserting itself with particular vigor. Its corollary, the wretched (moral and material) condition of the worker is indicated.

'The more mechanized labor becomes, the less value it has, and the more the individual must toil.' 'The value of labor decreases in the same proportion as the productivity of labor increases.'

At the same time, work becomes more boring: 'the worker's initiative is reduced to its lowest level'.

[1] Cf. *The poverty of philosophy*. London, Martin Lawrence, 1936. p. 47.

These two circumstances, the drop in the value of work (for which remuneration is therefore minimal) and the tedious nature of the work lead to stupefaction—the word is used deliberately. 'The worker's consciousness is degraded to the last stage of stupefaction.'

The process described earlier with regard to the objectification of creative work is now totally reversed. The greater the degree of control the worker has over nature, the greater his own self-degradation. *Work is therefore transformed from being the self-realization of the individual into his self-negation.* This leads to a real dehumanization, a bestialization of man, both the exploited and the exploiters being alike reduced to the level of animals within the universal system of exchange relationships: 'a vast system of communality and mutual interdependence', 'a moving life of the dead, moving of its own accord in a blind and elementary way, and like a wild animal calling for the firm hand of the master'.

These are the terms H. Marcuse uses to comment on this passage.

The tone and pathos of the descriptions point strikingly to Marx's *Capital*. It is not surprising to note that Hegel's manuscript breaks off with this picture, as if he was terrified by what his analysis of the commodity-producing society disclosed[1].

(c) Finally, as one might suppose, it is in the *Philosophy of right* that the most coherent analyses of the subject will be found, even though they are classed under various headings and treated in different ways.

(i) First, the author devotes a special chapter to alienation in its current, legal meaning, and this leads him to discuss inalienability, inalienable commodities, as would any legal handbook[2].

Then the inalienability of the person is put forward, and this is followed by the enumeration of the cases and the forms in which the alienation of the personality and its substantial being might be found, whether this alienation is produced unconsciously or deliberately. Examples of the alienation of the personality are: slavery, tangible property, the inability to be a property owner or to dispose freely of one's property. Then there is the alienation of the ability to act rationally and intelligently, the alienation of subjective or objective morality, of religion as manifested in superstition. Alienation is present, too, in the authority and the executive powers which I grant to others to determine and prescribe the actions I must perform. A deliberate decision to steal, to murder, or to commit some other crime, the duty imposed by conscience, religious truth, etc., these are all examples of the alienation of the personality.

This list is just an indication of some of the possibilities and is by no means exhaustive. We can, therefore, conclude from it that there exist

---

[1] However, Marcuse believes the last sentence is an appeal for the intervention of a strong powerful state, the first hint of a theme to be developed later. Marcuse, *Reason and revolution.* p. 79.

[2] As mentioned earlier, the German word used is not *Entfremdung* but *Veraüsserung*.

several types of alienation of the personality, that the extent of their duration can vary and, even, that they involve varying degrees of intensity, if for no other reason than that several alienations can occur together, the resulting situation usually being more burdensome for the individual than any one of the alienations on its own would be. It could also be assumed that the alienation resulting from slavery involves a more effective wearing down of the personality than that caused by superstition alone. . . . However, the author declines to pursue the matter, further having little incentive to do so, since his use of two different words[1] removed the necessity for defining the unifying factor behind the two concepts.

(ii) In an earlier part of the work (para 67) the author establishes that the relinquishing to another of the total ability to work and the quasi-totality of time is equivalent to the alienation (sale) of the personality itself (a point I made earlier).

(iii) When he touches upon the economic problem, Hegel insists, as he had done in the Jena manuscripts, on the division and mechanization of labor. Through the division of labor, the *work of the individual* becomes simpler; his *aptitude increases* correspondingly and, as a result, *the volume of commodities produced* is also increased.

From this point on, the process becomes irreversible and, finally, it is possible for the machine to replace man: *that the man is made redundant and is replaced by the machine* (para 198).

He returns to the subject in another paragraph, this time distinguishing between the positive and negative aspects.

On the one hand the *positive* aspect: progress, *a continuous, internal progress within population and industry* and the increased accumulation of wealth mainly as a result of *technological advances*.

Then the *negative* aspect: the consequences of the division and the limitation of labor are: the (growing) *dependence* and *misery* of the class *unable to escape from this work* (the industrial proletariat, Marx's laborers, are recognizable here, although the precise term is not used) coupled with the inability to experience enjoyment of other amenities, in particular the *spiritual advantages offered by society*, in short, what we would now call *cultural alienation* (para. 243).

(iv) Finally, the concrete description of alienation, of which a general outline had been given in para. 67, appears in the analysis (see para. 198) of the position of the poor, whose emergence as a class is a result of the growing disparity between incomes (para. 200).

The definition of the poor reveals that they have been

deprived of their natural resources, cut adrift from family ties (the family being seen as a clan), and that they are denied all social advantages:

---

[1] As mentioned earlier, the German word used here is not *Entfremdung* but *Veraüsserung*.

the possibility of self-improvement and the acquisition of culture, the enjoyment of the protection of the law, the benefits of a public health service and sometimes even the consolation of religion.

He goes even further and states that they dread their work and are inspired by feelings of malevolence (para. 241).

With not a little confusion, the author goes on to describe the formation of the *plebs*, the extent of their identification with, or difference from, the poor being difficult to discern. The emergence of this particular class demands two separate but connected conditions:

(a) that a great mass of people fall below the apparent level of subsistence 'necessary in the ordinary way for maintaining a single member of society'.

(I think this minimum must be higher than the remuneration absolutely necessary to conserve the physical strength of the worker [and his ability to work—the golden rule], for the author alludes to the worker's position as member of a society (which is, on the whole, worthy of that name) and not simply to his existence from the point of view of animal needs.)

(b) that, as an almost inevitable result, this mass of people 'loses its awareness of its legitimate right to, and the honor of, a life sustained by its own efforts and work' (para. 244).

This had already been said both about the poor and, in an immediately preceding section, about the workers whose jobs had been over mechanized.

But are these plebs still laborers, in which case the preceding definition still applies, or do they constitute a class of unemployed, idle, poverty-stricken people, similar to the so-called Roman 'wheat'[1] plebs, keeping body and soul together thanks to the generosity of the state?

This second interpretation would seem to be backed up in the analysis which follows (para. 245), which also reveals a fundamental pessimism about the possibility of remedying such a desperate situation. In fact, Hegel can envisage only two eventualities:

either the affluent classes discharge a charitable duty and allow the class of 'wretched' people to live without doing anything, which in normal circumstances is degrading;

or, in spite of everything, arrangements are made to provide work for them, which would result in a crisis of over-production. This is a clear foretaste of Marxism and the crisis theory (the actual word obviously is not used, but the allusion is unmistakable). Like Marx after him, Hegel did not foresee (and how can one blame him?) the possibility of balancing out surplus production by stimulating the purchasing power of the laboring masses.

[1] The 'wheat' plebs were that section of the poor classes at Rome who had to rely on *frumentation*, a public largesse of corn, for their subsistence. (Translator's note)

68

Finally, the least complicated solution is to abandon the poor to their fate and public charity as in Scotland (same paragraph), but the most acceptable solution would be for the corporations to intervene, serving as a sort of distribution agency of the conscience money donated by the rich: this is brought out in another paragraph (253):

> Within a corporation the aid received by the poor loses its humiliating character. By contributing, the rich man satisfies his sense of pride, but the poor man, who receives his money through the agency of the corporation, has no occasion to feel envious (the benefits are felt by everyone).

However, if you look at the problem from another angle, that of the absorption of the plebs into the mass of unemployed, an appropriate conclusion would be the mention of paragraph 244, according to which the formation of the plebs allows a greater concentration of wealth in the hands of a small group of people (do you not feel you are already reading the *Manifesto*?) an idea taken up again in paragraph 253 to the effect that the luxurious and wasteful habits of the industrial classes are directly connected with the emergence of the plebs. But it is not clear how the existence of a totally inactive proletariat could create wealth for anyone.

It can therefore be assumed that, with but scant concern for meticulous accuracy, Hegel estimated that the mechanization of labor would result in the creation of a proletariat split up into one group of workers, whose wages were kept to a minimum, and a group of unemployed men reduced to beggary, both groups being alike in a wretched material and moral condition, which cuts them off from society and dehumanizes and alienates them (although these are not the precise words used here).

This study reveals that, in spite of his taste for abstraction and his cult of obscurity, Hegel, for whom the reading of newspapers was a 'realistic morning prayer', was by no means incapable of picturing to himself, and depicting for us, the realities of existence or of observing, if need be, the human being in his everyday world; he prepares the ground in advance for the Marxist doctrine and gives us a foretaste of Marx's description of the proletariat. By foreseeing the continuous deterioration in the condition of the 'poor' and the 'plebs', by failing to outline any course of action to reverse or even to halt the trend, Hegel provides the necessary preliminary analysis prefiguring the inevitability of a radical solution, which, however, he does not formulate.

And yet how can the incurable harshness of the world of riches and the immutable tragedy of slavery, hinted at if not clearly stated in the *Philosophy of right*, be compatible with the view, expressed in the *Phenomenology of mind*, that the humblest task was a source of creative freedom? What has become of the slave's freedom from fear? Hegel sees no contradiction here. On the one hand, work in itself is not liberating, it simply creates the conditions in which the slave can resume the combat for self-recognition which, because of his earlier acute fear, he was afraid even to undertake. On the other hand, no one of the two actors in the Hegelian drama will ever succeed in ridding himself of his fraternal enemy: the Master and the Slave are bound to each other, and it will need the Modern State, powerful enough to accommodate division of the Idea, and having established that, ideally, all men are equal, to settle their dispute and effect their confrontation as partners within its organization. It is understandable that Marx should have regarded this solution as nothing more than a theoretical disalienation, as the perpetuation and consequent intensification of an alienation, as a deceptively calm description of a process which is really a cover for the seething turmoil of world revolution.

It is interesting to note that an unexpected chronological link between the work of Hegel and Marx is provided by the analogous views of A. de Tocqueville, an author of a very different stamp and who had no allegiance to their common ideology. It could even be said that it is Tocqueville who provides the most concrete definition of alienation without, however, actually employing the word itself.

When a workman has spent a considerable portion of his life in this fashion, [see Hegel] his mind ceases to function . . . his body has contracted certain fixed habits which it cannot shake off . . . in short, *he no longer belongs to himself* but to his chosen calling.

One cannot fail to see the similarity in the line of thought: effects of the division and specialization of labor. 'The craft improves, the craftsman slips back'; dehumanization: 'the former [the master] becomes more and more like the administrator of a huge empire, and the latter more like a brute beast'; degradation: 'Industrial science constantly lowers the standing of the working class', etc[1]. 'The worker becomes weaker, more limited, more dependent.'

In Marx

Marx's description of labor and the situation of the laborers does not differ in its essentials from that outlined in Hegel's writings, in particular the *Philosophy of right*. Work is uninteresting and purely mechanical; the worker has no understanding of what he is doing. The level of remuneration is extremely low, for the worker cannot play possible employers off against each other, a procedure which would allow him to accept the highest offer and to improve his lot as opportunities arose. Finally,

[1] See Tocqueville, A. de. *Democracy in America*, translated by George Lawrence. New York, Doubleday and Company, 1969. pp. 555-6.

because of the division of labor, the worker is condemned to endless drudgery from which there is no escape: 'Each man has a particular, exclusive sphere of activity, which is forced upon him and from which he cannot escape'.

However, this is not a case of a pure and simple rehash of the Hegelian analysis because, not only does Marx analyze labor in a precise situation within the history of capitalism, but also because the Marxist analysis occurs within the framework of a different conception of alienation. It is well known that, for Hegel, alienation is a starting point whereas, for Marx, it is the by-product of an original situation. Consequently, the description of alienated labor becomes obviously more striking, for, whereas work should be a humanizing factor in a man's life and should allow free play to his physical and mental energies, it does, in fact, dehumanize him. The process goes so far that man only feels he is a man in his animal functions —eating, drinking, procreation, whereas in his real human function, work, he feels like an animal. Thus, Marx's analysis is that of a radical perversion of the purpose of work; his description is that of a grossly distorted way of life.

Let us look first at the 1844 *Economic and philosophical manuscripts*. In them, Marx paints the picture of a double perversion. By rights, the laborer should express and find an outlet for his own personality in the products of his labor; in fact, the finished article confronts him like an alien entity, crushing him. By rights, his very activity should be a means of self-expression; in fact, this activity presents itself in the guise of a totally alien phenomenon; 'activity is inaction, force weakness, procreation castration'. Can the laborer escape? Probably not, for

> the more the laborer produces, the fewer the commodities for his own consumption; the more civilized the object produced, the more barbarian the laborer; the more efficient the work, the more impotent the laborer; the greater the degree of the spiritual content of the work, the greater the spiritual deprivation of the laborer and his enslavement to nature. . . .

However, there is still leisure, when man is restored to some degree of human dignity; but there is hardly any scope for it to be used other than for the satisfaction of elementary needs, man being pictured eating, drinking, or begetting (the latter being the reason for the old idea about the etymology of the world 'proletarian'—he who owns nothing but his issue). And yet why is this so? Obviously because, on the one hand, he lacks the means to use his leisure otherwise, for his wages have fallen to the absolute minimum and because, on the other hand, he is physically exhausted ('mortifies his body') and intellectually destroyed ('ruins his mind'). And so, as in Hegel, the couple (extreme poverty)+(dehumanization) puts in another appearance at this juncture.

Thus, it could be concluded that at this point Marx has no intention of picturing abstract man, alienated or not, to whom such frequent references are made, but 'living, active man', who, he was to say later, must not be lost from view in our consideration of the relationships between the classes. And, although it is becoming fashionable for writers to express a contrary view, in this one aspect *Capital* in no way represents a retraction of the views expressed in the *Economic and philosophical manuscripts*, in no way does it exclusively concentrate on the analysis of strictly economic categories, in no way does it display a lack of concern for the life of the individual. Just consider with me:

> The laborer is nothing else, his whole life through, than labor-power; all his available time is by nature and by law labor-time, to be devoted to the self-expansion of capital. Time for education, for intellectual development, for the fulfilling of social duties and for social intercourse, for the free play of his bodily and mental activity, even the rest time of Sunday, (and that in a country of Sabbatarians!), moonshine! But in its blind unrestrainable passion, its were-wolf hunger for surplus-labor, capital oversteps not only the moral, but even the merely physical maximum bounds of the working day. It usurps the time for growth, development and healthy maintenance of the body. It steals the time required for the enjoyment of fresh air and sunlight. It haggles over a meal-time, incorporating it where possible with the process of production itself, so that food is given to the laborer as a mere means of production, as coal is supplied to the boiler, grease and oil to machinery. It reduces the sound sleep needed for restoration and refreshment of the bodily powers to just so many hours of torpor as the revival of an absolutely exhausted organism renders essential[1].

Here we are faced with a tricky problem which I will just mention in passing. How far does limitation-alienation, the tangible by-product of socio-economic mechanisms, interfere with the process of objectification, which would have man the product of his own labor? It is no doubt possible to maintain that this function of labor persists, but the self-creation of man through alienated labor cannot but give deplorable results. 'The more the worker toils, the more powerful becomes the alien world of objects he produces to oppose him, and the poorer he himself becomes.' However, this pessimistic conclusion is justified only at the individual level, the idea of progress remaining valid on the collective level, humanity continues to advance through the sum total of the labor of all

[1] *Capital.* Translated from the third German edition by Samuel Moore and Edward Aveling, London, Swan Sonnenschen and Co., 1906. pp. 249–250.
If the epithet 'alienated' is applied in *Capital* to labor and not to the laborer, the meaning is still the same, for the laborer is seen as the 'man who sells himself'. *Op. cit.* p. 738.

men. Even the alienated individual benefits, in so far as he is a 'generic' being, from what we would now call macro-economic phenomena. 'History is the true natural history of man', his 'birth-certificate', the creation of mankind through human labor[1]. This explains Marx's constant insistence on the determining role played by the masses in history.

However, there still remains a certain degree of ambiguity in Marxist thought on this point. For Marx sometimes takes it for granted that the non-alienated laborer will no longer be tempted to seek self-fulfilment outside his labor; yet sometimes he also maintains, with increasing frequency, that the reign of freedom starts where work ends, and that, consequently, the development of the human faculties begins outside the harsh necessities of the labor situation and beyond the sphere of material production. This is why the Marx of *Capital* poses the reduction[2] of the working day as an essential prerequisite for the advent of the reign of liberty.

'The Marx of *Capital*' . . . Is there then more than one Marx (up to this point my study has sought to ignore such a possibility) as the most recent commentators, Louis Althusser in particular, would have us believe; a first Marx, who establishes with great clarity the concept of alienation, still encumbered with the humanism which is its inevitable corollary and, from 1845 on, a second Marx, this time a scientist determined to free himself from the philosophical trappings of a humanism at last recognized as a mere ideology. The transformation of one Marx into the other would be less the result of an evolution and the natural changes which occur in a living system of thought than of a 'cut', an absolute volte-face.

Absolute or made absolute by the critic? It is noticeable that the 'cut' in Marxist thought comes just in time to save the philosophical analysis from contamination by politics. It is understandable that L. Althusser should be tempted to banish all Marx's political theorizing (the description of alienation and the exhortation to abolish it) to a 'young Marx', i.e. an old Hegel. At one fell swoop it is easy for him to shake off—with what sense of relief we can but guess—the political implications of 'reading' Marx by

[1] *Economic and philosophical manuscripts.* pp. 111 and 158.

[2] However, neither in his early writings nor in any others, did he envisage the case where this reduction would be introduced into the capitalist system. Thus it is within the hypothesis of the classless society that he introduces a for once attractive picture of the life of the non-alienated laborer: 'In the communist society, where no one is condemned to one exclusive sphere of activity but can seek to acquire knowledge in any field whatsoever, society regulates production in general and thus gives me the chance of doing one thing today, something else tomorrow, to hunt in the morning, to fish in the afternoon, to raise sheep [sic] in the evening, to express critical opinions after meals, without ever becoming a hunter, fisherman, sheep-farmer, or critic, just as the fancy takes me'. But does this text taken from the *German ideology*, and therefore contemporary with the *Manuscripts*, represent anything more than a rather uninteresting Utopia in which pre-industrial revolution occupations are conjured up? The problem is taken up again in a much more thorough manner in the *Grundrisse*, translated from the German by D. McLellan. London, Macmillan and Co., 1971.

abandoning politics to the specialists. He is also tempted to keep for himself the Marx of *Capital*, sure in the knowledge, so dearly and so painfully acquired it is true, of his own scientific competence to analyze this Marx. It is so neat that it raises a suspicion in my mind: the stages of development which Althusser introduces into Marx's work, could they be the projection of stages of development in the critic's own life?

But this cannot be the true explanation. The world alienation is practically missing from *Capital*. And the phenomenon itself? It would be a distortion of the truth to say it had disappeared. Certainly, *Capital* abandons the spotlight (where the whole misery of alienated labor is displayed) for the wings (where what happens in real life can be seen plus, as it were, the machinery of the theatre).

To turn one's back on the stage where living men toil and suffer is surely to blur the essential features of the analysis. Nevertheless, we are the richer for it, for we are able to understand the inexorable character of the mechanism. Besides, does not capitalism itself transform human relationships into relationships between mere objects, give economic laws their falsely natural, apparently objective and, in any case, inexorable character? To observe the world of objects is not to forget man, whose alienated condition is always in the background of the system, both as a consequence of the system, in the case of individual destiny, and as the condition for our awareness of the very existence of the system. If the horror presented on the stage were not so inadmissible, who would have taken it into his head to look behind the scenes to discover its secret?

It is true though that, from this point onwards, Marx's reasoning is no longer deployed on the question of the (barely) living man, the man dying (from hunger) or begetting children (in utter misery), but rather on abstract ideas, the categories of class and property. He is concerned less with capitalism than with capital; less with the proletarian than with the labor-power available in the market; the representatives of the conflicting classes are often reduced to mere examples of economic categories. This gradual tendency (not a 'cut', for the basic problems have not changed) appearing in the course of the analysis seems to me a major flaw in the work, for it reduces to secondary importance the role of actual reality which is, however, the source of his thought.

13

Marx alienated by himself

That Marx should have considered the situation of the laborer as utterly wretched and that he should have been led to define it by the concept of alienated man, alienated in the absolute sense of the word, is perfectly understandable. Indeed, the situation of the worker was wretched, resulting in a virtual dehumanization, as seen in the analysis of the worker's condition given in the *Economic and philosophical manuscripts* and, although the terminology used is different, in *Capital*.

Moreover, that he should have considered this situation incapable of improvement (even subject to deterioration, although it is difficult to see how this would be possible in the case of such an absolute state) that, too, is perfectly normal, for similar views were held at the time by several thinkers, who had absolutely no interest in 'socialist' theory.

If, on these two points, the Marxist analysis seems well founded, considering when it was written, it, nevertheless, comes as a great shock to consider two other complementary aspects of the theory, according to which:

First, alienation is considered as a whole, indivisible entity; the idea of partial alienation, of a degree of alienation, is nowhere envisaged (the importance of this assumption is obvious, for if an alienation is only partial, its evolution should be possible in one of two directions, which would give rise to the possibility of reformist solutions).

Second, alienation is considered as a general, universal phenomenon, which affects everyone. This categorical view of alienation is even more surprising than the preceding one, and seems in direct contradiction with the law of evolution of the capitalist system as defined by Marx elsewhere. If, in fact, the capitalist system must gradually involve the proletarization—if only for a short time—of almost all the social classes, a few exploiters excluded (and even their numbers would be reduced by the evolution of the system itself), one should logically deduce that those sectors which are not yet proletarized are not yet, for that very reason, alienated. Either they are not alienated at all, in which case alienation is not general, or they are more or less alienated, in which case alienation is not an indivisible whole. This question is nowhere discussed; but, on the other hand, we see that the exploiters themselves are considered to be alienated. Since alienation is present at the two extremes, one should therefore assume (though it is not necessarily a logical consequence) that the intervening classes are inevitably affected by it.

These points seem sufficiently important to me to warrant further examination.

(a) The multiplicity of alienations

It would seem that Marx did not estimate there would be only one type of alienation, i.e. economic alienation; for he mentions at least one other type, religious alienation. This is, moreover, a very difficult problem, which cannot be dealt with here. It seems that, for Marx, religious alienation (and, no doubt, political and ideological alienation) are seen as a sort of monstrous growth on the body of economic alienation.

> Religious alienation has no other roots but historical ones, and the conditions for its disappearance have nothing to do with the field of religion. That is to say, the heavenly complement of an oppressive society will disappear of its own accord when the oppression disappears[1].

[1] According to Feuerbach's descriptions of religion, in fact—and this is what influenced Marx so much—the human being projects himself in the idea of God, at the risk of losing his own identity. But for Feuerbach, this projection, no doubt directed towards an image of something which does not exist, is, nevertheless, the condition for delivering that being from the narrow prison of individuality. Man must build up for himself and contemplate a divine essence before he can contemplate a human essence freed from the muddle and meanness of the individual's idiosyncrasies: and so the consciousness emerged from this necessary detour enriched; it makes up for its error about the existence of a divinity by attaining the truth of humanism. How can one fail to recognize in this description the process of objectification-alienation? Religion is a step to be transcended (and something is retained from it) and not to be eliminated. Marx thinks very differently on this point: for him, religion is the product of an unhappy, enfeebled consciousness, and not a transitional phase in the development of an enquiring consciousness. Religion provides no springboard from which one may attain the truth; it is to be eliminated, not transcended. He goes so far as to say that the only discoveries man can make about religion are absolutely negative and entirely critical. This is why, in my opinion, the theme of religious alienation is one of the least satisfactory in Marxist theory. Why must the religious man, to whom religion is explained, reject religion in order to transcend it? Would it not be possible to envisage the religious man using the process of assimilation to transcend religious ideas, which might, at the outset, be no more than mere conventions, and endowing them with a deeper meaning, in which his universal, human consciousness, far from being destroyed, would find consolation and a sense of the sublime? Many eminent thinkers, especially among Church dignitaries, have dismissed the traditional opposition between Marxism and religion as not relevant to Marxism and no longer applicable in the present day context. I myself think that Feuerbach's famous formula, 'The poor man has created a rich God', which was the starting point of Marx's argument, could be stood on its head today. Today are we not naturally led to think, as we see the changes taking place in the Church and among the types of men who adopt religion, that *the rich man could create a poor God?*

76

(b) The alienation of the exploited

However hard the conditions of the laborer at the time, it was impossible to believe that in every case they involved near famine and total dehumanization. In spite of the Silesian weavers and the sickening end of the working girl, Mary Anne Walkley, as lucid an observer as Marx could not really believe that all workers in every industry were condemned to die from exhaustion and to suffer a perpetual state of mindlessness.

However, even if Marx had believed this was true, he knew full well that not all the laborers were employed in industry, far from it. The life of that time was essentially rural, and no doubt hardships existed in the country (we know that the law concerning thefts of wood made a profound impression on him), but, still, it was not the same kind of hardship, and in some cases it was not a question of hardship at all. Why did he not attempt a description of the condition of the small land-owner, who employed labor, of the different sorts of farmer, or even of the farmhands? There was also the bourgeoisie, which was the dominant class in the German towns of that time. Can one deny that some members of the bourgeoisie led an active life, that they often worked under conditions which placed them, at least so it would seem, outside the relationships of exploitation? What about civil servants, teachers, soldiers, members of the clergy, journalists like Marx himself, and philosophers, whether revolutionary or not? If Marx had taken the trouble to consider these different categories, using the same approach, he would have been forced to admit that economic alienation can have different applications and, therefore, that there are different degrees of alienation. The laborer can be completely alienated or more or less alienated and, sometimes, without waiting for the joyful advent of the classless society, not alienated at all.

Marx paid for this over-simplification by a shower of paradoxes. Let us agree with him, for a moment, that the proletariat at least is placed in a situation of total alienation. How can one assume that the same is true of all the other classes? If we admit the hypothesis of the gradual absorption into the proletariat of those members of the population who are not completely alienated, which is to result in the decisive confrontation of the exploiters and the exploited, how can one assume that the laborers who have managed up to that point to escape the dead end of total alienation will allow themselves to be led like sheep into that state?

(c) The alienation of the exploiters

The alienation of the exploiters is derived from the Hegelian idea of the master, who enjoys no greater freedom than his slave. In Marx's writings, bosses and capitalists are themselves in the grip of alienation. This alienating whirlwind which, under the capitalist system, sweeps along all men, does it really, at the same time, sweep aside the differences which daily life creates between living, active individuals? For it is not the same thing to lose one's personal identity in a property one owns as to lose it in a property one does not own. It is not the same thing to suffer personally, on the physical and moral plane, oppression, poverty, and unemployment as to suffer on behalf of other people (although this kind of sympathetic suffering is only rarely experienced—otherwise the system would crumble). What is more, the exploiters are not subjected to the same constraint as the exploited in their *leisure time*—and this observation is equally valid, generally speaking, for the intermediary categories.

They can make profitable use of their free time; 'the man of an hour' of freedom is by definition, a non-alienated man. They can, according to the idyllic picture presented in the *Ideology*, hunt, fish, express their critical opinions (after meals . . .), more important still, they can, according to the considerable study devoted to this subject in the *Grundrisse*[1], turn to good account their hours of leisure, a time for self-creation which allows a man to consolidate himself as his own capital[2].

Besides, Marx certainly does not adopt a universal, mystical conception of alienation when, instead of forecasting what will happen, he concentrates on the political action to be undertaken as a consequence of forecasted developments. To accomplish the revolution, which he believes necessary, he makes no appeal to all-embracing philosophical alienation, a global phenomenon affecting everyone. He counts on the revolt, which will result from the worsening of economic alienation for those already subjected to it, and on the *extension* of economic alienation to an increasing number of those not yet subjected to it. It is not the revolution of the exploiters that he is prophesying, although they are by essence alienated. Neither is it a revolution of those who have religious faith, although they are alienated through their practice of religion, for then it would be a case of a theological revolution (examples of which are not unknown). The 'eschatological' role attributed to the proletariat is due, not to the fact that the proletariat is alienated like *everyone else*, but because it is alienated in its own particular way, in the most tangible everyday aspects of the wretched material conditions in which its members live. Is this not tantamount to admitting that the alienation of the alienator—and this is the most optimistic hypothesis—can only be of an intellectual and moral

[1] There does exist an English translation of the *Grundrisse*, published in 1904 under the title of *A contribution to the critique of political economy*. This edition is, however, difficult to find. References in this translation will be to the 1971 edition published under the title *Marx's Grundrisse*; for details, see p. 73, footnote 1. (Translator's note)

[2] From the standpoint of the immediate production process, free time may be considered as production of *fixed capital; fixed capital creates* man . . . Free time—for leisure as well as for higher activities—naturally transforms the man enjoying it into a different individual, who will then come forward to resume his role in the direct process of production. *Grundrisse*, p. 149.

order? No doubt it can be grasped as a philosophical concept, but, in this case, we are no longer dealing with real life. And if this is so, why talk about economics?

How can we explain these anomalies, one might almost say, these defects?

How could such a lucid thinker as Marx—he saw much further than Hegel and Tocqueville who, a little while before him, had admitted they saw no way in which the industrial worker could escape from the ghetto[1]— simply fail to admit the existence of a *partial* alienation while admitting, by implication, the mechanism of a gradual alienation; how could he lump all these alienations together in economic alienation, ignore or disdain discussion of the alienation of the intermediary categories and, finally, put the alienation of the alienated and the alienators on the same footing?

The key factor in this strange tangle is private property or, more exactly, the quasi-mystical interpretation he gives it by making it the embodiment of alienated work. This theory makes its first appearance in the *Economic and philosophical manuscripts*. It is quite easy to understand how, in this early work impregnated with Hegelianism and yet with an internal tension caused by his efforts to throw off the older doctrine, Marx should have failed to make a clear-cut distinction between philosophical speculation and concrete social analysis. But, in later works, although the word alienation is hardly used, the absolute, universal concept it originally applied to remains unchanged, thanks to the fetish of private property, which is amplified, magnified, embellished in the themes of reification (*Verdinglichung*) and fetishism (of commodities, of money).

Marx made of private property, seen as a separate, monolithic entity (after the fashion of his original conception of alienation itself, of which it is both the agent and the helper), the universal scourge which will dehumanize everyone, exploiters and exploited, producers and owners of commodities alike. This concept then enables him to solve all problems, or rather to hide their true nature. I will even go so far as to say, at the risk of being sacrilegious, (though why should this attack be more sacrilegious than that aimed by eminent but dissident Marxists against the mythicization and mystification of the messianic proletariat[2]?) that Marx's use of the concept of private property as an explanation of every evil is a colossal error on his part, which was to have a lasting, detrimental effect on the whole school of thought and to minimize the responsibility of history

[1] Marx gives the workers this chance by drawing up a plan for social evolution, which admittedly never materialized but for which substitutes have been found.
[2] 'The Marxist concept of the proletariat is a mythological concept.' Marcuse, H. *One-dimensional Man*. London, Routledge and Kegan Paul, 1964. p. 189.

(the cunning of history) for the accumulated reversals, which make up the burden that now weighs us down.

Why is it imperative to challenge the validity of the idea of the alienation of labor—crystallized, reified, made into a fetish in the form of private property, possessions, commodities, money—why must this all-too-convenient explanation be questioned?

Naturally, I am not attempting to deny the value of discussion of this subject as a generality, as a problem of ethics (it could just as well be a question of liberal ethics) or its validity in any specific field of application. I do not think it is being too bold to resume this considerable literary achievement (which sometimes reaches pure poetry) by expressions taken from colloquial speech, for example: 'You mustn't let your possessions rule you', or 'Money isn't everything', 'Money can't buy happiness', 'It's no sin to be poor', 'You can't take it with you', etc.

But let us return to a systematic analysis of the problem.

The worker has invested a certain part of his life, vitality, and personality in a task which has taken x hours, days or months, the end result of which is a tangible object (I am taking the example of a material commodity, because it is the most convenient and, at that time, would have been the most common result of labor). If he kept this object for himself he would be enriched in some way.

However, this object is handed over to someone else (or incorporated in some bigger manufactured object, which belongs to someone else). This is perfectly feasible in an industrial society. However, the laborer receives wages, the price of his labor. If his wages are to the exact value of the object produced (let us suppose it is equivalent in value to the time he spent at his task), he has not wasted his labor, his time, his life. He can, with the money received, obtain another commodity, over and above what is absolutely necessary for his bare existence (the latter type of object being immediately consumed). He has created something and he has enriched himself. This brings us back to the original problem.

But we know that, for Marx, it does not happen like that. The worker is dispossessed. Completely? No, for that would be contrary to the hypothetical social contract, however unjust it may be, and would constitute robbery. Besides, if the worker received nothing, he would not be able to eat, he would die. He is dispossessed of everything not absolutely necessary for his material existence for the time in question. He does not die, but he is not enriched, either materially or even morally, for the feeling of having conquered nature through the created object is taken away from him.

Such is the mechanism of a dispossession, which is not total but has the maximum possible effect, involving the *whole* of the surplus-value.

However, let us go on and imagine that the worker is only partially dispossessed, and that the amount by which he is dispossessed gradually decreases. Then, a greater or lesser degree of enrichment and self-creation is possible, though admittedly not for the whole labor-force the whole of the time.

Now, a society of advanced technology, which is the basis for the capitalist system, favors the gradual enrichment of all its citizens, a process which could go on indefinitely. The result is that the worker who is partially dispossessed, but also partly enriched, can find himself the owner of an object which is far superior in value to one which, in an economic system where dispossession was unheard of but where technological skills were hardly developed, he could have produced and kept for himself.

Thus, private property is bi-polar. If one assumes that the laborer is alienated by the property of the exploiter, would he be alienated in the same way by his own property, acquired in the multiple movement towards prosperity, where exploitation has its place, but is not the *whole* story?

Let us suppose that in an economy where alienation was unknown, the end product of a man's working day is one single pick-axe, of which he is the undisputed owner and which he exchanges for a shovel. In the capitalist technological system, he would manufacture 50 pick-axes, which he could exchange for a bicycle, even a car, although some of the surplus-value would pass out of his control.

One would have to live in cloud cuckoo land to believe that the laborer who has earned a car, which can travel faster than a horse, is more alienated than he would have been if, for the same amount of work, i.e. for the same period spent working, he had gained a shovel.

No doubt the regular improvement in the purchasing power of the worker is a relatively recent phenomenon, which could not have been foreseen when Marx was writing. However, it was not unheard of for workers to become property owners. And, in any case, the word property was no more than a term of convenience, which could be applied to a great variety of situations. It represents no more than a legal formula, one of the ways man has of clothing his mastery over material objects (an idea which Italian expresses more clearly than French, in the word *signoria*). This clothing of an idea itself can vary in cut, style, ornamentation and can be adapted to fit all different sizes. To talk of property in general is not very meaningful. To talk of private property, without reference to the specific piece of property in question, is no more helpful.

Can it be claimed that an individual's possession of a few cows is comparable to the possession of a trading fleet which sails the world? Is the ownership of a trust fund by 30 000 shareholders identical to its ownership by an individual, a group of local people, a university? What is the difference between this and the owership of the same fund by 30 000 workers or by 15 000 shareholders and 15 000 workers? Is the ownership of a piece of land, which can be disposed of as the owner thinks fit, comparable to ownership of the same piece of land when permission to build on it has been refused or the land has been zoned for agriculture? Is the ownership of a field for the cultivation of vines identical with the ownership of the same field when laws have been passed to forbid the planting of vines there, etc.?

The very definition gives rise to confusion. '*Private property*—detached from the idea of alienation it implies—is the existence of objects essential for man, both for his enjoyment and for the execution of his work.'

Did this definition have any real meaning, even in Marx's day? Here we are at the dawn of the industrial era as a result of which these problems occur. From the outset it became apparent that there was in existence a considerable amount of industrial plant, and it was possible to foresee that this amount would vastly increase. How can a man personally derive enjoyment from a blastfurnace—whether he be employed to operate it or not—if not through money, which is exactly what Marx was attempting to abolish. The (private) owner of 50 steamers will derive no enjoyment from them if he does not allow them to go to sea and his business is constantly in the red. On the other hand, is there any other way of ensuring that a coal-trimmer working on one of these steamers gets a just reward for his efforts if his material condition is not improved, if indeed he is not given a chance of possessing, thanks to his part in the share-out, some (private) property which is precisely what alienates him?

Indeed, the definition used can be applied appropriately to only one hypothesis—a curious one in view of Marx's general indifference to things agricultural—that is to the taking over of a portion of land by the laborer who works it, the area taken over depending directly on the amount of cultivation carried out by that particular laborer. In this case, in fact, labor and enjoyment indisputedly go hand in hand, the pleasure derived being indeed far deeper than mere satisfaction with security of employment. There exists, too, as everyone knows, an instinctive attachment to land which can have the intensity of a passion. Paradoxically, it is this example which prompts me to retain as a meaningful concept the term 'private property', although its defects are so rightly denounced!

This is no doubt the reason why the only successful revolutions have been agrarian revolutions and why the only way in which socialism could gain ground in Russia and China was to allow the peasants to take initial possession of the land for themselves.

Marx's mystical conception of private property has, with some justification, been compared to the doctrine of original sin. In the old days, there was a sort of Golden Age, and once sin is redeemed the second coming of Christ will be at hand. In more philosophical language, Marx was reproached with creating, with his concept of property, the first of a series of ontological categories—admissible in the case of labor (considered inseparable from the human essence) but not so in the case of the product of labor and even less so in the case of the consequent legal disposal of that product.

From this point on, Marx seems to have abandoned himself, as far as this particular problem is concerned, to the excesses of idealism for which he so rightly reproached Hegel. Just re-read the eloquent 'epigram' from the famous passage in *Capital*:

> The links uniting an individual's labor with that of other people appear not as direct social relationships between people, but for what they are, material relationships between people and social relationships between things.

What is it in this passage that most appeals to us? Surely, a symbolic use of language, which belongs more to the realm of poetry than to economics and politics.

In spite of all the defects of capitalism, how can relationships between people be material relationships? They are obviously social relationships, while Marx himself insisted often enough on the fact that, for man, the object was inseparable from a human relationship and social behavior.

As for social relationships between commodities, evidently these cannot possibly exist. There is always an element of human psychology involved, for example, the prominent place commodities hold in the minds of the men involved in the production cycle. The same problem is much more acute today, since the invention of computers. It has gone so far that it has been thought plausible to talk of the domination of man by the machine. Now this is just another example of language being wrongly used to powerful effect. Man cannot be slave to the machine, but only to other men whose domination operates through the agency of the machine.

And so it is not the Muse of History who must be put in the dock if absolute proletarization and pauperization have failed to materialize. It is not History, as some people have been absurd enough to say, that is deviationist. Rather it is Marx himself who has been unfaithful to his original vision. His fondness for the ethereal realms of abstract thought, a *penchant* so paradoxical in a philosopher who claimed as his prime preoccupation the depths where man toils in chains, marked him out as a victim of a common, fashionable, modern alienation: the alienation of language. Yet he seems to have been aware of this danger, for he included in his own definition of verbal alienation not only individual words themselves, but also verbalized concepts. The words property, reification, fetishism, employed with but little regard to the reality they signify, acquire a sort of independent life of their own, and this causes the work to betray both life itself and its own inner coherence.

Is this a matter of but little importance? Certainly not; for the concepts of the class struggle, reification, fetishism, social relationships between commodities and men as mere commodities to be bought and sold can quite easily become myths. Then, the analysis of a mythicized, absolute situation leads the philosopher to seek for an equally mythicized and absolute solution. Myth-problems lead directly to the myth-solution: revolution.

The revolution, a violent solution, is the answer to what criminologists call the dead-end complex[1]: the feeling that it is impossible to escape from an intolerable situation by any means other than the total destruction of that situation, the substitution of another radically different situation for the present one. Is this the solution to the untenable situation of the proletariat? It is more likely that the great dis-alienating proletarian revolution provides the solution to the untenable contradictions of Marxist thought. Could Marx have possibly imagined a more effective method of restoring some order to his unruly categories, his uncontrollable abstractions which seemed to have been released from a Pandora's box, than a universal upheaval in which his troublesome charges would be swallowed up?

[1] However appropriate this comparison might be, no moral similarity between revolutionary action and criminal activity is implied.

14

The painting of the dragon and the revolutionary myth

'Yegong covered his walls with paintings of the dragon, but the day the dragon, moved by his adoration, came down from Heaven to live with him, he made no attempt to welcome his visitor.'

Chinese legend[1]

There has been no working-class revolution in the industrially developed countries: it was highly improbable that there ever would be. Today, it is improbable that there will be a revolution. Is it really necessary to repeat these truisms? Emphatically yes, and for as long as many eminent thinkers, who are, however, free from any doctrinal taint, remain sensible to the fascination of revolution. It is not that they are unable to accept reality as it is or to bow to self-evident truths. Rather they seek to save what they believe to be the essential (about which they are making a big mistake, in my opinion). And so, deserted by the working class, now just another consumer and which no longer seems capable of instituting the Revolution, they place their hope in the underdeveloped peoples, the lumpen-proletariat, the coloreds, the intellectuals, and the students, or even in those obscure forces which the revolutionary spirit can sniff out intuitively, even before their activity has had time to blossom forth on the surface of a society (yet another angle on the legendary mole).

This is why it is a matter of no little importance to try to prise the less dogmatic Marxists away from the revolutionary myth[2] to which they still have a sentimental attachment; similarly too, it is imperative to put heart into those nominal Marxists within Socialist Parties, who are not revolutionaries, but who dare not admit it, even to themselves.

And so, let us return once again to the Marxist analysis and try to follow

[1] Quoted by Vandermeersch, L. 'La jeunesse Chinoise', in *Esprit*. 1 May 1969.

[2] Let me make it quite clear that when I speak here of the concept of revolution, I am in no way thinking only of its bloody and romantic image, which, on the whole, has ceased to attract any adherents. I understand the word in the widest sense of a radical attempt to change the status quo.

the major historical stages it distinguishes before the advent of the reign of the wage-earning classes. Throughout the development of history, the condition of the laborer, far from deteriorating, has improved thanks to continuous agitation and minor concessions, some real and some illusory, but not because of revolution. For example, there was no revolution to transform slaves (who were the private property of a master) into serfs (who were not, but were attached to an estate, and subject to personal, limited alienations). And yet, the abolition of a system which reduces man to the level of objects and of animals, which, literally and not just symbolically, *reifies* and *objectifies* him constitutes a major improvement in social relationships.

If someone like Marx had been writing at the time when societies were based on slave-labor, would he not have been led by the existence of this very real alienation to advocate the need for a radical, revolutionary change for the better? And yet the transformation came about so slowly and gradually, that historians of this era have great difficulty in disentangling the various threads.

Nor was there a revolution to transform the serfs into free laborers. In France, the liberation of the last serfs, the vassals of the Abbaye de Saint-Claude, was made possible thanks to the pamphlets of Voltaire and the lawyer Crispin and involved no revolutionary action. In Russia, the freeing of the serfs was put through very peacefully by an edict of that omnipotent autocrat, the Tzar, following a shift in public opinion, which itself originated, not just with the intellectuals and the liberals, but with the capitalists too, who saw the move as a means of modernizing labor relationships.

Under these conditions, why make a special case for the third step, the progression of the workers to a less alienating situation? Why, unlike the two earlier transformations, should this one demand revolution?

Let us go on. It seems to me that the economics of the revolutionary upheaval conform exactly to the socio-economic explanation of them given by Marx himself, and which the Soviet commentators, including Stalin, reiterate with such great care. Indeed, if one admits that the improvement of the forces of production demands at each stage a higher level of technical competence, such improvement can only be effected through the agency of a labor force, which progressively enjoys better conditions and a lesser degree of alienation. One can force the slave, a mere object endowed with speech, *instrumentum vocale*, to do any routine task, but force is not enough to persuade him to make the imaginative and creative effort necessary for a skilled job. How could you expect a wage-earner, who worked like an animal and had ceased to think for himself, to make a similar effort? It is strange that Marx should have envisaged the mechanization of labor as nothing more than the triumph of repetition and monotony and that he should not have seen it as a first step towards the improvement of technical skills, which he so rightly saw was the governing factor in different stages of production relationships.

However, history is in the process of justifying this analysis, even in the case of the wage-earner. Not only is the skilled worker, and following him, even the non-skilled worker, witnessing a regular and appreciable improvement in his material and legal position, but there are already signs of his social advancement. The laborer is no longer considered as a member of the proletariat but as a wage-earner, and now the most advanced members within the hierarchy of the wage-earning class can be seen to be moving towards contractualization, i.e. agreed rates of pay for specific jobs.

History has, therefore, tended to confirm, not invalidate, the essential broad outlines of the Marxist doctrine. It is not history, but Marx himself who, by entrusting to revolution the responsibility of the necessary step towards dis-alienation, which is inseparable from any improvement in the technical skills of production, is guilty of not taking his faith in his own analysis to its logical conclusion.

No doubt, one could retort that neither the slaves of antiquity, nor the serfs of the *Ancien Régime*, nor, to come nearer home, the serfs of the Tzar and the Negro slaves in the United States could achieve a conscious awareness of their class and of the class struggle, whereas the proletariat is capable of attaining this awareness. However, the homogeneity of an alienated social group is all the stronger if their alienation is concrete, imposed upon them and uniform; the great slave revolts of antiquity give a powerful example of the general struggle of an enslaved proletariat against an oppressive system. Without doubt, as the alienated laborers become more intelligent and better educated—a hypothesis which can hardly be reconciled with pauperization—they are more able to assimilate abstract ideas and a global view of history. But if their ability to understand their alienation increases, their willingness to tolerate it decreases, with the result that, paradoxically, the conclusion should be reached that class antagonisms can only come into play at the moment they are becoming attenuated.

But let us get back to the question of revolutions themselves and, changing our viewpoint, try to see whether they have brought about any structural changes in production relationships. Even if the word revolution is taken in its widest sense, the answer must be in the negative. Neither the Goths in Italy, nor the Vandals in Africa effected any lasting changes. The Renaissance, the Reformation, the Wars of Religion passed over Europe without changing the conditions of labor and commerce. Finally, the French Revolution, which exercised an almost magical influence over political philosophy in the first half of the nineteenty century and from which was expected to emerge a new definition of the situation of man in society, led to no improvements in the quality of life. There were quantitative changes, of which the most apparent was the great increase in the numbers of rural landowners. The fact that the bourgeoisie found it easier to accede to political power, although obviously connected with the earlier improvement in its financial condition, cannot be said to constitute a relationship of production.

The great social revolutions of the twentieth century serve no less to invalidate Marxist forecasts. First, because these revolutions have erupted, not in countries which have attained an advanced degree of material civilization, but in backward countries. This turns Marx's forecast completely on its head and also destroys the hope which accompanied it. *The advent of socialism was to mark the socialization not of the poor but of the wealthy*, whose riches would have been acquired thanks to the considerable expansion of capitalism which would precede the revolution[1].

Second, the change in the (social) relationships of production preceded—instead of following—the transformation of the (technical) forces of production.

In fact, the Russian and Chinese Revolutions were, like the French Revolution, agrarian revolutions. They were able to prolong their successes and gain a firm hold only thanks to the support of the peasant masses, who were eager to gain lasting possession of the land, which for them constituted their instrument of work, the horizons bounding their daily life, the objectification of their will to power. It is possible to give a historical recipe for successful revolution: a nucleus of an urban proletariat to get things moving (without which a peasant rebellion with no well drilled troops or leaders is doomed to degenerate into chaos) and a large supporting peasant force (without which the revolts are confined to the townships).

In a situation where industrial workers represent a large part of the population, where industrialization is advanced, the workers, who have been freed from the alienation of abject poverty, are keen to improve their lot, for they know from experience that this is possible (and their wives would take care to remind them of this fact if they showed a tendency to prefer daydreaming to action). Whether they like it or not, a kind of complicity grows up between them and the bosses (most of whom are no longer just capitalist owners) to withstand the other protagonists in the game: the buying public, the State, the banks, the customers, the suppliers.

In a situation where peasants are few in number, they are, for this reason alone, more prosperous, since the market is shared between fewer interested parties (the extreme example is England, where there is a huge gap between the farming population and the proletariat). These peasants will, for the most part, have succeeded in becoming property owners, because they will have been encouraged by the many and diversified

---

[1] Conforming to the logic of the system, before the Revolution the Russian Communists used every means in their power to encourage progress in industry and capitalism. They went so far, in fact, that some of them were accused of being over-zealous. (Berdiaeff)

opportunities for the investment of personal fortunes to invest their money in something other than the acquisition of basic necessities.

Having reached this point, let us try to assess the chances of the revolutionary myth at the present time and in the near future. Will there be other agrarian revolutions in the many countries of the Third World where the 'peons' are legion and industry unsure of itself? This possibility cannot be excluded, though the likelihood of it happening is becoming more and more remote. It will not be easy to find a combination of circumstances as propitious as that in China immediately after the war. Then again, what the peasants want is to own their own piece of land and not farm it collectively; the example of their brothers, who were initially tempted by the traditional myth of sharing but who then found themselves caught up in the cycle of a new form of dispossession, may dampen their ardor. The questionable economic success of the Communist countries is not calculated to revive their interest, while, in the long run, the material comforts of the American way of life exercise a more powerful attraction over them. Then again, the elements opposed to revolution, concentrated in national armies, often equipped and trained by the USA, with their officer technicians and their politically minded colonels, can nip subversive movements in the bud: *principiis obsta*. It is noticeable, and has often been remarked upon, that the Cuban revolution has not had the expected contagious effect on the whole of the South American continent.

At the end of his life, Lenin had intimated that the functions of the industrial proletariat, whose members had betrayed their Marxist calling, could be taken over by the huge populations of Asia and Africa, a hitherto little-known source of power. They could take up the running, and indeed they did so, especially where they became involved in a struggle for national liberation: whence the trend towards socialism and mutual understanding in Cairo and Algiers. However, hasty and almost general decolonization defused the time-bomb, and, in spite of Chinese reckoning, the fire is not spreading. To tell the truth it is on the wane: look at Indonesia. And if it were not for Vietnam ... Moreover, the setting up of semi-Communist regimes dependent upon Peking or Moscow cannot be compared to the dis-alienating revolutionary process which is the subject of our researches.

Some time ago now, there was put forward a romantic, exhilarating idea of an ethnic-economic class struggle between two opposing camps, this time on an international scale: on the one side there would be the economically underdeveloped, often colored, peoples, on the other, the industrial nations, confident in their economic wealth, their history exempt from humiliation, the (supposed) superiority of the white race. However, such an abstract scheme does not fit reality. The distribution of the races and the various levels of economic growth do not coincide; there are rich people among the poor nations and poor ones among the rich . . . And, in any case, this has nothing at all to do with Marxism.

Some observers see as their last hope (though one hardly dares to use such optimistic terminology) countries which, although industrialized, have not yet traveled the whole length of the road leading to an American-type consumer society. Such is the case in France and Italy in particular[1]. What is more, these countries have preserved a considerable agricultural population and a Catholic majority (which renders them, or so it is believed, more interested in the world of the spirit and therefore disdainful of present material gains). Finally, these two countries, with their influential Communist Parties, have at their disposal a large mass steeped in Marxist philosophy and in revolutionary doctrine. In this case, the observers concerned are counting on the new detonator provided by the activist students, the young workers, one section of the intelligentsia . . . even by the 'new working class', which some observers have described, made up of technicians, engineers, specialists, and scientists . . .[2] (something approaching the so-called New Left in America, but which would have, or so they believe, a greater chance of success in Europe). These new forces should manage to rouse the sleeping masses before they sink into an irreversible state of lethargy, and it is with this end in view that some encouragement is drawn from the May troubles in France and contemporary upheavals in Italy.

Now the absurdity of these calculations is manifest, for it is obvious that in industrialized countries, even if industrialization has only been achieved on a small scale, no revolutionary movement, whose aim was to destroy the political and economic regime, would have the slightest chance of success. It is unlikely that the Communist Party would lend a hand, for the Communists have no desire to witness a successful revolution engineered by someone else; neither do they want a revolution led by them to succeed. The ambition of the Communist Party is to be an influential, governing, democratic party of order, as it was after the war, and to become part of 'republican' coalitions in return for a few minor symbolic social or financial concessions. If, however, contrary to expectations, the Communist Party did support a Left-wing uprising, this strange alliance would have a polarizing effect and would unite the majority of the population, backed up by the combined resources of the State, to oppose it. The recently published notes of Trotsky read, 'The proletariat can only gain power through a national uprising coupled with a surge of nationalistic feeling.' When I read this, I would like to know whether this quotation has escaped the notice of certain enthusiastic Trotskyists.

Our young activists must be careful as they pursue their dreams. Dur-

[1] Cf. Marcuse, H. *One-dimensional man*. Introduction, p. 11.
[2] Cf. Marcuse, H. *Five lectures*, p. 85. (Translator's note)

ing my period in office, I was struck by the growth of a real movement of hatred against certain demonstrations in the colleges and schools. I was even more impressed when I read something written by Herbert Marcuse to the effect that he had seen the American police protect the demonstrators . . . from the workers[1].

Let us just reflect on it (especially the demonstrators). Many revolutions have failed, but many counter-revolutions have succeeded.

We are told, it is true, or rather we are led to understand that, 'We know full well that, in reality, no revolution is expected or will be attempted. But by adopting an extremist attitude we have a greater chance of obtaining the satisfaction of some of our demands.' It is then a case of the dummy revolution accepted as such: the painting of the dragon. *But its end result is to invalidate certain criticisms and claims,* which are partly justifiable and which are more often than not aimed at attaining some judicial right. They deprive reformism (why be afraid of the word?), true liberalism (again, why be afraid of the word?) of the support of the finest, resourceful, sincere people, who have been roused by the problems presented by the new society. The help of such people was sadly lacking when I was trying to transcend the problems specifically connected with the University and even the general field of education in order to evolve *a policy for the formation of modern man.* Such help must be forthcoming tomorrow, no, today! to those who will attempt similar reforms in this field and in others.

Since it has very justly been said that modernity is a substitute for revolution[2], since a new antagonism, bringing into conflict the forces of modernization and the conservatism of the old ways, has been substituted for the old capital-labor antagonism[3], it is imperative to rid our minds of a *conception of modernity which is already out of date.*

[1] Cf. Marcuse, *Five essays*, p. 83–108.
[2] Soubise, p. 234, quoting Lefebvre.
[3] Fougeyrollas, *Et maintenant ?*, article No. 16, quoted by Soubise, p. 119.

Conclusion

Having reached this point in my researches, it seems an opportune moment to take stock and to present, point by point, my provisional conclusions.

(a) The Hegelian analysis of objectification-alienation and its dialectical counter-movement, *transcendence*, finds its most tangible manifestation in the fact that man finally creates himself through his creative activity (through which he controls the external world). Unlike animals, man is a universal, generic being, each individual being the reflection of the entire race, which is, moreover, considered as a whole in its uninterrupted historical development. Such a concept implies the following:

the freedom of man envisaged as an end, not in the interest of this or that person or group, but in the interests of the whole species;

the solidarity of the species, so that it cannot be concluded that some men are (authentically) free when others (*their other selves*) are denied freedom;

the continuous, material, intellectual, and moral progress of humanity, man having necessarily to raise himself to the level of his own creations, this having a cumulative, progressive effect;

the recognition of the determining role of the masses (a point specially underlined in the Marxist analysis) in these changes and progress and in the activity of all men who labor.

(b) There is found in Hegel and Marx another concept of alienation (limitation) which corresponds substantially to the state of the industrial worker, reduced to a state of *dehumanizing*, alienating destitution, and bestialization by the uncertainty of employment, the unreasonable extension of working hours, the mechanical and repetitive nature of labor, and the extremely low rate of remuneration, which makes it impossible for the laborer to derive any advantage from his leisure hours. This state of alienation was extended, symbolically and confusedly, by Marx to all the social categories, including the exploiters themselves, by his use of the concepts of private property, reification of labor, fetishism of the exchange of commodities and money.

(c) The concept of alienation in its concrete form (limitation) corresponded, at that time, to the situation of most of the industrial workers.

Contrary to Marx's predictions, this state did not spread or harden. Today, it corresponds to the situation of a certain number of workers, either in the industrialized countries (but where it is a case of a *lumpenproletariat*, the result of immigration, whose situation is, in any case, generally not all that bad) or, more likely, in the underdeveloped countries (where it is a case of a rural proletariat, whose living conditions, although wretched, are very rarely conducive to the complete destruction of the personality).

(d) Since total alienation does not exist, it is possible to talk, in conventional terms, of a series of partial alienations (although this phrase is a contradiction in terms). In view of this, I would define alienation as follows:

> The general term alienation can be taken to mean all that imposes a limitation on man (considered as an individual or as part of a collective group), and which prevents him from expressing his opinions in a reasonable manner or from developing his personality, i.e. which limits his true freedom.

I will have occasion to comment upon this definition in a later section of this book.

I prefer this definition to that of L. Sebag which, although very interesting, is, in my opinion, too restricting (he is really defining betrayal-alienation[1]).

(e) The mystical concept of absolute alienation engendered by private property, and the ideas connected with the pauperization and proletarization of the intermediary classes, with the self-destructive mission of the proletariat as a class, with the inevitable revolution, etc., have not been realized in any historical form and must be seen as forming part of an ideological development whose useful life is over.

(f) All this in no way obviates the need to understand why the language of Marxism still strikes a chord, especially in the works of some of the most recent commentators, and with young people in particular. The energetic denunciation of alienation, even though couched in a too-rigid and now outmoded abstract conception of the exploitation of the wage-earner, will ensure that Marxism enjoys lasting credit with those who make it their business to combat the more modern, more diverse, more subtle, more underhand forms of the same threat to the personality. Thanks to

---

[1] 'I understood in this sense that alienation is identified neither with violence nor even with exploitation; it does not condemn a particular human group to perpetual opposition to the laws which must govern every authentic community. *Rather, it arises in a tangible form when the processes through which the historical energy of individuals and social groups manifests itself prove destructive of this very energy.*' Sebag, L. *Marxisme et structuralisme*. Paris, Payot, 1964. p. 76.

the humanist philosophy which inspired its first stirrings, Marxism retains the power to persuade, while the ineffectiveness of the ideological systems put forward by non-Marxist theorists and politicians cannot but work to its advantage. In truth, can we offer our contemporaries anything which Condorcet and Jefferson have not already offered to theirs? With the exception of a few lines by Stevenson, a few of Kennedy's speeches and, of course, the best pages written by General de Gaulle—which we will examine to see how they achieve their object, albeit imperfectly—what has been written during the last twenty years or so which even attempts to provide an answer to the basic questions posed by tormented consciousness?

(g) It is high time to put an end to the passionately held antiquated ideas and the inferiority complex which inhibit Western philosophical thought where Marxism is concerned. Although the most activist areas of Marxist thought have been disproved by history (an obvious failure which should, moreover, help to cure us of any panic reaction), the doctrine did undoubtedly mark a great step forward in basic political philosophy. It is important to recognize this fact without reservation. It is no disgrace for the believers in social democracy to accept the heritage of Marxism, to capitalize on this investment. It should be possible for modern theorists to look at the problems Marx raised, to learn from the certain truths he discovered as well as from his mistakes, and so be able, in their turn, to elaborate a new comprehensive political philosophy to suit the needs of modern man until the day when, naturally, this new system of thought will need to be revised too.

As L. Soubise so aptly writes, 'To transcend Marx is to admit his influence'. I have shown quite sufficiently how Marx has influenced me. All that remains now is for me to reveal why I think it imperative I should go further. As for Marx, the prophet of transcendence, who revealed through many ironic comments that he did not see his work as the untouchable sacred cow which it was to become for many commentators, he would undoubtedly have been the first to suggest it was time attempts were made to transcend it.

Part 3

The consumer society

15

Towards a definition
A first critical assessment

It is remarkable that the consumer society should be so frequently criticized, but so rarely defined. Critics usually rely on value judgments to help
them pinpoint its characteristics, but this is contrary to every scientific
principle. I know it is not going to help me much to say that the endless
discussions on this subject are a reflection of the confusion and difficulties
which it presents. It is clear that criticism which could conveniently be
defined as 'Left-wing', i.e. criticism whose aim is to improve and transcend
this type of society, is indistinguishable from 'Right-wing' criticism with
its pervading sense of nostalgia for the past and which, because it is
impossible to put back the clock, has really only one aim: to restrict the
access of the popular masses to a higher level of enjoyment of the good
things in life, especially where culture is concerned.

According to this view, culture should be reserved for an elite—rarity
being an essential defining characteristic of both culture and the elite. The
masses cannot 'authentically' benefit from culture, while culture, if it
comes into contact with the masses, loses its refinement, it breaks free
from the realm of quality to descend to the vulgar world of the quantitative. Perhaps, when these lines are read, there will be an outcry and protests will be made to the effect that no one has even said such a thing.
However, if we were to scratch the surface of certain pronouncements, I
am sure that it would not be long before something of this attitude, which
its proponents like to camouflage as much as possible, showed through.
Some critics even hide this attitude from themselves, and I know certain
'Left-wingers' who, upon close examination, would make fairly convincing
'Right-wingers'.

This ambivalence and overlapping of attitudes is strikingly displayed
in the so-called *anti-Utopian* works of fiction. Formerly, utopians, who
more often than not could also have been called *irénistes*[1], took delight in

---

[1] *Irénistes*—an untranslatable term taken from the name Charles Irénée Castel de
Saint-Pierre. In 1713, the Abbé de Saint-Pierre published a book called *A project for
perpetual peace*, which exercised considerable influence on the development of various
schemes for securing universal peace, culminating in the Holy Alliance. (Translator's
note)

describing for us wisely governed dream cities, which were infused, almost saturated, with a spirit of harmony, living proofs of perfection. More recently the great anxiety which seized the mind of man as he contemplated the astounding succession of his own triumphs, the *fear of the holocaust*, has given rise to nightmarish visions, cities where the absurd is law, the annihilation of man as he reaches the peak of his powers.

Social progressives like H. G. Wells—*When the sleeper awakes*—like Aldous Huxley—*Brave New World*—join reactionary writers like George Orwell—*1984*—in concocting these horrific yet anodyne portraits of future societies. Huxley fears eugenic standardization and indoctrination while the victim was asleep, but the only refuge he can offer is an imaginary island, whose economic independence is guaranteed by its gold mines, until the absence of military protection exposes the island to a catastrophic invasion. In a similar vein, Orwell imagined a world where thought is controlled by well-mounted television screens, and where physical torture is used to secure the gradual annihilation of the personality. The party, a minority group (2 per cent), supported by a band of helpers (10 to 15 per cent), keep the proletarian mass of the population (85 per cent) in a state of bondage; one is led to wonder whether the manipulators are not just as manipulated as the robots themselves. The conditioning mechanism makes it easy to persuade the guinea-pigs of the validity of the formula $2+2=5$ (though it is difficult to see what useful purpose this serves). However, we are forgetting that in some ancient societies (to say nothing of some modern ones), a good section of humanity did not even ask itself what the sum of $2+2$ might be.

In Russian society at the end of the nineteenth century, a society so cruelly described by Fedor Sologoub, the hero of *The Little Demon* allows himself to be easily seduced by a line of reasoning whose logic seems to him irrefutable: 'Since $2+2=4$, you will marry my sister'. Is it quite certain, then, that the dreaded manipulation bothered to wait for a great burst of progress and the general spreading of comfort before making its appearance?

This hallucinatory pessimism spills over into less famous, often attractive, works. A recent novel in the *Série Noire* presents us with a graphic picture of the superman type, the big business man with a finger in many pies, living in his car, riveted to his telephone, completely alienated in his giddy social whirl and answering to the name of Gascogne. Just before the May uprisings, French television was broadcasting for a second time, in weekly episodes, the saga of the *Prisoner*, the man who has remained intellectually himself, a living cipher among brainless ciphers, wandering in luxurious apartments and in the streets of an agreeable town, among contented idiots, controlled by invisible and unintelligible commands, a man condemned to an endless search for a plan of escape, a carefully contrived plan but one doomed to be thwarted each Sunday as we watched.

All this is the consumer society, no doubt about it; but having said that, are we any further forward?

In my preceding chapters, I have indicated certain ways of looking at the problem which arises when man and society cease to be regarded principally from the point of view of productive work and the organization of commodity production. However, that is just an approach and not a definition. It is now a question of deciding from which point in time, according to which characteristic landmarks, a social system calls for and provokes this change in interpretation.

Not claiming to write an exhaustive study, I propose to examine briefly the way in which this theme is treated by three authors who escape, as far as it is possible to do so, the suspicion of ideological ambivalence: Henri Lefebvre, Alain Touraine, and Herbert Marcuse.

With the talent for which he is well known, Henri Lefebvre attempted systematic research into the problem[1].

First of all, and I am fully in agreement with him here, he did away with the Saint-Simonian concept of the *industrial society*. He stated that there was not one, but several, societies which merit this general title. Moreover how was it possible to limit oneself to the idea of industrialization, when precisely what mattered was to transcend it? One of Lefebvre's favorite ideas, to which he attached great importance, was that of urban society, urbanization. Now this phenomenon, with all its modern connotations, is not just one variable within the concept of industrialization. The proof of this is that Marx, who based his theories on observations of the world about him, did not envisage it. Should we then talk of the technological society? But this raises the problem of how to wrap up the idea of the urban environment in that of the technological environment? How can you define the principal feature by a subsidiary one? Moreover, the much-vaunted supremacy of technology seems, to this philosopher of everyday life, somewhat suspect. 'The only benefit everyday reality derives from technology is an incidental one.'

And so this takes us back to our starting point as we contemplate the so-called society of superfluity, of *superfluity and wastage*. But can one seriously talk about a society of superfluity where there still exist some islands of poverty, even of downright wretchedness, and where the perpetual round of pauperization and proletarization is still apparent? Could it be called the society of leisure then? But, as H. Lefebvre rightly pointed out, things are not that simple. He divides the hours of a day (as important a concept to him as that of urban living and an inseparable adjunct of the first phenomenon) into three, not two, categories: *pledged*

[1] Lefebvre, H. *La vie quotidienne dans le monde moderne*. Paris, Gallimard, 1968. See especially parts 1 and 2.

time (non-professional labor), *free time* (leisure properly speaking), *unavoidable time* (traveling, necessary activities, and formalities).

I agree with him on this point, but it must be taken a step further. The tripartite subdivision is just as unsatisfactory as the traditional bipartite over-simplification. Evolution which leads, not only to the setting aside of a considerable and ever-increasing part of the day to be spent in activities other than work, but also to the establishment and prolongation of *non-working time*, in itself creates a diversity unimaginable at a time when it was simply a question of snatching a few hours of leisure in a day, a few years in a lifetime. One could distinguish a thousand other kinds of non-work in the time devoted to education, to leisure, to seeking information, or to family life.

This is how H. Lefebvre finally reaches the point where I was waiting for him, i.e. the consumer society. He begins by dismissing one very restrictive but nevertheless debatable definition, which he attributes to other authors, to the effect that the first step towards the consumer society would be the rationalization of production: from the moment when production escapes from the state of anarchy (commented upon by the first Marxists) and is geared to demand forecasts. Lefebvre prefers to concentrate on the emergence of an *ideology of consumption* and, desiring to link this with his key concept of 'everydayness', he puts forward a compound definition, which will provide the title of one part of his work: *the bureaucratic society of controlled consumption*.

This formula, which has the merit of being the result of scientific analysis, is nevertheless both complicated and inaccurate. Two distinct concepts, whose inter-relationship seems neither constant nor necessary, are confused. In the first place it is necessary to know what a bureaucratic society consists of and at what stage in the development of the bureaucracy the epithet bureaucratic should be applied to the society. Many societies were bureaucratic: almost all societies are to a certain extent. And then the link between bureaucracy and consumption must be understood. Ancient Egypt was a highly bureaucratic society, but it cannot be considered as a typical consumer society. On several occasions, Lefebvre places great emphasis on advertising as the inspiration and controller of consumption. And yet, is advertising a manifestation of bureaucracy? Not obviously so. The idea of controlled consumption does not seem particularly significant in itself. Consumption can be controlled and yet remain negligible, for example when rationing is in force. During the German occupation of France, consumption was bureaucratically controlled, since very few objects could be bought, and then usually only on the presentation of coupons or permits issued by the administrative authorities. Does this mean that France in 1943 was a typical example of a consumer society? What about Eastern European countries, where the state painstakingly shares out the limited resources, or China, where recently a card had to be presented to obtain vegetables? In the rest of his study, H. Lefebvre gives an eloquent description of all that to him seems characteristic and despicable in the society in question, but he makes hardly any attempt to clarify his initial definition.

The most remarkable part of H. Lefebvre's analysis for me is the two chapters devoted to the periods, beginning 1950 and 1960 respectively, whose dominant characteristics he delineates. The first of these is a new concept of the mechanisms of accumulation, which is no longer limited to capital properly speaking, but is extended to scientific knowledge and technology. (However, H. Lefebvre feels it necessary to mention population here, a strange and, in my opinion, inopportune harking back to the archaic population theory.) The other is linked with Galbraith's theories and the views of American economists on the role of the diffusion of knowledge in the development of the economy (the Denison Report). For the second period, he points out the dominating influence of the cybernetic revolution, linking it, as one might expect, to 'everydayness': 'The mechanization of society seen from the angle of everyday life'.

And so, let us remember these two themes (including the communications revolution) as being the dominant factors in the present problems of the society, which may or may not be called the consumer society. I shall return to them at a later stage.

In his recent work[1], Alain Touraine does not actually use the term 'consumer society' although he deals with this subject. He gives a cursory explanation for this:

> The idea of a society of pure consumption in which the secondary sector would occupy a very reduced place, in which labor problems would hardly raise a spark of interest among the wage-earners, all of whom would pass the greater part of their time in leisure pursuits, belongs to science fiction.

That goes without saying. However, in order to relegate the consumer society to the realm of science fiction, the author found he had to embellish this society with an arbitrarily chosen adjective. Whoever talked about *pure consumption*? The problem is to know whether there exists a type of society characterized by a new and determined role of consumption.

The author also rejects categories such as: mass societies, societies of rapid transition, societies where income is greater than expenditure, on the grounds that they are products of abstract theories far removed from historical reality. He puts forward the phrase *post-industrial* society, which provides him with his title. But the description he gives of this

[1] Touraine, A. *La société post-industrielle, naissance d'une sociéte*, Paris, Editions Denoël, 1969. p. 24.

society is a very guarded one. It is simply a question of 'measuring the distance which separates them [post-industrial societies] from the industrialized societies which preceded them, traces of these earlier societies still persisting in the new societies, both in their capitalist and socialist form'.

In what way are the new societies different then? What distance are we talking about?

A society cannot transcend the industrial phase unless it has first attained and welcomed wholeheartedly complete industrialization. Has this happened? Where? It would be a plausible hypothesis as far as the USA was concerned, provided its terms were more specific. At what point can America be considered as having reached the peak of industrialization? By what standards can this be judged? However reduced in size, the agricultural sector still produces a surplus. There are still many artisan-type or modest enterprises which could become industrialized, or, at least, more industrialized than they are now. No doubt, American economists admit as a general rule that the growth of trusts in no way implies the abolition of medium-size or small businesses (Lilienthal); however, it is probable that the trends characteristic of the large units of production will be pursued further and strengthened. How can one say that a society which is still pursuing industrialization has transcended it? And above all, how does one analyze the position of the principal European countries, especially France? If North American society is to be considered as a post-industrial society, presumably French society has not yet reached that phase, but has remained at the industrial stage. J.-J. Servan-Schreiber, who also uses the phrase post-industrial society, defines such a society by a straightforward reference to the level of national income. The convention he adopts has five group classifications: post-industrial society (in excess of 4000$), advanced industrial society (1500), industrial society (600), in process of industrialization (200), pre-industrial (from 50 to 200).

It is true that Alain Touraine backs up his definition with reference to two other characteristics of this society, each one corresponding to a different aspect of the whole. On the one hand, there is the *technocratic society* (considered from the point of view of executive power). On the other hand, *the programed society* (considered from the point of view of production and economic organization).

To me it seems a difficult task to define the type of society which I want to describe by a simple reference to technical competence in the management of public affairs. That is not a fundamental and causal prerequisite for this type of society, but simply a side-effect, a consequence of the technological changes in the economy. Besides, there are different degrees of technical competence, which can manifest itself in many and varied forms. Some of the governments of primitive societies, backed up by priests or the army, could be considered to be technocratic, for the knowledge of complicated rites and of the rules of combat constitute a kind of technical know how. On the other hand, it would be difficult to pretend that, in an industrial society, executive power is always entirely dependent upon technicians.

The concept of technocracy is in itself polyvalent, for it is connected with the concept of the technician, the expert, and the bureaucrat; A. Touraine very rightly distinguishes between these three categories of men, relying chiefly to do so on the concept of *techno-bureaucracy* as defined by Gurvich[1]. A man not possessed of any special qualifications might make an exemplary bureaucrat; a highly qualified politician might turn out to be a hopeless bureaucrat. Another point which the author makes is that, if no restraints are imposed upon the techno-bureaucracy, it tends towards totalitarianism, revealing itself most clearly in the absolute control of information. Now many so-called technocratic régimes do not go that far, and maintain a greater or lesser distance between them and this extreme. Thus, they cannot all be assessed in the same way and do not call for identical reactions; some can be modified by limited measures, others will only cede to a revolutionary uprising. If economic as well as political power is taken into account, the same observations are valid, for there is one part of economic activity which continues to be influenced by men or by groups (owners, customers, trade unions) which escape the control of the technocrats, who are not agreed upon concerted action in this field. Besides, as A. Touraine rightly points out: 'There is no reason for saying that a society in which the techno-bureaucratic threat exists is entirely analyzable from this one point of view'. From this point on, the definition he proposes seems to me quite ambiguous.

The idea of the *programed society*, which is the society the author favors, seems even more mysterious. I am tempted to see in it a prevailing attitude towards society similar to that expressed by H. Lefebvre in the concept of control: i.e. the idea of an economy freed from the anarchy which dogged the early stages of capitalism. But this development is but dimly perceived, for, with the possible exception of those planning organizations set up by socialist governments, the controls imposed upon modern economic systems are minimal. Some societies admit no kind of economic planning: others allow a flexible kind of planning based rather on forecasts than on the establishment of a norm. This is obviously what the author has in mind as his technical analysis reveals. For Touraine, a programed economy is essentially opposed to the accumulation of wealth;[2] and this statement cannot fail to surprise, until it is realized that the accumulation he is condemning is specifically the accumulation of private capital. This distinction does not seem valid to me, for the pheno-

[1] Cf. Gurvich, G. *Industrialization et technocratie*. Paris, Armand Colin, 1969. pp. 179–199.
[2] Cf. op. cit., pp. 65, 100, 102.

menon of the accumulation of capital is independent, in spite of the words used, of the existence of a capitalist regime. Socialist economies, in particular, place great emphasis on accumulation, which is a vital element for their progress. Lenin thought that the last stage before the advent of Socialism would be the general extension of State capitalism, which would necessarily involve an accumulation of State funds. If the objections to his definitions of various concepts are forgotten for a moment, although in his case it is not just a question of the use of terminology, it becomes clear that Touraine considers a society 'programed' if it allows some measure of planning: 'Where the State guarantees and directs an increasing percentage of economic investments' and where considerable emphasis is laid on social investments.

This is not a very sound base for explanation, for there are many intermediary steps in such an evolution; it is possible to conceive of a society where the State guarantees considerable social and collective investments but has no, or very little, interest in economic investments.

The most serious criticism I have to make of Touraine's analysis is that it fails to demonstrate how social programing could cause a society to be *alienating*; and yet the alienating nature of such a society is the principal tenet of the work and the chief subject of discussion.

The intervention of the State in the disorganized world of private investment must be seen as beneficial, since the State directs investments for the general good. Besides, any increase in the numbers of social workers, especially in the field of national education, seems to me calculated to contain rather than aggravate alienation:

'Our society is alienated, not because it reduces its members to a state of misery or because it imposes restrictive police control, but because it tempts, manipulates and integrates', and this leads alienated man to the situation excellently defined by the author as 'dependent participation'. In my opinion, such alienation is not attributable to an improvement in the field of education, which, on the contrary, gives the individual a better chance of resisting manipulation and of freely choosing social participation. A society with a lesser degree of programing would, by definition, contain many more ignorant people. Would they be any less alienated? I cannot believe that the author himself was convinced of this and, besides, in the very text in which he defines programing he compares development (through the medium of socio-cultural investments) with consumption. Referring to cultural manipulation in another passage he blames it, not on the influence of schooling but on that of the 'parallel school'[1].

Thus, even though it is possible to glean certain useful pointers from Touraine's theories, the idea of the programed society is no more likely to provide the magic key to the problem before us than were the concepts of technocracy and post-industrialization. Alain Touraine tried to avoid

[1] For more information, see the work of George Friedmann. (Translator's note)

the use of consumption as a yardstick, but he keeps coming back to it. 'Today it is consumption rather than production which dominates social problems and conflicts'[1]. 'The oppressed classes are no longer defined by the wretched condition in which they live, but by the level of their consumption of commodities and by the frequency with which their property is distrained.' 'Others manipulate man . . . in his social dealings, in his *consumption* pattern, in the organization of his working life . . .' In the final analysis, the comparison which I have already pointed out between *development* and *consumption* is very like Lefebvre's theories on *development* and *growth* (which, roughly speaking, is what gives rise to the consumer society).

And so these two authors agree upon the essentials. They both consider (modern) society as an alienated society, a society which has given rise to a new type of alienation, which no longer reveals itself in abject poverty or physical constraints but in a state of dependence, especially noticeable in the field of culture, in the widest sense of that word, politics included.

'Political activity is indistinguishable from political consumption', writes A. Touraine[2], while H. Lefebvre states, 'Alienation is taking on many different forms. It is affecting politics, ideology, technology, bureaucracy, city life'[3]. It seems natural that they should reach similar conclusions. H. Lefebvre advocates the cultural revolution; A. Touraine erects 'creative protest' as a weapon against 'dependent participation'.

But post-Marxism has found an even more eloquent advocate and the consumer society a more vehement prosecutor in the person of H. Marcuse.

[1] Op. cit., pp. 28, 103, 145.
[2] Idem., p. 38.
[3] Lefebvre, H., op. cit., p. 179.

16

A critical analysis of Herbert Marcuse's system
The new revolutionary myth

Herbert Marcuse has rejected the verbal concept, consumer society; as far as I am aware he never uses the term. He prefers the phrase *advanced industrial society*, as found in the sub-title of *One-dimensional man*, a society which he also designates the *society of abundance*. In view of the difficulty in ascertaining at precisely what point in its development an industrial society can be called advanced or at what stage abundance can be said to have been reached when some commodities are still scarce, the author provides two precise criteria to help us.

Firstly, this society is a society in which the technical apparatus of production and distribution (including the sector of automation) does not constitute a sum-total of mere instruments which can be isolated from their political effects. Thus, right from the outset, Marcuse himself has yielded to the temptation of introducing subjective and controversial critical criteria into a supposedly scientific definition.

Secondly, he maintains that this society does not exist as an absolute, indivisible entity. Rather his analysis is concerned with trends which have varying degrees of influence in different contemporary societies. This reservation made, the author's general line of argument is to assume that there is no difference between American and Western European society. He simply poses the question of whether the latter, and more particularly French and Italian society, has a better revolutionary chance, because, in these two countries, the working-class movement has not yet been integrated into the system, not yet been 'brought into line'. However, he does not entertain very high hopes in this direction for 'the force of militant factions is undermined by technological rationalization and by the rapid growth of authoritarian political control'. He would never dream of passing a less severe, even favorable, judgment on some countries in view of their colonial dis-engagement, nor does he give France credit for her anti-imperialist stand, especially on the Vietnam question.

According to the logic of this system unfolded for us, a better name for the advanced society or the society of abundance would be the *technological society*.

This is the concept to which the author constantly refers and which he explores in depth. The universe, rationality, man, order, nature, oppression, planning, etc., are all referred to by reference to technology, i.e. they are either pre- or post-technological. This is the crux of the matter, for it is in a frenzied analysis of the relationship between science and technology, in the very idea of the 'technologization' of science that Marcuse finds, or so he believes, the key to his main preoccupation, the 'closed' nature of social relationships (closed society, the closing of the political universe, the closing of the universe of discourse).

It is interesting to note that, at one time, Marcuse was going to give his book the title, *The technology of self-consumption* while retaining the same subtitle and thus resuming the two dominating themes of his work in its title . . .[1].

Whatever its formal definition might be, Marcuse's society is simply and strikingly characterized by the fact that it has at its disposal the necessary means to ensure man's happiness but which it stubbornly refuses to use for that end. On the contrary, it uses these same means, or allied ones, to thwart human aspirations and to deny authentic needs which it could and should satisfy, thus denying itself the realization of a historic mission which would secure for it lasting glory and peace.

And yet, what demands are made of it? The formula presented to us in the design for a 'transcendental project' has nothing of revolutionary delirium about it. Two objectives are stipulated: the *pacification of existence* and the *free development of human needs and human capabilities*. Pope Paul VI might be speaking. And yet 'society' is bitterly and irrevocably opposed to these ends. *Abhorret*. Man has only one weapon against society's total rejection of his cherished ambitions, that is the total rejection of society, *the great refusal*. But his success in the venture is nothing if not uncertain. As he can no longer rely on the support of the mythological proletariat, which has long since been integrated into society and transformed into a conservative popular class, he has at his disposition only two sources of strength, the one completely uneducated, the other very well informed. The uneducated force is that made up of the social pariahs, the unemployed, the coloreds. The other is that of the more far-seeing intellectuals. A union of 'the most evolved form of human consciousness and the most exploited human body'. What will be the result? Who knows? 'There is nothing to prove that there will be a happy ending.' On the other hand, 'It is only for the sake of those without hope that hope is given to us'[2].

Herbert Marcuse is a pessimistic idealist. An idealist in the commonly

[1] Information taken from the preface of the Vintage Edition of *Eros and Civilization*. New York, Random House, 1955. p. viii.
[2] The book ends with this quotation from Walter Benjamin.

accepted meaning of the word, as is apparent from every page of his works, but also in the philosophical sense, if his aversion for 'concreteness' and his liking for 'universal concepts' (though he tries to distinguish them from logical categories) are anything to go by. And he is a pessimist of the like unknown since Malthus, for he postulates what is to him an apparently insoluble problem, insoluble even by revolutionary methods, or for which, at the very best, there is a fifty-fifty chance of reaching a solution. We are a long way from the bland optimism of orthodox economists, from the reasoned optimism of the social planners, even from the severe optimism of the Marxists, who entertain no illusions about the difficult time ahead, but who take comfort in their belief in the happy end. In order to impress upon the reader's mind the conclusions reached in his great work, Marcuse uses a quotation from Walter Benjamin. Personally, I would prefer the poem which Freiligrath addressed to Marx during the dark days following the 1849 fiasco:

> Farewell, but not for ever farewell!
> They can *not* kill the spirit, my brother!
> In thunder I'll rise on the field where I fell,
> More boldly to fight out another [1].

The 'advanced' society, as depicted by Marcuse, appears to me as a being endowed with both thought and will, attributes which it uses for evil ends. I have the feeling that the philosopher has an anthropomorphic conception of society rather like that which man often has of God or of a god. It could also be said that he turns society into a supernatural being, the God of Evil or the God of Hell (an expression which he, moreover, uses to talk of the society of abundance). And yet, why should he do this?

On several occasions, he makes it quite clear that vested interests of private individuals are opposed to the general good and to the 'transcendental project'. But Communist society, where the private interests of the exploiting classes have been abolished, are still included in the general definition; this society is not judged free of evil practices for, if this were so, the simplest solution would be for us all to join the Communist Party. Now, not only is the capitalist system of exploitation unknown in the Soviet Union and the so-called popular democracies, but also some of the principal mechanisms of manipulation denounced by the author are conspicuous by their absence. Where are the ravages of advertising, the sexy salesgirls, the wastage inseparable from the massive consumption of unnecessary commodities? The first explanation proffered is that the regime born of revolution has not yet attained its definitive phase (to each according to his needs) and that the need to compete with the capitalist powers engenders imitation of them until such time that the new order is

[1] Freiligrath, *Farewell of the New Rhenish Gazette*, May 1849. Translated from the German by Ernest Jones, Leipzig, Bernard Tauchnitz, 1869. p. 228. (Translator's note)

established. Is there any hope that one day things will be otherwise? On this point Marcuse is very evasive. He emphasizes that the governing forces are separated from the production processes (i.e. the ruling politicians are not agents for powerful economic interests) but still he does not envisage that *technological progress plus nationalization* can *automatically* take society out of the impasse it is in. Moreover, he believes that the well established bureaucracy would, in this case, take over the role left vacant by the abolition of the vested interest of private individuals. The need to perpetuate antagonism against the capitalist world can provide this bureaucracy indefinitely with an excuse to resist all *qualitative* evolution.

This is obviously the weakest link in Marcuse's argument. It opens up a rift in his own logic. Moreover, one senses that he was unwilling to tackle this subject at all, and the difference between the two worlds will not be mentioned in his conclusion. This discrepancy destroys Marxist theory, not only in its claims to represent actual reality, but also in its basic principles. It forces the author to recognize that economic repression and class domination play but little part in dehumanizing society. For it would seem that in those societies where class domination does not exist the process is exactly the same, and any bureaucracy, which comes to power, thanks to a quirk of fate, can be authoritarian and as powerful as capitalism with all its accumulated wealth of surplus-value. The need for Soviet Communism to withstand competition or threat from outside explains nothing; for the Soviet rulers could still behave in as humane a way as possible, taking into account the exigencies of competition and national defense. Since they are unable to implement a policy of planned waste, they could at least justify austerity. The exigencies of the game do not require that they imitate the opposing side, but that they should be as different from them as possible in all aspects of material life. Why should it not be the same for the spiritual life? If the authentic forces of liberation were not thwarted, manipulated, or misused, they could certainly be mobilized to serve this spartan humanism, and the attack on capitalist materialism, grotesquely epitomized by the society of abundance, could be made under the impressive banner of a crusade for higher values.

If classless regimes are considered to block freedom, according to Marcuse's logic, one is forced to conclude that freedom itself is unfreedom. Men capable of making a free choice since, hypothetically speaking, they would never have lived under the capitalist system and would never have been subject to constraint, would tend of their own volition in the direction of maximum possible growth, towards the peaks reached by the most advanced technological societies. Their reactions then would be identical with those of manipulated men, although they are free from manipulation. This is likely to cause some scepticism as to the determining character of the manipulation itself. Is it not true that men's prime goal is the attainment of the optimal level of consumption, whatever the price? Only two categories of men escape this tropism, thereby conforming to the author's thesis which, on this particular point, goes from strength to strength: they are those whose intellectual powers and disinterestedness override all other considerations, and those whose income is so low that they can see no possibility of their attaining an acceptable level of consumption. This would suggest that the chances of there occurring a combination of circumstances favorable to revolution, a possibility Marcuse dreams of, are highly remote; for although it may be impossible to drive idealists off course, nothing is easier than to improve the fare of the needy.

And yet, there is really an explanation for this, which is that the offensive and repressive methods employed by the society of well-being are so skilfully camouflaged that their presence is undetected until it is too late, and the rebel finds himself alone out on a limb. But even this explanation gives food for thought. For how could humanity as a whole accept such a prolonged and artificial betrayal of its own destiny?

However, this is how Marcuse's comments on the capitalist world confirm the impressions which can be drawn from his views on the communist world. In this last society, private interests persist: but how? In order to justify exploitation, the exploiters are led to distribute the profits it brings in more and more widely[1]. This is how the trade unions, for example, are won over. The manipulators try to discover in advance what demands the workers are likely to make in order to surprise them agreeably[2]. This is the 'voluntary integration' Serge Mallet talks about. Ultimately, a vast body of exploiters or at least accomplices and beneficiaries of exploitation is created. The conclusion to be drawn from this is that it would be better to look for the secret of the inexorable mainspring of society somewhere other than in the permanent complicity of a cynical dominant class. Besides, how could one explain that exploiters, who show themselves more and more disposed to share their profits with everyone, should allow their own greed to precipitate them into a catastrophe on a universal scale, from which there could be no guarantee that they themselves would escape?

Although Marcuse is reluctant to reject entirely the class struggle as an explanation, although he continues to speak the language of a Church whose dogma he has rejected, his analysis leaves us with the image of an uncontrollable, baneful force, which might be that of an almighty will but which, in reality is not based on will at all; rather its source lies in the interplay of a system of ungovernable dynamic forces. This is perhaps what makes it so frightening, but it also makes it vulnerable. For it is unlikely that lucid, thinking beings could not master a blind and truly 'inanimate'

---

[1] By exploiting ever more efficiently the natural and mental resources *and distributing the benefits of this exploitation on an ever-larger scale*, p. 144. It is noticeable that the author makes no mention of the exploiters here (which I have done in order to get to the heart of the problem), but prefers the term 'society'.

[2] Cf., for example, p. 31, note 20.

mass of energy, however overwhelming its size. The only deadly, pitiless foe man has to fear is man. If my interpretation is correct, Herbert Marcuse should not be as pessimistic as he professes to be.

Inanimate or not, 'society', this social monster which jealously guards its hierarchical structures, manipulated or not, this colossal manipulator demands immediate investigation. By what mechanisms does it assure its unruffled supremacy; how does it wreck the initiatives towards a freedom whose secret lies within its grasp and for which it could take all the credit?

At the risk of simplifying a complex system of thought, it seems to me that the typical Marcusan method of argument is to employ long illustrations, sometimes digressive, sometimes reiterating an earlier point, sometimes anticipating a future development, to confront the reader initially with completely plausible ideas, whose validity very few people would challenge. He then takes the logical consequences of these ideas to extremes, to the very limit of what is acceptable, to the verge of Utopia. Finally, he proposes an explanation, which is sometimes of an ontological character, sometimes of a mystical nature, sometimes a combination of the two.

First stage (realistic)

Since the technological society brings in its wake great changes and opens up vast possibilities, it is henceforth impossible for us to be satisfied with certain ideas, which were accepted without question in an earlier stage of the development of society or production. Neither freedom, nor art, nor love and eroticism can be the same today as they were yesterday.

Thus, in earlier days, art was an expression of:

a revolt against constraint; now such constraints no longer exist; they have been replaced by others which are inapprehensible;

a (dangerous) statement of the refusal to conform; now such a statement is no longer dangerous; scandal has lost its power to shock—henceforth to reject conformity is to conform;

a search for an 'estrangement effect' (*Verfremdungseffekt*) a means of escapism from painful reality; now reality has become agreeable, there is no longer any reason to withdraw from it, etc.

Similarly, attitudes towards love and eroticism were governed by a host of, now defunct, prohibitions and taboos, which have become counter-taboos, etc.

There is nothing here to surprise or which can be disputed in principle. I have made only brief mention of the problems relating to art and eroticism and will henceforth concentrate on the discussion of freedom.

Second stage (from realism to the edge of idealism)

This is where the Marcusan method could be represented by the figure of an impossible triangle, one side being the end to be attained, another the means, and the third the negation of the end by the means.

It is the problem of freedom that is going to stretch realism to its furthest limit.

(a) The objective. Economic and political freedom must reach that extreme point where man is liberated not just *within* the economic and political sphere, but *from* economics and politics.

This means that man must be able to be free, not only to work less but even not to work at all. As for politics, the implication here is that, not only is it imperative to remove the *makers of public opinion* (which is possible, though difficult), but public opinion itself must cease to exist.

Marcuse defends himself against the charge of idealism. However, the question might be asked as to what would happen in the post-technological society if men wanted to use their freedom to do nothing at all. But, let us admit that this is an outrageous hypothesis and suppose that the author's concern is rather a general reduction in working hours. The desirability of such a course of action is made even more attractive by the powerful description Marcuse gives of the wretchedness of actual working conditions. The former painful physical effort demanded of muscles has been transformed into something worse, into the nervous tension demanded by specialized jobs: 'an exhausting, brutalizing, inhuman slavery'. The Hegelian-Marxist analysis is therefore still valid not only for the workers in the industrial sectors who feel the effects of automation, but also for 'the typist, the bank teller, the high-pressure salesman or saleswoman', even . . . 'the television announcer'. Here, as in the case of a world without work, the spirit of systematic exaggeration with which the author exploits a situation, which at first seemed perfectly plausible and reasonable, is evident.

(b) The *means*. The liberation from work, or more accurately, liberation *in relation to work* having been postulated as an objective, and a realizable one at that, the only question remaining is how this end can be attained in practical terms. Taking into consideration the breathtaking possibilities for *productivity* provided by *automation*, nothing could be easier. Here we hit upon the essential difference between two categories of consumption, those concerned with vital needs, and then the others.

Thus, this ultra-modern author agrees with classical economists that a distinction can be made between the consumption of essential commodities and that of luxury goods. The difference is that, in Marcuse's reasoning, the consumption of vital commodities should be within the reach of men

112

who had chosen to be idle and not just the prerogative of those who had chosen to work.

The vital needs are nourishment, lodging, clothing[1]. On the whole they can be satisfied by a marginal labor time[2]. These indications taken together with the statement about freedom to choose not to work lead to the logical conclusion that the consumption of these items would be freely guaranteed, a conclusion which partly anticipates the last stage of communism (to each according to his needs); this is similar, too, to the way of thinking which, a few years ago, led China to introduce the policy of the six guarantees (which, however, did not include either lodging or clothing but which did include medical and funeral expenses, hairdressing, and cinema visits, as well as rice and vegetables. This undertaking was abandoned and no one can be found who remembers it: only the written records remain).

It is advisable to note that Marcuse did not say in so many words that vital commodities would be provided free. Therefore, in spite of his categorical pronouncements about non-work, perhaps we should accept the hypothesis that these commodities would be procured with very little exertion on the part of the individual (marginal labor).

However, in order to attain this objective and to ensure that the execution of labor is the result of a completely free choice on the part of those who spontaneously feel the desire to do something, the technological society would have to:

make full use of the techniques of automation, whose progress is hampered at the present time, usually because the employers give in to the trade unions who oppose automation;

avoid the wastage of the production forces, a result achieved by a (blatant or camouflaged) war economy or by the manufacture of a great number of useless commodities for which an artificial market must be created (by psychological conditioning).

(c) *The resistance of the means to the end,* the containment of (authentic) affluence by the (artificial) affluent society.

The advanced society, not content with just refusing to adopt a course of action, which would permit the liberation of man, and persisting with the wasteful 'stop-go' economic policies I have just mentioned, actually expends great energy and guile actively to thwart and repress the demand for freedom, to dehumanize men, who will then forget to react like human beings and will cease to press their claims for their human rights.

As I once said, 'The very idea of escape becomes itself a prisoner'[3]. What is worse, in this case the idea is dismissed as though it were no more

[1] One-dimensional man. p. 5.
[2] *Ibid.* p. 16.
[3] Faure, E. *La condition humaine sous la domination nazie.* Paris, Service d'information des crimes de guerre, Office français d'édition, 1946.

than a mere passing whim. These offensive methods (I use the term offensive to distinguish them from the negative, abstentionist tactics mentioned earlier) are among others:

(a) the suppression of antagonisms which might rouse a critical spirit. Thus, business and organized labor are as thick as thieves, the political parties agree, tacitly or openly, to a bipartite system, etc.

(b) the individual is swallowed up in the team and the worker tends to become integrated in his plant, to become interested in its concerns (thus, in the Marcusan analysis, the social participation of the producer is considered as a factor of alienation).

(c) Advertising, using the most questionable methods (notably the arousing of the sexual interest through its methods of presentation or by the charms of the salesgirl, even of the salesman), by playing on people's vanity and the desire to conform, incites the buying public to acquire articles for which it has no real need, to run into debt, and to regard the execution of an arduous task in order to obtain a spurious satisfaction as the most normal thing in the world, although both the task and the object obtained as a reward could easily be dispensed with.

(d) Political indoctrination, which is the result not only of overt political manoeuvres, but also of the general climate created in all the non-political aspects of life, i.e. advertising (see above), stereotyped forms of art and culture, the general use of the mass media—in short, the political effects of the procedures of depoliticization.

(e) Drawing chiefly on the work of Roland Barthes, Marcuse includes in his condemnation of political conditioning in general an evolution or, as I would prefer to say, a distorting involution of language, a general misuse of terminology, which blocks the channels of the mind. Included in the catalog of evils are the excessive use of clichés, endless repetition whose purpose is to impose biased opinions upon the public, the analytic predication (the 'free world' so much talked of in the West, the 'construction of Socialism' in the East), what psychiatrists call auto-intoxication through the use of language.

Marcuse goes even further and denounces as a manipulation technique the search for a concrete expression, 'concreteness', which hides the concept behind its operational definition. Here, he seems to me to be contradicting the views expressed by Korzybski in his *General semantics* as well as H. Lefebvre's theory of meta-language[1].

1 [A] Korzybski's main contention is the need to transcend Aristotelean logic, itself based on the principle of identity (which ties it up with the theory of the dialectic). This logic can no longer be considered satisfactory in a world where science has transcended the stage of so-called Newtonian physics. As far as language is concerned, Korzybski makes the three following observations:

(a) the word is not what it represents;
(b) the word does not represent the whole of reality;
(c) language is auto-reflective.

114

Does not the danger lie, as these two last-mentioned authors believe, in the fact that the concept is detached from its real applications and is transformed into a myth? Marcuse criticizes the use of the hyphen while Korzybski, on the other hand, recommends it as a means of preventing alienation through language and the dangers of auto-reflective language.

Marcuse calls this kind of language 'Orwellian', but he also uses the epithet 'Aesopian' to describe it, which raises some doubts as to its modernity and the specific use to which it is now put. Is the use of expressions like 'the politician with the heavy eyebrows' so worrying? What about 'Berthe with the big feet'[1], Scipio Nasica, the appropriateness of some names, and Pyrenean villages where nicknames are carved in the grey stone of steles?

All these types of conditioning together create one-dimensional man, i.e. man deprived of his internal dimension, determined by external factors, extro-determined according to the expression used by Riesman in *The lonely crowd*[2].

(f) Finally, the whole sphere of thought is impaired by industrial society, which tends to tie thought down to concrete situations. Concepts are threatened by a mounting wave of the instrumental and the operational; their universal and abstract potential, which is nevertheless always closely related to the synthesis of lived experience (for this is not Kantism, but . . .), will be submerged.

Even philosophy itself cannot escape the indignity of enslavement and manipulation. It is reduced to an inoffensive non-entity with a grovelling gait, for which Wittgenstein presents a complacent and derisory justification in his Anti-philosophy.

The whole of this section of Marcuse's work reveals the transition from

---

Whence the tendency to confuse mere words with realities, which results in, for one thing, a 'seizure' of thought and, for another, different forms of *elementalism*, which separate ideas from facts and people. Whence the threat of a 'schizophrenia', a lack of synchronism between the evolution of the real and the social on the one hand and of language on the other. This *décalage* also presents an opportunity for a semantic revolution (the phrase is taken from Bachelard) and for some pedantic linguistic engineering tending, contrary to Marcuse's wishes, to tie the use of words and concepts to their concrete, operational application: numerical indices, an obsession with data, the use of inverted commas, etc. Cf. Korzybski, *Science and sanity*, Lancaster, International Non-Aristotelean Library Publishing Co., 1933; Chisholm, F. P. *Introductory lecture on general semantics*.

[B] In his study devoted to *language phenomena* and *meta-language*, H. Lefebvre takes a different situation as his starting point; he chooses the disappearance of what he calls the referential system, a phenomenon which he dates from the beginning of the twentieth century. Language tends to become its own referential: 'the signifiers and signified' are 'divorced from reality'. Eventually cultural consumption is affected; it degenerates into a 'consumption of signs', The consumer laps up meta-language'. (*La vie quotodiene dans le monde moderne*)

1 See Villon, F. *Ballade des dames du temps jadis.* (Translator's note)
2 Riesman, D. *The lonely crowd.* New Haven, Yale University Press, 1961. (Translator's note)

the accurate observation of the facts to the excesses of theoretical interpretation bordering on madness.

There will be further discussion of some of the problems raised here when I come to analyze the main characteristics of the consumer society on my own account. For the moment, I shall simply reiterate that I disagree with the imputation underlying Marcuse's general presentation of the facts and the use to which he puts it in his attempts to reach a positive conclusion and to suggest a practical course of action.

Imputation: What Marcuse is really doing is to impute to the society, which his own efforts have made into a living, personalized being, a constant vigilance and unwavering ingenuity, which it deploys with the express intention of thwarting freedom. However, unless you believe in a plot hatched up by the exploiters, a hypothesis which Marcuse does not seem to entertain seriously in spite of the occasional reference to it, the various defects of this society, between which there would appear to be a certain degree of coordination (but is it really all that effective?), are but effects, consequences, epiphenomena, the results of the development of a certain type of economy and its attendant social relationships. They are neither efficient causes nor legally constituted, accepted norms. Their negative aspects must not blind us to their merits, which even Marcuse has the grace to recognize. Consequently, one is perfectly entitled to believe that it is not beyond human capabilities to rectify and reform the existing state of affairs, for man succeeded in overcoming many other obstacles in order to create the basic situation or, more accurately, to create the dynamism, which incidentally gives rise to these more or less troublesome, but literally secondary, phenomena.

As for the *conclusion* which his analysis draws, it is quite simply to destroy the base and stem the dynamism. In Marcuse's eyes, the only way out of the dead end, to which he condemns both the reader and himself, is to arrest expansion: 'The expansion which perpetuates and shores up the system'.

In the words of Mao Tse-Tung, is this not to kill the patient in order to cure the illness? Is it not the teaching of the dialectic that movement can not be suspended in a vacuum and that it can only be neutralized by reversing its course? Is it not this very expansion which can liberate man from much, if not all, of his labor and from many, if not all, constraints? For Marcuse, the Romantic world, which he salutes briefly in tones of resigned nostalgia, was a historical necessity of progress. If the destruction of expansion involved that of progress too, would there not be a risk of returning to a world which was not even Romantic? Marcuse states 'the welfare society' is inseparable from 'a warfare economy' [1], but would not the first result of the upheaval he recommends—and to which the 'intellectual

---

[1] See Marcuse, H. *Eros and civilization*. (Translator's note)

labor' he is undertaking would tend—be to destroy effectively man's well-being in all-out warfare?

That is not the last of my worries. It would be impossible to envisage the prospect of a definitive end to expansion without feeling some apprehension. If later expansion were to start up again—and, according to all the evidence, it would start up again from a lower level than that already reached—how could the same causes be prevented from producing the same effects; how could the monster of technological rationality, the monster whose supremacy would be admitted all the more easily because it would have been longed for, waited for, called back, and restored to favor, be prevented from unleashing anew the forces of its relentless machinery? At great expense, after taking great risks and with untold damage done, we would have returned to our starting place and to the exact situation of the earlier problem, until a new Marcuse, a new Faure, perhaps, would try, above the abyss, to knit up again the threads of the interrupted controversy.

It would be impossible to bring this section to an end without mentioning the author's daring and significant investigation into the question of whether pure science is not about to be identified with applied science, if 'operationalized' science is not based on technology. Because of the importance and the difficult nature of this part of the book, I do not think I can conveniently resume it here. I can only recommend that the reader read it for himself. However, I would like to express my personal misgivings about the constant insistence on the rationality of technology, about which I feel he should make at least some reservations. For, even if this rationality is apparent from the outset and can make its imprint on the whole of the social organization allied to the technological world, it is not an integral part of the internal structure of this organization. It seems to me that Marcuse has not paid sufficient attention to the latest researches which have brought out the determining role of the irrational in technical innovation and which tend to identify scientific creativity with artistic creativity. The author points out 'According to the Greeks, there exists an affinity between art and technical know-how'. However, he interprets this relationship by the presence of a specific rationality in art and ignores the irrationality—true artistic irrationality—which is at the heart of all technical innovation, of all technology. The affinity perceived by the Greeks seems to us today even more intense and more strongly motivated. For this reason, the reconciliation between technological society and an aesthetic vision 'guiding the establishment towards freedom' does not seem to me such a remote possibility. It constitutes a sufficient reason for me to want to go beyond both Marcuse's theories and the pessimism they inspire.

17

The (technological) consumer society

My survey of what I regard as the more important theoretical works has convinced me that I have chosen the right terms of reference, but I realize I must also give my own personal views on this subject. I would now like to try to define the consumer society fairly, without bias either in its favor or to its detriment and without an unwarranted degree of pessimism or optimism. I certainly do not intend to submerge the whole social organization under the one aspect of consumption, nor do I intend to limit my study to one single or a few particular aspects of so-called industrial society[1].

My problem is to discover how and why it is now possible to bandy about the term 'consumer society', which was unheard of in earlier days, and to ascertain how and why this concept can, in the modern situation, be used to take still further Marxist ideas about man in a situation of non-work.

The first image which comes to mind logically when thinking of a con-

[1] Take, for example, the opinions expressed in the number of *La Nef* devoted to this subject. There it will be seen that J. D. Bredin, having first reminded us that this subject is like a Spanish inn, each man finds in it the things that he himself has brought there, chose to concentrate on the theme of false needs and artificially stimulated consumption. Raoul Ergmann condemns industrial society out of hand as an infernal machine. André Amar, quite rightly, sees that it is characteristic of this society for consumption to be at too low a level; why is it called the consumer society then? Evelyne Sullerot tackles it from the angle of the stimulation of production and defines the consumer society as a society in which the selling of goods presents a more formidable problem than their manufacture. Finally, Jean Duvignaud, whose views are closest to my own and who is largely responsible for putting me on the right path, defines the consumer society as a society which provides, at low prices and for a large proportion of the population, a large number of products or objects hitherto reserved for a restricted class of privileged people. He rightly sees this society as a corrective to individualistic society, an anathema to the socialistic doctrines of the last century, but, like the authors mentioned earlier, he places great emphasis on the idea of the 'prefabrication' of wants and needs. Finally, let me mention, just for the record, that Walter Rostow, whose work tends towards a totally different view, states that the 'mass consumer society' constitutes the fifth stage of economic growth. For him the main characteristic of this society is the fact that the population as a whole can afford consumer durables such as cars, televisions, radios, washing-machines, refrigerators, etc. The USA reached this stage in a kind of leap forward beginning, according to Rostow, just before the First World War with the launching of the Ford motor car and ending somewhere between 1946 and 1956. Western Europe and Japan entered this stage fully around 1950.

sumer society, even more so in the case of an affluent society, is that of a socio-economic state in which everyone enjoys a high—perhaps too high, but in any case adequate—level of consumption. Now obviously, this occurs nowhere, and no one can seriously imagine that we have attained that stage in the development of communist society where to each it is granted according to his needs. The invalidity of this assumption is immediately apparent when one considers two aspects of a very common phenomenon. On the one hand, no quantitative definition of the consumer society can be valid, at one and the same time, for both North America and the European industrial societies, because the *per capita* income and, therefore, automatically the 'consumption' level in North America is at least twice as high as in Europe. If then the *European* consumption level is high enough to merit calling European societies 'consumer societies', it must be concluded that American society reached this stage long ago and that the problem is an older one than was believed. It is only surprising that no one brought it up before. If, however, it is the American consumption level which is the determining factor, then it must be admitted that the problem has not yet arisen in Europe and that, even given the most favorable conditions possible, it will be a good 15 years before European society reaches that stage. As a corollary to this, I would have to admit that, as my book is not confined to a study of American society, it should be classed as science fiction.

Secondly, it is just as easy to make the point that nowhere can the consumption level be considered adequate even if, by a complicated and entirely artificial exercise in abstraction, one takes into account only the satisfaction of moderate needs and completely ignores the luxury market (in itself a very elastic and fluctuating concept). In fact, American statisticians put the number of people who could be classified as poor between 25 and 30 million. Moreover, several of these are in a state even worse than poverty: they live in abject misery. Then again, it must be remembered that a certain proportion of the remainder of the American population are certainly not comfortably off. Taking this wider view, L. Keyserling estimated that in 1962[1] there were 77 million poor people, making up two-fifths of the nation. To salve my conscience, I will take a look at the case of France (obviously the total consumption of goods is at a lower level than in America, though it is perhaps more fairly distributed over the whole population) but I will confine myself to only one example, which I was able to study closely during my period of office as Minister for Agriculture, the example of the current consumption of foodstuffs, in particular milk products (milk as such, butter, and cheese). The figures examined show that 7 per cent of homes are totally or partly deprived of liquid milk, the most necessary basic product, and that in more than 30 per cent of those homes in which milk was drunk the consumption of milk products, i.e. butter and

[1] *Poverty and deprivation in the USA. The plight of two-fifths of a nation.* 1962

119

cheese, was restricted or eliminated altogether. If I were to consider only the sectors of primary consumption mentioned by Marcuse, I would undoubtedly find that there was an acute shortage as far as clothing is concerned, while, as for housing, the low level of consumption in this sector is due not just, as in the other sectors, to the low income level which limits demand, but to a general shortage of available houses.

Since no quantitative measure, not even a rough and ready guide, of an adequate consumption level exists, I find myself drawn quite naturally to the idea of growth, in actual fact to a quite rapid growth, which is what is taking place. But this is not the whole answer to the question: at what point can this growth influence the type of society to such a degree that it may be qualified a consumer society? At what point should a growing but *by no means adequate* level of consumption be judged to have passed the crucial point? If modern French society can be termed a consumer society, what name will have to be given, in *x* years, to a society where everyone could at least consume enough milk? Would this constitute a society of hyper-consumption?

It is impossible, then, to escape a certain degree of difficulty and it is this difficulty which leads the more conscientious critics either to confine themselves to the realms of social or moral criticism or to be satisfied with peripheral criteria, with a mere by-product of the main phenomenon. All you have to do when dealing with this problem is to make a choice or even to avoid the issue altogether. It is possible to say that in this society, where consumption is growing, greater indignation is raised by the fact that some people enjoy a high, too high, much too high level of consumption while others, etc. However, this situation has always existed, and the very fact of growth tends to reduce these disparities; the poorest members of this society dare to hope for speedy deliverance, a hope completely denied to them in earlier times. It is possible to complain about sales methods, but they are a direct result of increases in production. Complaints can be made about high-pressure selling, but this presupposes an improvement in the financial position of the buyer, etc.

An objective, historical definition of the consumer society, which would justify our claims that it emerged for the first time in our own age and which would account for the inductive importance of this phenomenon, must not be sought for either in the consumption level or in its growth; nor will it be found in the consequences of the rise in consumption. The answer lies elsewhere in a *relational dynamism*. The consumer society is born when the phenomenon, known by classical economists as *the production-consumption balance*, is established. When consumption rises with the (growth) movement of production and, in so doing, sustains the movement, in reality giving it a fresh impetus to launch it anew. When an almost constant function can be established between the factors: total production (national income), consumption (in the home and in public welfare services), investment (in production, defense, etc.). It is precisely the definition of a society of expansion, considered both in its characteristic aspect and in one of its efficient causes. The consumer society is another name for a *society where crises are unknown*, a society free of the crises resulting from over-production, which used to interrupt and even reverse the growth rhythm. Crises are no longer *inevitable*, thanks to the outlet offered by consumption.

Now, this is a recent situation, both novel in itself and in the *idea we have of it*, so new and recent that some people still doubt its existence. *Scientifically* in the socialist camp where there still persists the view that this type of society (as observed in the capitalist world) is constantly threatened and has not long to live. *Instinctively and mnemonically* in the liberal camp, where many still believe that crises are inevitable, and where others, who no longer hold this view, act as though they did. Besides, it cannot be said that up to now definitive proof of the end of the inevitable crisis has yet been given.

This situation and the idea we have of it date only from the post-war years, more accurately from the period 1950 to 1960. Its characteristics did not begin to be clearly distinguishable until after 1960. Its consequences have not yet been clearly worked out in all parts of the world. Whence the tendency to employ vague adjectives to describe it; to confuse causes and effects; to set up secondary effects as prime causes, to attribute permanence to phenomena which will disappear when the period of adjustment is over, to become obsessed with defects which could be corrected, to the point of ignoring the essential good points; finally, as has been pointed out, to propose definitive—because lethal—remedies for fleeting or curable ills.

In order to get a clear picture of the novelty and of the importance of the consumer society and also to be able to present fully the problems it poses, I think that a brief historical survey would not come amiss.

The first results of the industrial revolution gave the early nineteenth century economists food for thought on two fronts, the boom in production and the extreme poverty of the workers. This was particularly true in England, simply because that country was so advanced, and the terrible destitution of the Nottingham hosiers had the same striking effect on the development of Sismondi's thought as the Silesian weavers' revolt had had on that of the young Marx. From now on, those with a public conscience were faced with the problem of a fairer distribution of incomes, while for those whose only interest was their profit margin the problem was the infamous production-consumption balance. Controversies arose between out-and-out pessimists (Malthus), optimistic pessimists (Sismondi) who believed that the situation would get better though not of its own accord, and the optimists (Say, Ricardo, MacCulloch, von Kirschmann) faithful disciples of the liberalism of the happy end and who believed that everything would turn out for the best.

However, none of them ever dreamed that one of the steps towards a solution would be an increase in the consumption level of the working masses themselves, made possible by a rise in the level of real wages. They imagined expansion would continue, either according to the totally abstract concept that sales outlets would automatically be guaranteed by the products themselves, or by an increase in the total number of workers (the sole possibility envisaged for any increase in the total money earned by the wage-earners), or by an increase in the level of consumption of luxury goods by just the capitalists (although this was a market which could represent only 1 per cent of the total, as Sismondi pointed out), or, sometimes by rather bizarre means, through the consumption of the intermediary social categories. Thus, Sismondi[1] placed great store by the possibilities offered by the rural nobility and the clergy 'with their unlimited capacity for wealth and luxury'. 'The church with a capacious maw is blest'[2], was Rosa Luxembourg's ironic remark on this subject, though this did not prevent her from taking up a similar theme in 1913, and she extended the list of those with welcome appetites to include civil servants, the army, the clergy, the scientists, and the artists[3].

We have to wait for Rodbertus to witness the emergence of a remarkable, if formally rather naive, set of ideas which anticipate the work of Keynes. Rodbertus fixes his sights on national income, considered as a whole, and suggests that the State should take the necessary steps to ensure that the wage-earners receive a certain invariable proportion of the gross national revenue in order to guarantee their continuing ability to buy consumer goods: 'an absurd, childish Utopia' according to the socialists.

At the end of the nineteenth century and beginning of the twentieth, those Marxists, who were said to stick to the letter of the law, dreamed up some weird and wonderful economic systems. Tugan-Baranovsky maintained that the production of capital equipment coupled with the consumption of the same would be sufficient to ensure continued expansion. Voronstov proposed amassing all unsaleable surplus goods and distributing them free. Fritz Sternberg was the only one to take the trouble to point out that, contrary to all that had seemed probable and in contradiction with all forecasts made, the purchasing power of the working class had increased. However, he refrained from working out the logical consequences of this strange phenomenon and never dreamed that the impetus provided by this new class of consumers would be sufficient to guarantee

[1] Faure is mistaken here. It was not Sismondi but Malthus to whom Rosa Luxembourg attributes these particular views.

[2] This remark was actually made by Malthus and is simply quoted by Rosa Luxembourg, see p. 222 of work quoted below. (Translator's notes)

[3] Cf. Rosa Luxembourg, *The accumulation of capital*, translated from the German by Agnes Schwarzschild, London, Routledge and Kegan Paul, 1951. pp. 222 and 454–455.

an acceptable growth level in the processes of the accumulation and production of capital.

As for orthodox Marxists, we know that they think there are only two social classes worth consideration: the capitalists and the workers, the other classes being content to obtain their income at the expense of the wage-earners or from surplus-value, as they wait for their complete absorption into the proletariat. That the level of real wages might rise is completely out of the question. This means that for them it is unthinkable that consumption should follow the rhythm of production, and, anyway, such a system would necessarily lead to periodic crises of over-production, culminating in the final catastrophic crisis, for which Marx and Engels tirelessly laid in wait for year after year. This rigid, 'catastrophic' view was complemented and strengthened by the theory, put forward in *Capital*, of the two sectors of production: the production of capital equipment and that of consumer goods[1]. Now the first sector, employing workers who transform their labor into non-consumable goods, had necessarily to be supported by the second sector, and as the first sector grew bigger, this too led to a dead end. This is the point in his theoretical writings where Marx appears to have felt a fundamental doubt. We know that *Capital* was never finished. To their amazement, his disciples discovered that the last example Marx put forward and supported by statistics resulted in a balance and that consequently it could have been deduced scientifically that capitalism might continue indefinitely, with the sole proviso that the proportion between the production of capital equipment and consumer goods be respected. They examined the figures again (Otto Bauer), juggled with ideas, but could find no way out.

Moreover, it would seem that on several occasions both Marx, and even more so Engels, experienced doubts about the categorical assertion that there existed a ceiling for real wages. It was precisely these doubts which allowed later political theorists to defend them against the charge of dogmatism. However, these doubts found no real expression beyond Engel's extremely reserved attitude, at the Erfurt Congress in 1891, on the subject of pauperization. He criticized the unqualified assertion that the poverty of the workers would continue to get worse. On the same lines, Lenin requested in 1902 that the Party Program should no longer talk of the *absolute worsening of poverty and destitution*. And so the definitive text was toned down to read 'The relative, sometimes absolute, worsening of the situation of the working class.'

From then on, the Marxist doctrine and, therefore, after the Revolution, Soviet Marxist doctrine, has constantly retained as an article of faith the pauperization, either absolute, or in any case relative, of the working class.

[1] Here there is no question of anything other than the *production* of commodities, but this prospect virtually includes the possibility, the probability even, of an increase in consumption itself.

Strange as that may seem, the concept of *absolute pauperization* had its proponents for a long time. It seems that it still has some today! In 1958, the Russian scholar, I. Kuz'minov, maintained, with all the gravity in the world, that in England the level of the workers' real wages *had fallen* in comparison with the 1938 and even the 1900 level. This is how far the concept of *secular absolute pauperization* will go.

A more perceptive economist, Eugene Varga, who criticized these untenable theories very severely, was content to base his theories on relative pauperization, which he defined quite simply as *the reduction of the working classes' stake in the national income.*

Whether it is a question of absolute, or even just relative, pauperization, it is obvious that its existence would be sufficient to make the likelihood of a so-called *consumer* society unimaginable under a capitalist régime!

It is therefore surprising that analogous ideas should have found adherents right up to the second half of the twentieth century. But there are historical justifications for this.

Expansion, balanced accumulation as a general phenomenon, was not yet perceptible in 1914. A year earlier, Rosa Luxembourg was making strenuous efforts both to justify and to qualify the orthodox doctrine in her great work, *The accumulation of capital.* The outbreak of war seemed to the Marxists a striking verification of the prophetic announcement that, failing a great economic crisis, capitalism would founder and be destroyed in an imperialist war. After the Russian Revolution, other revolutions were expected. Then, when revolutions failed to materialize or proved to be abortive, everyone was waiting for the crash. It came with Wall Street's 'Black Thursday' and the chain reaction of catastrophes that ensued.

The period from 1929 to 1938 can be considered on the whole, not as a recession properly speaking, but as a long period of stagnation. The total production of the capitalist countries, taken as a whole, achieved only a 4 per cent increase over a period of ten years, i.e. 0·4 per cent per annum. This was not enough for there to be a sudden leap forward in the consuming power of the masses. France held the record for recession, the national income falling by 30 per cent. Such was the success of financial policies inspired by orthodox economic theories and the 'fear of the holocaust'. The Second World War seemed to confirm yet again the idea that the inevitable resurgence of imperialism would trigger off the inevitable war. Stalin's attitude over the German-Soviet Treaty is only too understandable, coming as it does from a man brought up on these doctrines. Since the capitalist world must bear within it the seeds of war, it was imperative to remain aloof and let the prophecy come true. Stalin's convictions on this point never wavered; they account for the whole of his post-war foreign policy. In 1952, he was still proclaiming that war was inevitable between, on the one hand, the European powers Britain, France, West Germany, plus possibly Japan and, on the other hand, the USA, whose economic stranglehold had become intolerable to its partners in the capitalist world[1].

On this point too, the twentieth Congress of the Soviet Communist Party was to initiate a new policy by abandoning the dogmatic insistence on the inevitability of war.

This ideological revision has not yet been extended to economic crises.

After 1945, Soviet economists were waiting for the crisis in the capitalist world. They are still waiting. They like to think that the advent of war disturbed the normal movement of the cycle.

Even today, the monetary difficulties of Western society, the extraordinary inability of its political leaders to put an end to a system whose absurdity continues and whose maleficence is increasing can, as the poet says, 'give them food for thought to while away their wait'.

Can we face the future with complete assurance?

However, it is now quite clear that the link between production and consumption is firmly established. The capitalists, or rather those who pull the strings, the techno-structures within big business, now understand that the interests of the workers are not inimical to their own. In accordance with the wishes of Rodbertus and the recommendations of Keynes, the liberal State has abandoned its reserve and intervenes in economic affairs. The far-sighted Varga himself points out that crisis, in the present age, no longer reveals itself in an explosion, in the sudden brutal transition from prosperity to recession, but rather in a period of *marking time*. Indeed, in the course of recent economic history and in the European countries in particular, we have witnessed that the semi-crises, attributed to the overheating of the economy do not result in a collapse but simply in a period of stagnation. To be even more precise, they have resulted in the growth rate falling to a level lower than that to which we had become pleasantly accustomed but which would still be counted as a very substantial growth rate by pre-war standards.

E. Varga adds, however, that this marking time will be followed in its turn by a definite collapse, the crash, but this is more a case of paying ritual homage to the doctrine and a concession made to prevent the demoralization, if not to fend off the anger, . . . of the orthodox[2].

And this Soviet economist (during a discussion on the European Common Market, too) puts the crucial question very succinctly, *Is it possible to achieve a permanent or, more accurately, a durable, non-cyclic extension of the consumption power of the population*?

[1] Varga, E. *Politico-economic problems of capitalism*. Moscow, Progress Publishers, 1968. p. 79. Stalin, J. *Economic problems in the USSR*. Moscow, Foreign Languages Publishing House, 1952.

[2] Cf. *ibid.*, pp. 235–236. Generally speaking, this over-objective and over-competent economist 'smacks of heresy' as is evident from the reservations expressed by the anonymous writer of the preface to the recent French edition. [This would be the 1968 French edition of the *Politico-economic problems of capitalism*—Translator's note]

The consumer society is the name given to the affirmative answer to this question.

I can therefore conclude this chapter with the following observations.

(a) the consumer society can be defined as a distinct, newly emerged style of society, endowed with a number of coherent characteristics all connected with the growth of consumption;

(b) no doubt another name could be chosen for it. None of those attributed to it are suitable; other possible names are the 'society of crisisless expansion' or the 'society of continuous development', but I think it is preferable to retain the explicit reference to consumption which has substantial advantages;

(c) by emphasizing that the consumer society is precisely a society of expansion, the role of consumption as a motive force equal to that of production is indicated. The danger of considering consumption as a *consequence* of expansion when it is really the *substance* is avoided. We must be careful not to think of this society as a train, driven by a separate engine, from which one or two coaches could be detached according to the demands of the situation. Let us rather think of it as a train whose engine could not move forward without the coaches and of which no constituent element can be suppressed without the whole grinding to a halt, with the added risk of it being more difficult to set it in motion again than was believed;

(d) the emergence of the consumer society and in particular its official recognition have an important consequence for the confrontation of political ideologies and can therefore influence the so-called *political chessboard*. Now that so-called imperialist wars are no longer inevitable, the disappearance of the inevitable crisis has put an end to the irrevocable hostility between socialism and liberalism. The two rival types of society now both admit the validity of planning (with certain differences, of course) and structural problems, such as nationalization, no longer create an unbridgeable rift. Finally, the fact that crises are no longer inevitable proscribes revolution for, as Marx emphasized from the outset, revolution could be contemplated only as the result of a crisis;[1]

(e) it is quite obvious that the indispensable element represented by the growth of production could not be ignored, but the growth of production is implicit in that of consumption, whereas the reverse formula is not true. Besides, the growth of production at a rate compatible with the emergence of the characteristic traits of the consumer society is not a chance phen-

[1] 'In a period of general prosperity during which the productive forces of bourgeois society expand and proliferate to the fullest possible extent within the framework of bourgeois relationships, there can be no question of a true revolution. A new revolution will only be possible after a new crisis, but it is as inevitable as the crisis itself.' Mehring, F. *Aus dem literarischen Nachlass von Karl Marx, Friedrich Engels und Ferdinand Lasalle*. Stuttgart, J.H.W. Dietz Nachf (GmbH), 1902. pp. 467–468.

omenon appearing of its own accord. It is the result of scientific progress incorporated in technology, which assures the infusion of fundamental discoveries into the real life of society. If one wishes to get a complete picture of modern society in all its aspects, it could be summed up adequately as the *technological consumer society*. These two determining factors complement each other. No other is really significant or indispensable.

18

A critique of superficial critical analysis

Current criticism levelled against the consumer society can be qualified as superficial on two counts. It concentrates on external signs, superficial phenomena, a procedure which allows it to isolate them one from another, to pick and choose, to classify, and to wage war against either advertising or the importance accorded to consumption, against the mass media or dehumanization, etc.

Secondly, this type of criticism, concerned only with isolated phenomena, makes hardly any attempt at a thorough analysis; it makes no attempt to discover causes, to get to the root of the problem. Then again, it nearly always declines to offer positive solutions, or if it does deign to propose a solution it is either unrealizable or catastrophic.

Without daring to admit as much, even to itself, nostalgic criticism is inspired by the venerable concept of luxury articles[1], luxury consumption, which found expression so often in the course of history in sumptuary laws and which was the focal point of the controversial arguments between nineteenth century economists. Our contemporaries have not yet got used to the idea that the laboring classes can afford to purchase expensive items instead of being content with simply assuring for themselves a 'decent' standard of living, decent in two meanings of the word (for if it is indecent to see a man reduced to misery, it is no less so to see him rising above his

---

[1] The distinction between necessity and luxury consumption being nowadays obsolete, in the course of my analysis I shall employ other categories, inspired partly by Rostow. Thus I distinguish between:

(a) basic consumption (food, clothes, housing, articles of everyday use);
(b) household equipment (including the car, since it is principally or partly intended for private use);
(c) the consumption of services;
(d) marginal consumption including those products, whether expensive or not, which would not fit in to the preceding categories;
(e) the consumption of cultural merchandise.

Finally, there is indeed another category, which I am tempted to include on the list but which implies a completely different angle on the problem; I shall be content with just mentioning it here: *it is the consumption of time* which is the key to the real problem confronting every type of society, i.e. its relationship with man.

proper station in life!) and with putting by the eventual surplus of his earnings to secure his future.

It is easy to discern in these criticisms a longing for the good old days, which even authors like Lefebvre and Marcuse do not attempt to hide.

If their tale were to be told it would recount how the people lived, in wretched conditions but in an atmosphere of great warmth and friendliness. Much progress has been made since these good old days[1].

True this romantic pre-technical world was permeated with misery, toil and filth and these in turn were the background of all pleasure and joy. Still, there was a 'landscape', a medium for libidinal experience which no longer exists[2].

(a) The critique of inadequate consumption

The first thing that strikes one when one tries, as I have done, to define the consumer society, is that the level of consumption in such a society is in fact inadequate and that there may be some isolated sectors of the population living in absolute poverty, while a greater or lesser proportion of the others will find their consumption of even basic commodities is curtailed. Surely, these are adequate grounds for a justifiable sense of indignation.

However, a moment's thought will reveal that this is not a characteristic of the consumer society as such. It is a characteristic of all types of society in which the incomes of certain people are too low to ensure a decent standard of living.

The difference between the consumer society and societies which have preceded it is, for one thing, that the zones of inadequate consumption are smaller in the consumer society, and, for another, they tend to diminish instead of remaining constant or increasing.

In the consumer society, an inadequate level of consumption of essential commodities is not, as a general rule, the result of the faulty distribution of the commodities available for consumption, but of the unequal distribution of incomes. The mere fact of limiting the consumption of the wealthier people would not, *in itself*, have any effect on the consumption level of the poorer people (unless, of course, it was a question of fiscal and budgetary measures taken to adjust the distribution of incomes; but this is not the aspect of the problem with which I am concerned here). If, on the other hand, we envisage the limitation of (supposedly excessive) consumption by cutting back the production of certain 'superfluous' commodities, this method by no means guarantees the promotion of the consumption of vital commodities by those whose consumption of them is inadequate.

It is not by producing fewer cars, refrigerators, televisions, etc., that one

[1] Lefebvre, *La vie quotidienne dans le monde moderne*. p. 147.
[2] Marcuse, H. *One-dimensional man*. p. 73.

will guarantee an extra ration of butter or cheese to those who are deprived of these foodstuffs. The production of necessary articles everywhere exceeds the demand or at least could be stepped up, and there is no need (nor indeed any real possibility) of transferring the workers in the electronics industry to work on farms, nor even to manufacture cloth. Quite the contrary, in fact; the only result of cutting back the production of cars, and the activities of the second, third, and fourth sectors generally, would be to reduce total income and to limit purchasing power still further.

Taking the best hypothesis open to us, those whose purchasing power is abnormally low can hope for nothing more than to preserve it at the present level, with no prospect of it being improved. Then again, the chance of conserving income at its present level may not always be granted, for during a slump it is the lower incomes that are the most affected, especially as a result of unemployment or short-time working.

There is, however, only one way to remedy this state of affairs: that is to accentuate the characteristics of the consumer society, a society where technology favors the rapid rise of the level of production accompanied by a corresponding rise in the level of consumption. At the same time we could, as far as it is technically possible, redistribute income in favor of the most underprivileged sectors.

This is what has been done, on a greater or lesser scale depending on the country, thanks to institutions such as the minimum wage, unemployment benefits, social security, old-age pensions, scholarships, etc. These achievements have been made possible by the consumer society with its growth economy and, as this society develops, further progress could be made in these fields within its framework. These measures have not been brought about in spite of the consumer society, but because of it and for it, for a more equal distribution of income and *especially the raising of the lowest incomes is a condition for growth.*

And so, far from filling us with a feeling of righteous indignation against a type of society which tolerates them, the excessive disparities, which society has not yet abolished, should urge us to strengthen, accelerate, and make fullest use of the movement of expansion and to implement further the social planning, which goes hand in hand with it or, more precisely, which is an integral part of it.

I must make particular reference to the problem of housing. If housing, along with food and clothing, is one of the three articles of basic consumption, in this case the increased production of available units poses technical difficulties completely out of proportion with those presented by the other sectors. However, in this case too, it would be a grave mistake to believe that increased production of housing units would be guaranteed by cutting back the production of cars. The feasibility of a building program is determined by a combination of circumstances, the availability of the materials and a labor force and, equally important, the methods in which

130

the undertaking is financed, which are themselves dependent on the income level of the prospective customers. The suppression of other fields of production would not ensure an increased supply of building materials, and could go only a little way towards providing the industry with unskilled workers. Conversely, a fall in total income has never led to a boom in the building industry. On the other hand, in this field, there can exist a certain degree of competition between the different demand sectors. Given a certain operational budget, which is neither indefinitely extensible nor really elastic, it might be advisable to utilize some of the available money for social measures favoring the needy. But, this question does not affect the consumer society as such. The charge of implementing a building program with the wrong social priorities could not be levelled at the society I am analyzing: it can even be said that such a program is not normally a characteristic of this society. It is a political not a structural problem.

(b) Non-essential consumption

This is the area in which those who regret the good old days really let themselves go, their bitterness and confusion being all the greater because they cannot find the slightest reason or plausible justification to support their emotional hysteria. Moreover, they are joined in their chorus of woe by those Left-wingers whose hope is all in the future and who are deeply discontented at seeing the masses, having drawn back from the revolutionary impasse, being rescued and integrated, the masses whom they now look upon as both betrayed and betrayers. How can the worker be made to understand that the acquisition of the evil triad—car/refrigerator/radio—is proof of the fact he has been totally despoiled of the surplus-value inherent in his labor?

Here we are then, surrounded by useless objects, or at least objects which are not 'authentically' useful. We are obsessed by them, they prey on our minds, they devour us, they feed on our substance. Indeed, was it not the demon of consumption that was in Paul Valéry's mind when he wrote these famous lines:

> Sa dent secrète est de moi si prochaine . . .
> Ma chair lui plaît, et jusque sur ma couche
> À ce vivant je vis d'appartenir?[1]

[1] See Valéry, P. Le cimetière marin. Pléiade edition of the complete works. Vol. I. 1957, p. 151.
Translation:

> His secret tooth is so intimate with me. . . .
> My flesh delights him, even upon my couch
> I live but as a morsel of his life.

Day Lewis, C. The graveyard by the sea. London, Martin Secker and Warburg, 1945. (Translator's note)

However, let us take a closer look at what we are dealing with. The evil triad and the other commodities which go with it are neither essential for existence, like the vital commodities, nor do they uplift the mind, like (true) cultural commodities. However, neither are they incompatible with the first or the second objective, and anyone prepared to look at the problem with a modicum of good faith will admit that, on average or perhaps taking the algebraic sum, they create favorable conditions for the attainment of the two objectives. If exception is made of accidents (which are relatively rare occasions) the man who possesses a car and other consumer durables eats better, is better dressed, takes better care of himself (consumption of services), rests easier, and for this reason lives longer, which is the one condition *sine qua non* for the consumption of essential or cultural commodities. The possession of a car facilitates visits to museums and to the theater; the car owner can look at the world about him, in particular at its cultural and historical aspects. The motorist is encouraged to learn mechanical skills, which are a form of culture—no offense intended to the advocates of knowledge devoid of practical applications. As for the mass media, how could one deny their value as a source of knowledge? But I shall return to this point later.

Earlier societies were already acquainted with the large-scale consumption of capital equipment and so-called luxury objects. Instead of cars, there were horses and carriages, and the deification of the car will never reach the heights scaled in the apotheosis of the horse. True, the animal has the advantage of being a living thing; a bond of affection can spring up between it and man; Chekov's cabman could tell his secrets to his old horse. But it is also true that some cars have been endowed with a personality of their own. Films have been made on the subject. However, let us concede that mechanized transport deprives us of a certain warmth of feeling (which is hardly a consideration to be taken seriously), for it must not be forgotten that the chief effect of mechanization has been to free some human slaves, a consideration of great importance. The comparative level of luxury spending is falling not rising. Just think of the huge sums of money spent on monuments and temples in the Ancient World, buildings which were, for the most part, just as standardized as modern buildings of minor importance. Think of the quantity of armor and weapons, of the number of servants and carriages in royalist France. The only difference is that these luxury articles were available to the privileged classes only, whereas their equivalents today, although not available to every social class, are more or less available to the majority of the population. If that is what these philosophers deplore, they must say so. But, if that is the case, they must not claim that too much emphasis is placed on non-essential consumption but that they think it deplorable that non-essential articles are not reserved for a social élite. This being so, they will have to concede that their views coincide with those of MacCulloch, von Krischmann, and

132

even Rosa Luxembourg, who found it impossible to imagine the working class being interested in fine clothes or even in eating raisins.

(c) Standardization and the critique of quality

Here we have yet another fashionable idea. The extensive consumption of capital equipment and marginal objects could jeopardize quality control and consequently impair the finer side of life. Yet another sophism! How can quality depend on availability? Is it impossible for *quality* objects, even people of *quality*, to exist in *quantity*? Why confuse quality and rarity? This criterion only applies from an economist's point of view, where exchange value is more important than use value. It is possible to imagine an abundance of gold and diamonds in an area where bread was rationed. How would this impair the brilliance and beauty of the gold and diamonds, even though, in such a situation, they would naturally lose their (relative) exchange value?

Does the meeting of the hundred best skiers in the world, between whose performances there is a difference of only a few fractions of a second, afford less sporting quality than the meeting of the same number of amateurs, brought together by chance in an out-of-the-way mountain resort, where the champions are head and shoulders above the rest of the field? Is the French Academy qualitatively inferior to a body made up of one educated man and thirty-nine morons?

The car is standardized: good. How, and since when? There are many different automobile companies; each company produces many different models; there are seasonal variations in the finish; the customer can demand a certain type of bodywork. I read in a recent article, 'The Rolls come off the production line, one after another, and each one is unique'. The enthusiast says, 'I already have a white convertible Rolls with two doors, but it is inconvenient when I go to a gala occasion dressed in a cloak and an evening suit. And so, I would like you to make me the same model, but this time with four doors.' The reply: 'The Beatles were refused this model; it is only made for heads of State'. However, if this model were to be mass-produced, how would this affect its elegance, comfort, and beautiful lines? Not at all. There would be one slight change; the self-esteem and the selfish pleasure conferred upon the owner by the possession of a unique piece of machinery and the feeling of being placed on a par with a head of State, which he is not, would diminish in quality or rather in intensity. A standardized quality-object is the same quality-object made available to a greater number of users. To be intent upon maintaining a so-called refinement in the consumption of luxury articles by making them scarce only serves to encourage the stupid and pointless delight experienced by some people, who have no sense of social democracy, at being a cut above the common herd.

133

(d) The critique of planned waste

Besides, all those who cling to the idea that exclusivity and rarity are indispensable attributes of quality can be completely reassured. The extended distribution of articles of a specific quality gives rise, as it were automatically, to the creation of a higher quality where rarity value once more comes into play, and so the process is repeated *ad infinitum*. It is possible for this perpetual search for innovation-rarity to concentrate on unimportant details, while the users' frivolity may cause them to seek to acquire objects of no real use. Whence a new criticism, the criticism of planned waste. There is some justification for criticism of this type; many people certainly do feel a spurious need to change their car, shaver, etc. at a time when they could make do with the old ones with no appreciable inconvenience to themselves. And yet, what is being wasted? This question merits unbiased analysis. Materials? Labor? Energy? This wastage also produces an inflow of capital, which allows new sectors of the population to acquire, with no wastage involved, products of prime necessity or the most ordinary household equipment. How could one ensure that individuals buy only products for which they have a genuine need and, at the same time, that the general movement of the economy is in no way impaired? It would take miracles of psychology and genius in economic management.

Must we focus attention on the producer? Will he be told whether innovations are permissible? Will decisions be made as to whether such and such an improvement is worthy of consideration or not? Will a new product be banned on the grounds that it is but little improvement on an already existing one? Innovation is part of the general climate of opinion: by discouraging frivolity there is a risk of stifling the spirit of competition, of invention even. Prosperity must be seen as a whole: if some businesses were prevented from maintaining their sales on the grounds that the need for their particular commodity was temporarily satisfied, how could employment be maintained and taxes paid, how could one ensure that the manufacture and sales of other essential commodities would not be impaired? I feel some qualms at insisting upon such obvious points. But these are precisely the points raised by nostalgic criticism; they must be dealt with exhaustively once and for all.

Should attention, therefore, be focused on the purchaser? Will he have to ask permission to change his car before a certain period of time has elapsed? Can he be forbidden to discard a serviceable shaver to buy an apparently, though not necessarily, much improved one? What relevant documents will he have to produce? What bureaucracy will have to be set up? The final result would certainly be the same: the progressive asphyxiation of the production cycle.

The mania to possess more commodities gives rise to just as much sarcasm as the desire to renew them.

134

In *Brave new world*, Aldous Huxley asks whether the possession of two television sets is guaranteed to ensure twice as much happiness as the possession of one? The answer is in doubt; the likelihood of securing happiness by such means seems improbable. Perhaps the owner of two televisions is just a little happier, perhaps there is no difference at all; anyway, all that is certain is that no one is made unhappier. The presence of several televisions in one household permits each person living there to watch a different program at one particular time, depending on his own tastes. Is this to be sneezed at? The reason for providing several different channels is that it is considered necessary to vary what is on offer. It therefore goes without saying that the largest audience possible should benefit from this. If not, it must be argued that one television channel is sufficient; from this it would be an easy step to maintain that television itself is an unnecessary refinement, radio being enough on its own, etc. It is easier to stem progress altogether than to contain it.

I remember some sarcastic comments made about a report on the difficulties of agriculture, in the South-West of France I think, because a young farmer, who had aired his grievances, had two cars in his yard: he had, however, demonstrated very convincingly that one of his cars was indispensable to the running of the farm and that his wife needed the other to drive the children to school, to do the shopping, to play her share in running the farm, etc. Moreover, these cars represented a very small proportion of the cost of running his business. His job would have been made more difficult if he had deprived himself of this convenience, and by buying second-hand cars he helped the people from whom he bought them to buy new vehicles and the factory wheels to continue to turn.

It is a well known fact that the collectivist economies of the Eastern bloc offer fewer opportunities for, and less diversification in, consumption. In their case, there is no planned waste, or rather their wastage is of a different kind. It is the result of an inefficient bureaucratic machine, which sees to it that for long periods at a time the only shoes available on the market are in impractical sizes, etc. But is there another brighter side to this austerity? Is there less work, more pleasure in life? Not at all. Since the Apollo program, it is impossible to claim that a Spartan administration of domestic consumption guarantees superiority in great collective ventures.

In so far as this is a rational objective, there are only two ways of avoiding wastage. On the sales side, production of the essential commodities can be promoted and encouraged by non-restrictive, selective methods of granting credit and by investment, or, on the purchasing side, there is what is known as the 'education' of the consumer.

This point leads naturally to an examination of the next type of criticism, and this is a field where critics are at their most acrimonious: the field of supposedly artificially induced consumption.

(e) Artificially induced consumption. The case against advertising

We are told that the consumer society would be perfectly blameless if no pressure were brought to bear upon the consumer and he was free to choose for himself. But this is not the case. He is 'conditioned', hypnotized, manipulated, 'alienated'. Not because he abandons his personality of his own accord, but because external aggressions violate his psychological frontiers and instil in him desires and needs which are not really his. A whole garrison takes up residence in his head. Endless demands are made for food and supplies, his money is allocated for him, his mental processes are taken over. A simple man is transformed into a complicated, demanding being; he used to be humble, he is now forced to court ostentation; timid, now he is arrogant. Was he discreet? Soon he will be a show-off. Was he virtuous? Already he is a cynic. . . . Was he happy? Now he is a paranoiac. Never satisfied with what he has, he wears himself out in a ceaseless derisory search. While ostensibly offering him repose, society reduces him to a state of exhaustion; while claiming to offer a change of scene, it exposes him to the vertiginous precipice of instability. He used to sleep well: now he is taking sleeping tablets. Did he enjoy good health? Now he is looking for a fashionable illness with a view to doctoring it by the newest course of treatment, waiting to contract a second illness to ward off a third. In earlier times, lives were lost earning a living; now earning a living is big business, but the risk of losing life has gone, simply because we never really begin to live. In marked contrast to these horrific pictures of the infernal modern world, how healthy, natural, not to say 'authentic', even heavenly the everyday life of the noble savage seems! There is only one slightly disturbing aspect about his life; he tended to die at a much earlier age than we do.

How does this conditioning work? Obviously, in several different ways; chiefly by imitation, by playing upon the instinct to conform, etc; but the principal agent, in legal jargon the principal in the first degree, is advertising with its prodigious deployment of novel gimmicks, the most diabolical of these being the stimulation of eroticism and the indoctrination of sexuality with the express purpose of making us buy a number of commodities which may, however, have no connection with the emotions of the heart or the stimulation of the instinct.

Though not defending certain excesses which are, moreover, rarer than one might think and which could be eliminated by minor adjustments in the law, I would like to go on record as saying that this conventional indictment of advertising is, in my opinion, both unjust and superficial.

(i) Advertising does not normally create needs; it simply provides the agreeable revelation that needs can be satisfied. At the very most it facilitates a clearer awareness of our needs.

(ii) Advertising can never guarantee the success of a product, for which there is no real demand and which does not give the user satisfaction. Marcuse himself points out that an expensive venture geared to selling atomic shelters ended in a dreadful fiasco[1].

(iii) Advertising cannot reorientate a need, felt by the consumer, towards another product. Thus, American automobile manufacturers have never been able to convince customers, who want small cars, to buy big ones; this was demonstrated very clearly when the importation of foreign cars revealed a sector of the buying public which had remained hostile to every incitement to buy a big car. Some spectacular advertising campaigns, often based on the findings of thorough preliminary market surveys, have resulted in a failure as striking as it was unexpected, simply because the consumer refused to be convinced, having no prior disposition towards the product.

(iv) An evolution whose daily progress can actually be observed does not seem to indicate that the purchaser is being conditioned by the vendor: quite the opposite, in fact. It is the all-powerful purchaser who conditions the manufacturer, the future vendor. To an increasing degree, the manufacturer is using marketing techniques to see what the customer wants, what he is looking for, so that his own manufacturing processes and his proposed new products may be adapted to meet the demand.

Besides, all this is perfectly understandable. For, as Galbraith succinctly puts it, the large-scale manufacture of a mass-produced article demands a colossal outlay in terms of capital, time, and research. Our age, apparently so fast-moving, has in certain respects slowed down. A one-off car could be knocked up in a few days for a customer who had the money to pay. A new prototype of a model for mass production demands 18 months' development. No doubt this leads to a great burst of advertising activity, but the first step is a meticulous analysis of the state of the market. Advertising merely retransmits to the consumer his own wishes and demands; it speaks his language, for it has taken the trouble to learn it. It is reflexive. Although it uses aggressive techniques, its inspiration and message are quite harmless.

The consumer is becoming less and less of a dupe: he is becoming the master.

(v) *Finally, high-pressure advertising in the old style is unknown today. The practice of fraud through advertising is rarer than it used to be.*

For advertising has always existed. It did not wait for the invention of neon billboards and television. It used to be inseparable from the actual sale itself and worked by appealing directly to the customer. They are a disappearing race, those cheap-jacks of my childhood, who set up their

[1] Marcuse, H. *One-dimensional man.* pp. 89–90.

one-cent[1] bazaar (for the goods always cost one cent) on the public highway. But, just imagine how their patter and glib eloquence could make people forget themselves so far that they would be willing to buy unnecessary articles and to acquire worthless, useless trinkets, making great inroads into their meagre financial resources. And yet these traders had no direct power over people's minds. But there were other vendors who did, for example the innumerable salesmen, hawkers, agents, canvassers, pedlars, and gipsies, who marched in droves over the countryside, some of them (almost fraudulently) taking unfair advantage of the credulity of the village people, to whom they laid siege in their own kitchens. Before the war, when I was practicing as a lawyer, I often had occasion to witness the extent of this kind of financial trickery (it was round about this time that laws were passed to bring it under control). How many rural cantons were 'conditioned' to purchase title deeds sold to them by individuals, deeds whose value was in inverse proportion to the richness of the embellishment and the fineness of the magnificent parchment on which they were written.

In comparison with practices such as these, how pure our much maligned advertising seems with its brazen, open campaigns! If there were not more court cases involving advertising in earlier days, it is not because of a lack of initiative or ingenuity on the part of the advertisers, but because people had less purchasing power. Nowadays, the consumer enjoys a much greater degree of protection, respect, and consideration than formerly. Moreover, thanks to the abundance of lawsuits brought against advertisers, he is much better-informed than before; he is no longer likely to be persuaded by the categorical assertions of hawkers or the whispered blandishments of an old woman, but is capable of making up his own mind, having first examined the conflicting advertising matter of competitors, and, because of the very diversity of products, he is in no way disposed to put up indefinitely with unsatisfactory goods. When I read Jean-Francis Held's amusing reflection, 'If the economy depended on the manufacture of rollers, willy-nilly we would all have to have waved hair'[2], I did not believe it. For, if such a situation arose, there would be at least one more product, with just as striking an advertising campaign to promote it, which would find a market among bald people at the very least. If the outlay required is equal and the advertising similar, a more useful object will easily be preferred. Manipulation would be much more dangerous if advertising were a monopolistic concern rather than a competitive one. Moreover, the limit of the magical effect of pseudo-erotic images is apparent in the growing success of mail-order sales, which do not use this type of advertising.

Besides, and this thought is valid for the whole of this chapter, if the consumer was the mentally defective idiot he is made out to be, he would

---

[1] The French text has *carante* here, which is a corruption of *quarante* meaning 40. The goods displayed were all sold for the paltry sum of 40 *sous*, more or less equivalent to the English old penny and the American cent. (Translator's note)

[2] *La Nef. op. cit.* p. 132.

get into debt more. He would be hypnotized into wanting goods in a price-bracket way above what he could afford. Now, I know that the proportion of defaulters among those who buy on credit is very low, in the region of 1 per cent.

However, in so far as superficial criticism contains any truth at all, it is not the consumer society that is to blame, but man's relative failure to adapt himself to new circumstances, whose certain and peculiar advantages demand a corresponding psychological development. They demand education, education of the intelligence and of the character, together with a rise in the general level of knowledge. The real problem of every type of society is the man of that society. A progressive civilization needs a progressive man. A more open-handed world needs a man of greater substance. This will be clearly seen in what follows.

19

The culture boom

'Your numbers alone constitute a crime in his eyes.'
Stephan George

It is with the consumption of culture, the mass consumption of cultural articles, that I shall run the gauntlet of the bitterest and most concerted attacks of other critics, for this is just the subject on which there is some measure of agreement between superficial and radical critics. This is where the problem is revealed in all its complexity, although my viewpoint is rather different from that of other critics.

The charges levelled against the cultural consumer society have become classic, just like the charges levelled against 'the modern age' in the oratory of the pulpit. There is a very common, not to say preponderant feeling that mass culture is both mindless and inane, both degrading and degraded[1].

Such a point of view, in my opinion a rather extreme one, ignores two of the essential elements of the subject: on the one hand, the (growing) number of converts to culture; on the other, the (equally growing) richness and diversity of the fields of learning and intellectual activities, which are lumped together under this one heading.

The number of converts

Short of implying the existence of a dichotomy within the species, how is it possible to take seriously the idea that culture can be appreciated only at the level experienced by a restricted number of people? That in order to determine the progress made by culture, to see whether it is stagnating or has regressed, it is necessary to draw a sort of high-water mark constituted by a line joining all the points represented by the men who, throughout the ages, have reached this degree of excellence?

If present day industrial society is compared with the ancient civilizations of the East, of Egypt, of Greece, of Renaissance Europe, the most obvious difference is that the number and proportion of educated men, men who

---

[1] Even Henri Lefebvre writes: 'A general crisis in the value of ideas, philosophy, art, culture'. 'Through what remains of culture', etc.

are aware of what must be called cultural values, is infinitely greater in modern society. Moreover, I believe that there are just as many, if not more, 'geniuses' in our society as in earlier ones; but this is a point to which I will return. Can it be said that the objective of human progress is to produce, in each successive age, a few Aristotles, a few Leonardos? Will we be satisfied with one Pushkin more, in despair over one Shakespeare less? Obviously, this is not a problem to be taken seriously.

In fact, when dealing with the question of an élite, we make the acquaintance once more of an old friend of ours, the false criterion of rarity. There is a tendency to believe, at least one often hears it said, that in a society where everyone is well-educated, no one is well-educated. Now, the idea of an élite does not in itself imply rarity, but some members of an élite may derive an additional pleasure from thinking of themselves as rather rare birds.

This is where the great sophism is trotted out. The masses were happier, or so we are told, when they were uneducated, nay, when they were completely ignorant. The man without a shirt to his back was also without a dictionary: does this mean he had no problems? Such a pipe-dream costs nothing. Is the barbarian happy? Has he no problems? The only men capable of envisaging this possibility are those who are in the habit of asking themselves questions, men who are, by definition, unhappy. Like Voltaire's Brahmin, only the wise are capable of asking themselves if a state of ignorance would be preferable to their knowledge, and since they can appreciate only one of the elements in the comparison, they will never receive an answer to their question. To put it more simply, I will just say, and this is my own opinion, that I refuse to admit that any man can derive happiness from any source other than the consciousness of being a man, i.e. of having a place within the spectrum of the human condition as it exists at that time.

But a more serious difficulty will present itself. If it is difficult to recommend, openly at least, the maintaining of the masses in a state of ignorance in order to guarantee their happiness, it is possible to try to make a distinction between intellectual and spiritual life and the acquisition of knowledge. Must one believe that in a slower, less turbulent world, select beings, either by a life of meditation or even by securing for themselves a certain degree of isolation within their society, could attain a level of knowledge, a nobleness of soul which, today, it would be more difficult to attain and whose achievement is therefore rarer?

There have always been individuals tempted by this kind of ambition; no doubt there are some today. More or fewer than formerly? It is hard to tell. What must be emphasized is that isolation from the world, or within the world, with the aim of individual improvement presupposes a knowledge of the world. Meditation supposes an awareness of the whole field of knowledge. Deep thought on the great problems confronting man is possible only when one is truly a man, i.e. when one has reached an intellectual level which will allow meditation and reflection to come to fruition. The hermits of Port-Royal were the cleverest men of their age (along with the Jesuits, of course). It is no doubt desirable that as many people as possible, and not just restricted groups, should be capable of withstanding the whirlwind of the consumer society. But for the nobility and the usefulness of this effort to be understood, for any kind of enthusiasm in the undertaking to be aroused, it is imperative that the diffusion and availability of culture be on the widest scale possible.

What is culture?

The man who deplores the debilitation and insipidness of culture is yielding to the incredible preconceived idea that culture comprises only two branches: literature and the fine arts. Personally, I do not believe that, even taking into consideration these two lone fields, such complaints are in any way justified. Besides, we live in a scientific technological age. Science is culture. Technology is culture, even technical know-how is culture. Surely the discovery of the breathtaking secrets of life, of the composition of organic matter, the splitting of the atom, our intimate knowledge of astral spaces, constitute cultural values, which are just as valid as Latin grammar, fifteenth-century Italian painting, a profound knowledge of Corneille's plays, or an understanding of Robbe-Grillet.

If Pascal returned to earth, Pascal who had conceived of the atom as a divisible particle, who experienced the trauma of the contemplation of the two infinites, would he not feel that he had been enriched culturally by the great strides made in the two polarized fields of learning which had been the source of his own anxiety? Can you imagine a modern Pascal who would have no interest in cybernetics, who would be content with just . . . reading Pascal?

Surely, the discovery of the mechanism of our thought processes is a supreme cultural achievement; and what of the great strides made in the science of logic, thanks to the new mathematics, which have opened up to each and everyone of us the techniques of probability analysis, linear programming, operations research? This 'super-logic' transcends the field of scientific research proper (to which, nevertheless, it has opened up new horizons); it constitutes a major step forward in thought itself, and the gain it represents for man has rightly been compared with those which other species obtain by bio-genetic mutations.

Jacques Bureau suggests that *the calculation of the exact size of the universe* will be the ultimate challenge for tomorrow's man. Is the fact that such a project is even thinkable indicative of the disintegration of the cultural values of our society?

To sum up, I think I can safely make three assertions:

First, that there are today many more educated men than there ever were before, and that their numbers will probably increase daily.

Second, that the educated men of our time are much better-educated than were their counterparts of earlier times, because modern scholars reap the benefits from a general extension of the field of human knowledge.

Third, that modern man is intellectually and, therefore, culturally superior to the man of the so-called pre-logical age[1].

I must now examine more thoroughly the more important secondary objections levelled at mass culture.

(a) Some well-disposed people admit that the spread of culture to the 'popular masses' is not without its advantages; it is, in any case, inevitable. However, it pains them to think that the number of 'geniuses' will, as a result, be reduced and, what is worse, that those geniuses who manage to survive will be, dare I say it, less 'genial'.

Long before the emergence of the 'true' consumer society, this idea found a remarkable advocate in the person of Tocqueville, who already feared that social and economic progress would lead to vulgarization. He notes that the new type of society tended to withdraw from the extremes, both of good and evil. He writes, 'Rarely does one meet with either a truly well-educated man or an abysmally ignorant group of people. Genius becomes rarer and generalized knowledge more common'[2].

However, Tocqueville wisely points out that what seems a deterioration to him is perhaps a sign of progress, and that care must be taken not to judge nascent societies according to criteria inspired by defunct civilizations. This piece of advice is still relevant today. But I do not believe that mass culture necessarily leads to genius becoming rarer. On the contrary, I find Turgot's observations more convincing. He thought that the percentage of geniuses produced depended more or less on the extent of education, and he draws an analogy with the process of extracting gold from a mine: the more ore you take out the greater the percentage of precious metal obtained[3].

In fact, those who believe in the devaluation of genius are simply restricting their observations to the field of the 'arts' in the widest sense of the word and ignoring the field opened up to modern geniuses by science. Similarly, they are unaware of, or prefer to ignore, the emergence in the

[1] For more information on all these problems, see Jacques Bureau's remarkable work: *L'Ère logique*. Paris, Robert Laffont, 1969.

[2] Tocqueville, A. de. *Democracy in America*. p. 55.

[3] *Oeuvres de Turgot* edited in 5 volumes by Gustave Schelle, Paris, 1913–1923. Volume I. p. 118: 'Genius permeates the human race rather like gold in a mine. The more mineral taken out, the greater the quantity of precious metal obtained'. Cf. p. 117: 'Nature distributes a certain number of geniuses at almost equal intervals throughout time and space. Whether these be encouraged or relegated to obscurity depends on the hazards of education and circumstance'.

modern world of collective works of genius. Great discoveries are not always the work of a single individual, and our age has demonstrated that it is possible to be a genius without being a recluse. Besides, if one refused to be limited to the definition of 'geniuses' in the strict and, moreover, indefinable sense of the word, it is quite clear that, if education is more widely available, then the number of gifted and extremely able people increases as a result. The raising of the masses to the level of the élite favours the creation of 'super-élites'. And why fear a large élite body in an age of extreme specialization, where a group of élites may be sub-divided in to several smaller élite groups, each group being qualified in a different area of invention and research? The contribution to progress which could formerly be expected of a single man now demands the group, the team, the vast interplay of complementary talents and syntheses, as we shall see when I deal with synectics.

But, on the other hand, there is nothing to prove that the quality we call genius necessarily follows, among those lucky enough to possess it, an ascending rhythm in accordance with the growth rate of the economy or with the general widening of the whole field of knowledge. Perhaps the Ancient World did produce some geniuses who may be emulated but not surpassed. The superiority of mental and material means available to men of genius cannot be adapted to all branches of creation. I made a decision not to deal with artistic problems in this book. I would like to point out, however, that the preceding observation is particularly applicable to works of art. The intensity of a work of art depends more on the relationship between the artist and the society in which he lives than on the general level of that society itself. Marx made this quite clear in the remarkable passage in the *Introduction to the critique of political economy* devoted to Greek art:

> A man cannot become a child again unless he becomes childish. But does he not enjoy the artless ways of the child, and must he not strive to reproduce its truth on a higher plane? Why should the social childhood of mankind, where it had obtained its most beautiful development, not extend an eternal charm as an age that will never return?... The charm of their [the Greeks'] art for us does not conflict with the primitive social order from which it had sprung. It is rather the product of the latter, and is rather due to the fact that the unripe social conditions, under which the art arose and under which it could alone appear, can never return[1].

(b) This said, there is nothing to indicate that artistic creation in the consumer society is condemned to mediocrity, and here I am answering yet another objection often directed against mass culture. Contrary to

[1] See Marx, K. *Introduction to the critique of political economy*. New York, The International Publishing Co., 1904. pp. 311–312.

what some critics would have us believe, it is not a typical characteristic of mass culture to vulgarize art and make it immediately comprehensible. The popularity of non-figurative painting and of the modern novel demonstrates that the creators in our society seek to flatter neither the public's basest instincts, nor the instincts of the basest public, that art remains an arduous and demanding search. Will the objection be made that the more difficult works still appeal to only a limited audience? Not all that limited: an audience no doubt wider than that in other ages obtained by the most facile creative works.

The counter-proof is provided by communist societies, where the characteristics of the consumer society are much less marked in economic dealings. In these societies, there is little planned waste of commodities, few consumer durables for the masses and, as for cultural consumption, here austerity is the order of the day. Now, what are the effects on the artistic world? Its impotence cannot be denied. The type of painting favored, as depicted so strikingly in Ehrenburg's *The Thaw*, is conventional in the extreme. True, their literature does not incite to murder or sin, but it is deadly dull. This is the main reason for the surprising success enjoyed in the Soviet Union by translations of foreign works, even those with the dullest plots, for example Victor Hugo's collected letters.

(c) Since mass culture does not necessarily entail a dearth of cultural 'production', the pessimists and the élitists concentrate their gloomy forecasts on the mass 'buying public'.

According to them, the man of common extraction would, by definition, be cheated out of pure aesthetic enjoyment which can never be the prerogative of any but the happy few. If I object and say that modern reproduction techniques allow hordes of amateurs to become acquainted with the great masters of the art world, a world which would have been closed to them before, I shall be told that if the contact with the work of art itself is missing, nothing has been gained, and that the most faithful copy can never have the instructive and stimulating qualities of the original.

The replies which could be made to this stubborn pessimism are legion. The problem is not one of establishing a comparison between the joy felt by a rich man as he explores the Angkor ruins and the pleasure felt by a poorer man looking at them on film at his leisure. What should be our concern is to compare the merits of the film with those of a written description of the ruins and, most important of all, to contrast ignorance of the Angkor temple's existence with the knowledge, however imperfect, of its existence, knowledge gained through the medium of film. Besides, do I have to point out yet again that the museums opened up by making culture accessible to the 'masses' are not just imaginary ones; that the consumer society, which makes travelling much easier, which gives the public access to works of art, where man's chances to communicate with beautiful objects are multiplied, is constantly engaged in a process of making 'direct contacts' without which, according to some critics, no real joy or advantage is possible, both more numerous and less arduous?

With all due deference to those anguished souls, I must point out that mass culture has made fantastic progress. I have in mind the difficulties we had as students in getting to grips with those great books, which were then available only from libraries, open for just a few short hours a day, where requests for books (no more than two at a time!) had to be meticulously filled in. We never even dreamed that it might be possible to acquire these books cheaply for ourselves, to take them home with us, to annotate them in the subway. Nowadays, many titles have already appeared in paperback or in cheap collections. I had no difficulty at all in finding Hegel's *Philosophy of right* in a bookshop in a medium-sized town. As the gaze takes in the revolving bookstands, a breath of air from the sublime heights is already stealing over the reader. (On this particular point I must give credit to the Soviet Union, although I have just been criticizing that country. In Russia, scientific works are published in great numbers and sold, even in foreign countries, at exceptionally low prices.)

Because of the interplay between all the various branches of culture, the 'general' level of culture is definitely rising perceptibly. For example, it has been possible to note a marked upsurge in interest in exhibitions of painting among those people who have owned a television set for more than five years.

True, the mass consumer may fall easy prey to cultural products of inferior quality. There are plenty of these about. So-called 'light' literature is going great guns. Better than before? Without doubt. But remember, there are more readers now. It is not Hegel, and certainly not Sartre, nor even Marcuse, who are being robbed of their eager readers. The circulation figures for Marcuse's works would have been remarkable even for the *Médecin des pauvres* and the *Porteuse de pain*[1]. Light literature is turning non-readers into readers. Gradually, the unpretentious writers of light fiction will guide their readers, as if up a ramp, towards other more serious preoccupations. They must not be hurried. The demand must be spontaneous. It will come of its own accord. Our task is to help it along. Besides, even these lesser works vary in quality, although the élitists dismiss them with equal contempt. Simenon has raised the detective novel to the status of a literary genre. He has started a fashion. Like many others, I love suspense stories, and I do not limit myself to the big names. In some very mediocre works, I have often found an observation, a quotation, a useful piece of information. It is not true that the novels sold on station bookstands are all trash. And, it is very important that the books of Sartre, Camus, and Malraux should be found on these bookstalls.

[1] The *Médecin des pauvres* and the *Porteuse de pain*, titles of two popular, highly melodramatic novels which enjoyed a great vogue in the 'thirties, the *Porteuse de pain* even being made into a pre-war film. (Translator's note)

146

As for the mass media, which are so unjustly accused of being responsible for stupefying the masses, one would have to be extraordinarily biased to deny the remarkable progress achieved in this field in the course of the last few years. The newest programs, which have replaced the stumbling series of the early days of television, are often of a very high quality. Broadcasts of great cultural significance are put on. Do I hear someone say, 'Yes, but at off-peak times'? Here again we must not force people. So-called mass culture changes gradually. In turn, man, as he becomes educated, will change the face of culture, and all this more quickly than was thought.

(d) Finally—and this is the spectre at the feast—*conformity*. Conformity does not necessarily preclude quality: that doubtless is the danger. At one and the same time everyone is receiving the same message. Consequently, everyone has exactly the same views as everyone else on everything. . . .

And yet look at our departure point. Is the passion to conform a new illness? Were the societies which preceded ours non-conformist? Surely a conformity of non-conformity represents some progress compared with an age when Baudelaire was condemned under French law and Darwin, posthumously, under American law.

Here again, Tocqueville is a mine of information. He writes,

> Freedom of mind is non-existent in America, the majority lives in perpetual adoration of itself . . . one might suppose that all American minds had been fashioned after the same model, so exactly do they follow along the same paths. . . . The majority has enclosed thought within a formidable fence' [1].

After these remarks, written in the last century, we can hardly claim that the typical pattern of conformity, as existing in the USA dates from the advent of television. No more than does conformity in France.

The student movements which rocked Europe, and in particular France in 1968, are a useful yardstick to measure the degree of conformity. In one sense, it would be tempting to see the student revolts as a demonstration of the stifling character of the consumer society, the instinct to conform being so strong, so forceful in this society, that it incites to revolt. On the other hand, it could equally well be pointed out that if the students really had been indoctrinated and automatically conditioned, they would have been unaware of it. If it is a characteristic of a repressive society to subjugate minds, it must be admitted that minds have not been subjugated [2]. In any case, this revolt of the young, however one judges its different aspects, provides a worthwhile refutation of Huxley's jaundiced views, for Huxley

[1] Tocqueville, *op. cit.* p. 255. (Translator's note)
[2] Cf. Marcuse, H. *Eros and civilization*, 'The defense consists chiefly in a strengthening of controls not so much over instincts as over consciousness, which, if left free, etc.' London, Sphere Books Ltd, 1970. p. 85.

believed that the young were only interested in having a 'good time', while allowing themselves to be controlled by the oligarchy of experts[1].

Pessimism can sometimes cloud a man's judgment.

Thus, of all the objections levelled against mass culture, none seem determinative. More often than not, in my opinion they seem simply to serve to disguise a feeling of regret, regret for a cultural aristocracy, in the confines of which beautiful minds could meet, express their mutual admiration and argue. For them, quality is not the only hallmark of an élite, but rarity as well. Hence the tendency to defend rarity as one of the prime requirements for quality and, whether consciously or unconsciously, to defend privileges, the most sublime of all being the privileges of the mind, without realizing or without admitting that these privileges correspond largely to social privileges.

But in order to 'disalienate' culture, it is not enough simply to reject an élitist conception which would reserve it for the 'best people'. The knowledge so freely offered to all must not in itself be of a nature to constitute an instrument of alienation.

Now, by a paradox which is easily explained, within any society the system for transmitting knowledge usually constitutes one of the most impregnable bastions of the past, one of the most obstinate rejections of the challenge presented by the future. This was the case in France. The fault does not lie with the teachers: experience has constantly proved that their initiative, their efforts to breathe new life into education have foundered with depressing regularity on the rock of a certain conception of education, a conception common to all administrations whether of the Left or of the Right, a conception so common in fact that it seems endemic to all societies everywhere.

According to this conception, the transmission of culture is the transmission to a *certain* limited number of individuals of a *certain* well founded and unvarying type of knowledge, according to *certain* well defined and well tried methods. This *system* with its fixed objectives, methods, and 'audience' seems closed; if its essential lines have not been perfected, they are at least in an arrested stage of development. It is a system which will admit only the occasional, prudent, minor adjustment. Its aim is well known: the formation of a certain type of man epitomized to perfection by those members of the middle class, whether of upper middle class extraction or newly arrived members of the lower middle class, who are products of the famous establishments[2] of higher education or who have gone through the usual essential channels at university. Placed at the levers of command,

[1] Huxley, A. *Brave New World*. London, Penguin Books, 1971. p. 185.

[2] The French has *grandes écoles* here. *Les grandes écoles* is the collective name given to the 'prestige' higher education establishments, such as the École Normale or the École Polytechnique. The cream of the French teaching profession and civil service was probably educated at one of the *grandes écoles*. (Translator's note)

148

this type of man sees to it, consciously or instinctively, that the supremacy of his own type is perpetuated. He passes on the recipes for success which he has learned. The force of the weight of the past on the whole educational system is all the more effective because the privileged ones who have passed through the system now claim the right to run it. They have it in their grasp and are the only ones powerful enough to hang on to it, and their grasp seems unshakable. Thus, twentieth century man, with an eye to his own interests and on the whole satisfied with his lot, runs the risk of impeding the progress of twenty-first century man. Twentieth century man usually refuses to admit that he is conservative by nature. He is not always a political conservative. Nor is he always conservative in his social life; at least, he tries not to be. But he would never imagine or would not admit that the educational system, of which he is a product, could become old-fashioned. And so he intends to pass on his knowledge to his son by the very methods which were used to educate him. Thus, the one permanent characteristic of education, which is by nature a process of change, adaptation and renewal, has been its conservatism, capable of withstanding all attempts at reform carried out under all types of administration. In the confusion of constantly changing conditions, all necessary concessions are made, provided that the essential remains the same. Experience has shown this very clearly. Up to last year, never had so many reforms guaranteed so much immobility.

But the élitist conception of culture does not only tend to defend a culture for the sons of gentlefolk, geared to the privileged social classes. It also tends to assure, in every branch of learning, the *immobility of the knowledge passed on*. Classical culture, which is largely concerned with the humanities, constitutes a complete world. The knowledge it implies admits of very little innovation. Thus, the past claims the right to set limits to the knowledge of future generations. This resistance to change wreaked no serious damage as long as knowledge developed or was modified at a slow rate, i.e. up to the middle of the nineteenth century. Then the acceleration and the diversification of scientific progress presented our education system with a few ultimatums. Educational syllabuses have had to make room for new forms of knowledge. This they have done, more often than not, by a process of *accumulation*.

But this does not mean that the struggle to retain a certain conception of culture has been abandoned. It has simply shifted its ground. Now its tack is to *freeze* education in its branches, i.e. to dignify with the name of learning only those old, well tried, non-controversial branches of knowledge. Thus, the constant innovations in the scientific field and the changes which they involve in the literary field are retarded or completely neglected in the name of prudence and loyalty, which really provide a cover for ignorance, for an exclusive attachment to the old forms of learning or, sometimes, for a deliberate rejection of the modern world.

And it is *technical skill*, the natural daughter of science, which has to bear the brunt of the attack launched by conservatism. Whether openly or under cover, these attacks are made for the sake of preserving the distinction between noble subjects and those minor ones which are more suitable for study by the children of the poorer classes. In this way, social prejudice saddles children, whose natural tastes and aptitudes fit them for technical jobs, with literary or law studies. But can the son of a teacher, doctor, barrister, or attorney devote his life to mechanics or electricity without suffering a loss of consequence? For the member of the ruling élite, a worthless diploma, obtained after years of effort, is of more value than the humble execution of a useful technical skill. It is the old, endlessly debated quarrel between general culture and applied knowledge, which is responsible for the thousands of misfits in our society, misfits who have almost no general culture at all and who are condemned to be failures.

But just look at the new methods, offered by the modern world. The publishing and distribution of books is big business and, consequently, its efficiency is always improving. The moving image (cinema, television) presents us with an ever-increasing capacity to broadcast happenings at almost the moment they occur. Finally, the computer opens up a huge, largely unexplored world. But here too, the culture of the landed gentry offers some resistance.

There are several reasons for this resistance. Some are instinctive ones: distrust when confronted by any innovation, prudence in the face of untried methods. Some are the products of conscious thought: the new methods reduce the sphere of action of the old ways to just those areas where they cannot be replaced. Threatened in its supremacy, the lesson delivered orally becomes, like Latin, a symbol. It seems inseparable from 'culture', i.e. from the old, stable, well tried branches of learning, in the struggle to resist the new, elusive forms of knowledge. The latter demand new, contemporary teaching methods, which are often the best vehicle for them. Nuclear physics, organic chemistry, sociology, cry out for the newest, most diverse methods. But it is felt that to teach the history of Louis XVI's times, to unveil the marvels of the *Aeneid*, to initiate pupils in Romanticism, there is no need to employ new methods. That is a debatable point, and I am personally quite convinced that modern scientific methods have a positive contribution to make to the study of traditional subjects. And so, for better or worse, classical culture seems to go hand in hand with the old methods, while the new branches of knowledge rely upon all kinds of teaching methods: the lesson on the Punic Wars delivered by a teacher seems to hurl defiance at the computer age. Other methods might worm their way into teaching, other branches of learning might overrun the old building, but the old methods will not cede an inch, will not make any concessions.

Finally, conservatism endows 'culture' with two characteristics which are both barriers to its adaptation to the modern world. The first is that education is individualistic. Success is individualistic. Effort is individualistic. The system of grading and examinations serve to confirm and magnify victory and defeat. Each individual, in his appointed place, does his paper, writes down what he has learned, receives his reward or punishment. This system, which is strongly inspired by the individualism inherent in French society, a system which exploits to the utmost the spirit of aggression and competition, pride in success and the natural egoism of those at whom it is aimed, finds its clearest expression in the great competitive examinations[1], which are recruiting stations for the élite and which often have a lasting effect on those who were forced to sacrifice their childhood and adolescence to them. Now this organization is in open conflict with the modern world where the great undertakings are collective ones, a world which makes endless demands for a greater degree of concerted action from complementary abilities, which demands more team spirit to draw together allied skills. But our whole cultural system, which is entirely based on the spirit of competition, is highly suspicious of the collective work. The spurious reasons for discrediting it are legion. How can each individual's contribution to the work be measured and individual merit be assessed? (And there are yet more examples of individualistic comments: a collective work cannot exist, it has no real value; the part played by each individual, the value of the contribution made by each member of the team must be clearly demonstrable.) Does not a collective work run the risk of encouraging those who know how to get others to do their work for them to be lazy? Is it not possible for the great individual virtues, invention, imagination, will-power to be neglected and therefore diminished? These arguments and others like them serve to keep up the illusion, an illusion largely supported by contemplation of the past, to the effect that knowledge and merit are individual things, that the great human achievements are products of individual effort. The progression from the epic story of Alexander the Great to the Apollo XI mission represents a complete upheaval in human destiny. But our culture has its eyes firmly fixed on Alexander the Great.

Moreover, the past cannot rid itself of the idea that education, by nature or necessity, must be a boring, sad affair. Each stage in the process of acquiring knowledge must be accomplished with much irksome effort and attendant pain. It is not the teachers' fault, for they are the slaves of the education they themselves have received, of the syllabuses they must follow, and of the methods they must apply. It is largely the fault of the conception our society has of education, seeing it as a process of instruction rather than a real education, as a lesson to be learned rather than a pattern for a life-style. Memory is the supreme faculty to which education is geared; intelligence and reason must give way before it. It means nothing

[1] Faure means the examinations for entry into the *grandes écoles*. See p. 148, footnote 2. (Translator's note)

to have learned Théramène's[1] speech; forty pages of a historical account and the list of irregular verbs must also be recited by rote. It is of no consequence that a child has read and liked Tacitus and Virgil, he must have recited twenty lines of the Latin text without faltering. Thus, the syllabuses based on the accumulation of facts, the methods geared to memory training, would seem to imply that knowledge can only be attained with considerable effort.

Suffering and boredom do not only appear an inevitable necessity. They seem to be the very objectives of learning. Most French families, when questioned, would confirm this masochistic conception of culture. Learning is a matter of asceticism, of discipline; it is a test. Several proofs of this are to be found in the French education system. Detention, refusal of permission to go out, 'punishment' are the penalties for unsatisfactory work as well as for misconduct. Conversely, a child punished for unruliness will have to learn forty lines of Racine by heart. Examinations are the supreme achievement of those who believe the road to culture should be strewn with stumbling blocks. They are a form of punishment.

This way of thinking about education is responsible for the instinctive mistrust engendered by all those branches of learning and teaching methods which might arouse interest. That the medium of film should be used to transmit knowledge, or that the minds of children and adolescents should be opened to the social and economic reality of the world, this is enough to make hordes of well meaning people worried. The only teaching methods they will admit as valid are lectures and lessons, i.e. those methods incorporating the simplest, the most austere, and sometimes the most irksome relationship between the teacher and the pupil. The only branches of knowledge to which they are prepared to accord any dignity are the difficult ones. If physical education and the teaching of the plastic arts have not had the place they merited, it is largely because they arouse interest, animation, and joy; they involve the assertion of the personality through play and a pleasurable confirmation of individual progress. For many people, the name of knowledge can be accorded to only difficult, frightening subjects, and then only on condition that they be taught in the most arid way possible.

These prejudices are the result of the accumulated weight of social conservatism and more particularly of cultural conservatism, which is a much more robust, much more aggressive, force than social conservatism. For having had the finger of accusation pointed at it for years, social conservatism has developed an uneasy conscience which is not shared by cultural conservatism. Once its real nature is understood, cultural conservatism must be fought: it is not enough to dis-alienate access to knowledge; dis-alienation must be extended to knowledge itself, to the need and the desire to know, and, through them to man's development as a human being.

[1] Théramène, a character in Racine's *Phèdre*. (Translator's note)

Part 4

Dis-alienation

20

From superficial critical analysis to an analysis in depth

Studying the consumption of culture, mass culture (which does not necessarily imply the vulgarization of culture) and, finally, the dis-alienation of knowledge has thus led me from superficial critical analysis (and its refutation) to radical critical analysis and to an examination in depth of a type of society, which is already upon us and whose characteristics, whatever we might say, can only become more pronounced in the near future.

The sole aim of the early part of this book, to which I deliberately gave a systematic turn, was to eliminate a certain number of irrelevant points, irrelevancies due for the most part to the psychology of 'refusal' in its timorous and conservative form, while in later chapters I have tried to eliminate the 'great refusal' in its passionate, revolutionary, and visionary form.

But it was not my intention to devote my study to an apology for the consumer society nor to take pleasure in absolving it of its sins. The technological consumer society exists, it can only advance. Please God, let it continue to exist but let it not take it into its head to retrace its steps! I wanted to dispense with the impossible dreams if not with the curious angels. But the positive aspects of this society dialectically imply its negative ones. It is our task to extract, according to the golden rule of 'negation of the negation', the productive and beneficial consequences from this negativity. The new society contains many threats, brings many dangers, but these dangers and threats should be welcomed light-heartedly, for they signify that economic growth, advances in pure and applied science, and with them man's own progress, are still continuing; without them we would have to pull in our horns, live more cheaply and less dangerously but deprived of all dynamism and hope, and withdraw into a static society, a state of affairs which would soon degenerate into the rout of triumphant man.

An authentic analysis, and not just one which is at the mercy of changes in mood and nostalgia, reveals that the negative aspects of the consumer society are many. I will concentrate on those which seem to me the most characteristic.

(a) **An inconsistent society**

In the first place it is an *inconsistent society*. Like all societies, you say? No doubt. But in a society on the move, inconsistencies are more apparent and more violent than in a peaceful, stagnant, and declining society. These inconsistencies are capable of presenting a strong challenge to any methods utilized to lessen their effects or to remove them altogether (which does not mean that they are to be ignored, quite the contrary; nor should we be overwhelmed by them or take refuge in the lachrymose state of idleness occasioned by a feeling of helplessness). There is the fundamental inconsistency existing between consumption and non-consumption, between a society, which is designated the affluent society, and the persistence of real misery; world famine, underdevelopment. We are so moved by the problems—and yet we are not moved enough—and rightly so too, for our emotion is tempered by the degree of realism we can bring to the problem, by our ability to stop dreaming idle dreams and to get to work, bridging the gap between (ineffective and—it must be said—alienating) charity and (practical, modest, dedicated) friendship. What must not be said is that the advanced type of society is doomed, because it has not resolved the problems of the backward countries; what must be said is that the advanced world should strain every sinew and devote all its resources to procuring for the underdeveloped world, not compassion, but a solution to its problems. A solution long in coming, no doubt, perhaps desperately slow, a solution which seems to make, alas, infinitesimal progress, but a solution ultimately realizable, because it has begun to be imaginable. A solution which depends on will-power, on imagination in the most precise meaning of the word. Let the prosperous man imagine the plight of the poor man (who might be he); let the man weighed down by the education he has received imagine what it would be like to be completely ignorant (which he might be); let the modern man whose suffering is caused by so many problems just think of the man whose suffering is caused by everything except problems, and let him think or imagine that this man could be he and he could be that man. Let advanced humanity—the humanity of the masters—for even those who think they are slaves could be masters compared with *real* slaves (who are often not the slaves of anything tangible or of any person—but are slaves by essence, incapable even of dreaming of being free men) imagine that it has changed places with inferior humanity for a few days. Then it will all seem much easier. And most important of all the decision to act, the key to the whole problem, will be easier.

No less overwhelming, perhaps even more so, seems the discrepancy between the affluent world—where antagonisms must be suppressed—and the world where war born of poverty and ignorance still exists, war which outlives its causes in its absurd atrocity. No doubt our young people feel this particular inconsistency more keenly than we do. Instead of condemning a society, which must outlaw war because it has the means to wage it, why do they not concentrate their energies on demanding that this society employ the money spent on military hardware to end poverty in the underdeveloped world? It is not by replacing affluence with poverty that affluence will be forced to do its duty. When affluence has disappeared, what demands can be made of it? Force it to justify its existence and to fulfil its destiny. This is your task, young people. And also the task of a number of older people who are children in so far as this objective is concerned.

(b) The society of saturation

The second negative characteristic, doubtless the most negative one of all, is that the consumer society is all too often a *society of saturation*. I believe that the considerable opportunities the technological society offers for progress are never harmful in themselves; it is our irresponsible use of them which may make them harmful: but this is not the fault of science and technology, it is the fault of the men who employ them. A comfortable home is not an evil in itself, a skyscraper is not a crime, the automobile is not a vice. But the concentration of homes, skyscrapers, and cars in a restricted area, surrounded by a complete desert is an absurdity all the more shocking because it could easily be avoided and because, although this is more difficult to do, it could be corrected. The amazing development of the equipment which is now used for the construction of monstrous city complexes, for the production of too many cars, for the despoilation of the atmosphere, for the pollution of lakes and rivers and for the rape of nature could, if only these developments were put to better use, just as easily give us the power to site towns in suitable locations, to safeguard natural resources and to preserve for man, if not his most precious possession, at least the organic condition for the existence of all other treasures: the environment.

Many other examples could be given. I will simply mention the one which seems the most important, *the saturation of time*, which leads inevitably to the most typical modern *alienation*.

(c) A society of alienation

The new society is thus a *society of alienation*, more precisely of alienations. Could it ever be otherwise? All societies are the same. Our alienations are more numerous and more irritating, consequently they are capable of arousing a greater sense of anguish; but it is precisely because they are numerous and varied that they do not constitute the total universal alienation according to the Marxist conception. By that very fact they can be cured more easily.

157

In all this, the problem is not one of society (technological, consumer society, etc.). It is a problem of *the man of this society*.

We have eliminated the elementary, biological fear which gripped the entrails of past generations of man, clouded his nascent reasoning faculties, thwarted his first faltering steps towards knowledge. We no longer make gods of animals and winds, we no longer live surrounded by capricious guardian spirits, whose benevolence we implore. If we imagine a divinity, it is no longer in the image of a fickle man but as the purest form of the spirit of which we have received a spark. Are we going to personalize, deify, *anthropomorphize*, be afraid of, revere, or curse a society which is nothing but a reflection of ourselves? If we make it into a hell, let us be proud of ourselves: it is our creation. Our closed door has no guardian; we hold the keys. We can lock it or unlock it. We are all equally responsible.

The only necessary conditions for the exercise of responsibility are self-disciplining and aspiration towards that end.

21

Creative man in logical society

Life in a technological society. The education of the whole man. The communications revolution. Transmission and reception.

'Psychologically premature at birth, man only grows to maturity by the practical assimilation of the human patrimony, which is given objective reality in the historical development of society.'

Lucien Sève

I now propose to reconsider the problem, which I had undertaken to tackle, in the light of a goal I will define thus: how is it possible to 'dis-alienate' man, to reaffirm and extend his creativity, without rejecting the irreversible and largely beneficial characteristics of the technological society? Because this new society brings great changes in its wake, it is inevitable and quite natural that man should be affected by it, not only in the external circumstances of his life and in his behavior, but also in his essential being. Society presents him with new problems. It forces him to run new risks. It demands of him new efforts. In order to resolve these efforts successfully, man must change within himself.

We are presented with three phenomena. The first is technology in general. The second and the third are connected with the two 'revolutions' which dominate the twentieth century (it would perhaps be maintained that they represent two different aspects of the same revolution), the revolution which has occurred in the field of the immediate communication of thought, the so-called Marconi or transistor revolution, and the cybernetic revolution, the revolution of the so-called 'thinking machines'. Indeed, the methods by which technological and economic expansion are achieved are matters of vital importance. Each of these revolutions implies consequences for man quite different from those, for example, connected with the first Industrial Revolution, which occurred in eighteenth century England. In other words, it is not absurd to suppose that considerable and continuous progress in prolonging the development of the first industrial revolution could have been accomplished, thanks to the discovery of the different forms of energy, without the intervention of the transistor or the computer. The discovery and utilization of new sources of energy, petrol after coal, atomic power after motor-fuel, are already considerable achievements; but they are all of a piece. It is possible to conceive of a society which, having discovered the different modern sources of energy, could derive from them a high growth rate, one high enough even to create a society of mass consumption, but which, however, would have at its disposal neither transistors nor computers. Now, such a society, even supposing that its possibilities for growth were absolutely identical with those in our own society, *would not present the same problems in human terms*.

(a) Generally speaking, since he lives in the technological age—a fact which no one disputes—modern man must know and understand technology. This implies that he has attained a certain level of education. It is not simply a question of the knowledge which he may have received, stored, and accumulated, nor even of knowledge which he has assimilated and rethought for himself. He must be given something else: a *technological approach*, that is the ability to make practical application of the basic knowledge he has learned. It is imperative to ensure the achievement of a sufficiently high level of attainment in this two-fold ability (absorbed instruction and the mastery of the techniques for putting it into practice) to enable a man to assimilate, not only a certain number of established facts, depending on the state of knowledge at the time when he completes his education, but also to keep up to date with later developments.

(i) This means, therefore, that the young must be educated with a very ambitious view as to the level to be attained. Moreover, education must be such that it can constantly be brought up to date. A comparable effort is necessary, too, in the field of adult education, with various retraining programs and with opportunities for a 'second chance'; in fact, education must be a permanent process continuing throughout life.

(ii) It means that the considerable activity and innovation in the field of education (in the widest sense) must not be managed or restricted according to the purely utilitarian criterion of the immediate need to fill statistically available job vacancies. The man of the technological age must belong to his age and see to it that, whatever job he may be called upon to fill, his age belongs to him. If he does this, he will be able to choose a job to his own satisfaction, to change that job at a later date, an eventuality which will become more and more necessary, and to pursue interesting activities during his leisure hours which, as Marx had foreseen, will play an increasingly important part in his life.

But on this point care must be taken to avoid the kind of confused thinking which the Malthusians and the élitists are so prone to employ. There can be no question of encouraging all young people to obtain diplomas, nor of producing too many aspirants to those professions which seem to imply the attainment of a superior level of culture. The question of diplomas, to which our society attaches so much importance, is in fact a very minor one, or, at least, it will have to be considered in a completely different light (as will the question of access to those professions, where applicants have to submit to screening in the public interest, and for which a kind of Lloyd's Register has to be established). The analysis of future needs will not always entail a relatively empirical process to grade the various degrees of intelligence, a process rather similar to that used to sort peas and based on inadequate criteria; it will not always have the traumatic character of the wager or the test, but will be integrated into a policy of continuous vocational guidance. No longer will training for a career be seen as a painful ordeal to be endured but as a constructive and stimulating experience. Who would not derive satisfaction from the knowledge that he had been put on the right path? Who would not be pleased at discovering for himself, with the necessary help, the vocation which is right for him, a vocation in which he can exercise those abilities, which had been despised and neglected for so long, simply because they were not immediately apparent?

The educational system will tend constantly to become more open, to encourage interplay between the various disciplines, to be less geared to concrete objectives. Examinations and diplomas will no longer be barriers; a lack of paper qualifications will no longer imprison an individual within a certain sector of activity or at a certain level of culture.

It is a mistake to protest that the extension of knowledge and culture will culminate in overburdening the professions, for the simple reason that culture must be detached, once and for all, from the restrictive conception of 'professionalism'. If at the present time certain careers are over-subscribed, this is partly due to a lack of awareness of other possible openings (a situation which can be remedied), but it is mostly due to the preconceived idea that all cultivated and well educated men should be shared out among a certain number of 'professions', the practice of which is proof of the attainment of a superior culture or of some outstanding quality of mind, and that if they were removed from their particular sphere of activity they would go into a decline. If one believes and behaves as though all educated men must be teachers, engineers, doctors, and lawyers, everyone, in effect, will want to be teachers, engineers, doctors, or lawyers, for everyone will want to be thought well educated.

Any apprenticeship for a profession, any 'professional training' should be nothing more than an off-shoot of the main axis of a general 'cultural' education. To make education and culture dependent on possible job opportunities is merely to aggravate, not resolve, present ills. On the contrary, the problem is to ensure that culture ceases to be mere professional 'training', which traps a man in a particular job, makes him resistant to change and, to all intents and purposes, couples his intellectual level to his social level. The worst feature of the system we actually live under is that one can deduce a man's level of knowledge and culture, his class and position in society, simply by knowing what job he does, and since no other culture is open to him except that which allows the outsider to pinpoint his job with such accuracy, he is shackled to that one job. The whole of social conservatism rests upon the apparently modern conception of basing the need for knowledge on the need for employment, thereby irrevocably linking a particular type of culture with a particular job.

(iii) Since the problem is to form, really to create, technological man, his education must be multi-disciplined. The belief that economic know-how is the exclusive prerogative of the economists, scientific knowledge of the scientists, an awareness of social problems of the sociologists, etc. is a very common and pernicious error. The separation of the different branches of knowledge into watertight compartments makes a man believe that, since his normal sphere of activity is restricted to one specialized subject, he himself has no means of access to other branches of knowledge, that he can neither know nor have an opinion on anything outside his own particular field, and that he must rely on others for anything unconnected with his specialized skills. This is an obvious breeding ground for alienation and exploitation. For indeed, the excuse that modern skills are so complex and so specialized is good enough to confine each individual within the narrow bounds of his own particular speciality, of his own particular job. The individual becomes set in an intellectually submissive frame of mind, and thus he obeys orders willingly.

May I quote just one example? The general ignorance of the French public about anything concerned with economic affairs is one of the most persistent causes of a series of financial setbacks. Their particular susceptibility to inflation is not, as it is so often said, due to the irresistible attraction this feverish state of affairs has for the French people, to the reflex action of a drug addict, but simply to the fact that the French public believes it can see inflation where it does not exist and is incapable of recognizing it when it does. The French public is, therefore, inclined to treat the illness with remedies which simply serve to aggravate the situation. I think I was one of the first to maintain that inflation was not incompatible with recession, a fact which is now generally admitted, although the full consequences of this are not always realized. Because it has been so often told so in the past and is still told so today, the public believes that inflation is due to expansion. Thus, when inflation seems to reach alarming proportions, the public accepts a brake on expansion as the inevitable cure. But, since the French public is becoming ever more acutely aware of the need for expansion, it will sometimes, in desperation, agree to run the risks of really inflationary procedures, the nature of which it does not understand. In France, they have already had a long experience of this kind of thing and, judging by contemporary events, it would seem that they have not seen the last of it yet. There exists a powerful temptation for politicians to believe that the public is incapable of understanding economic problems, and the full effects of this pernicious belief have not yet been fully measured.

If a working knowledge of science, of the practical application of basic science in technical skills, of technology, and of economics is indispensable to the education of a modern man, if this man must be capable of constantly bringing what he has learned up to date, then, obviously he must also acquire the necessary mental apparatus to cope with general ideas. He must be able to conceive of historical evolution; he must be acquainted with, and able to withstand, developments in foreign countries; he must be capable of evolving a certain philosophy of life from the things around him: all this points to the necessity for so-called general culture, sometimes so wrongly considered incompatible with scientific and technical culture. Multi-disciplined education is not a revival of a humanism adapted to modern tastes. It is not another name for the monstrous accumulation of unconnected bits of knowledge. It simply affirms the right to make a choice; modern man, however specialized his professional activity may be, is not a man of a single discipline. And it indicates a trend: one major field of study is enriched and is seen in a new light through contact with other fields of study. Behind the phrase multi-disciplined education (the choice of terminology may not be a happy one), there lies a new conception of education whose avowed aim is not so much to impart bits of knowledge as to provide the pupils with tools, not so much to pass on mere book learning as to discern and develop capabilities. To dis-alienate man is to refuse to imprison him in one field of knowledge, 'his' field, to prevent him being caught in the stranglehold of his own learning to their mutual destruction.

(b) My second line of thought concerns the 'communications revolution'.

The immediate transmission of news (in the widest sense of the word), particularly through the mass media, in itself presents a problem totally independent of the *content* of the news.

This problem finds expression, in fact, in an entirely new phenomenon, namely the extraordinary disparity between the mental faculties needed for transmitting and receiving communication.

In earlier times, we spoke and listened to each other, though some men and, more particularly, some women kept quiet throughout the whole of their lives. But it was always more or less a question of individual personality and choice. In the representation of dialogue, whether written or spoken, each protagonist was aware of the existence of the other as a real physical entity.

'Reading' did nothing to change this attitude. The decision to begin

163

to read and to continue reading is a conscious, constantly repeated one. The book or the newspaper can be laid aside or taken up again: one can resume reading. Writing as, Lefebvre so rightly says, is a *recurrent* activity.

Today the pattern has completely changed.

The idea of an individual's first meeting with water will be seen from a different viewpoint if the water in question is contained in a carafe rather than being present in the form of a flood.

We are the victims of an invasion. We are under constant attack from a flood of broadcasting which assails us with massive strength. It is possible to maintain that it is our own decision whether or not we 'receive', but it is equally possible to maintain that the decision is not ours. One can hold a book open before one and yet not read; but a radio cannot be left on without being heard. One is aware of television without really watching it. Turning the knob to the off position demands a definite act, a decision; it demands physical effort and a little daring. One wonders vaguely whether one is committing a minor offence. Here, there come into play social conformity coupled with the constraints placed upon us by our tendency to imitate others and by habit; but there is, too, an element of duty and the feeling that we may derive some useful information from the program. This invasion, this attack could be beneficial. In fact, taking the algebraic mean, on the whole its effects probably are. That is not the problem at issue. The programs may be of an excellent standard, the material broadcast may be completely accurate, interesting, a source of aesthetic pleasure; they may, in fact, be of the very highest quality. But, however good the transmission might be, the feeling still remains that the audience is constantly being inundated by a relentless wave, before which the listener is condemned to impassivity, for he has no chance of answering back or of expressing his own opinions. To this one might also add McLuhan's observations on the peculiar effects of television, a *cool medium*, working by trans-lumination rather than il-lumination and demanding a more intense degree of participation on the part of the audience. But to explore this channel would lead me away from the point and would add nothing to the general tenor of my researches. It matters little whether it is television or just radio; the superabundance of programs bombarding us have a quasi-permanent and totally unilateral character. We are endowed with a receptive personality, reduced to the role of a mere listener or spectator, like a confidant in a play, who never answers back.

Thus, our intellectual reactions are thwarted and contained, and the conception we have of ourselves, in the depths of the collective conscience, as stations capable of both transmitting and receiving communication is weakened. This no doubt accounts for our inability to free ourselves of subconscious worries through speech, a phenomenon which Michel de Certeau calls the 'seizing up of speech'[1].

[1] *Prise de parole* in French. (Translator's note)

Conversely, it is noticeable that a certain number of opportunities for spoken communication, for arguing, which existed formerly, have now been curtailed. My farmer friends have often spoken to me of the difference in life-style resulting from the decrease in the number of work units needed nowadays to run a modern farm, even a very large one. Formerly, the farm hands sat down at the same table as the boss for their midday meal. They talked to each other, whereas now the day slips by in silence. Then there were social evenings. There were great gatherings for the corn threshing, to which the women would come bringing food. All kinds of topics would be discussed, and certain astute electoral condidates, canvassing for votes at local elections, would drop in on informal friendly visits. Now the number of cultivators who make use of the itinerant threshing-machine is decreasing as is, too, the number of people who used to come to take part in this disappearing ritual. Generally speaking, rural life and life in small towns used to offer, sometimes it still does, opportunities for a protracted discussion, for dialogue between equals; each man could take the floor and tell a story or sing his song. All this has not completely disappeared, but it is becoming rarer, as too are club dinners, weddings spread over several days, political meetings, and shows, all pleasures denied those who have migrated towards the large towns.

It is the same in city complexes. The opportunities for chatting with small shop-keepers are disappearing as the shop-keepers give way before the supermarkets with their policy of self-service. Chance encounters in the street are rarer, for we all walk less. There are fewer discussions among friends after work, for all are in a hurry to get back to a home which is further from the work place than formerly; people no longer drink coffee together, for we are rapidly returning to the passive state in which we can only 'receive'.

Some would add to this list the decline of courtly love with its opportunities for long speeches and short poems, for carefully concocted letters and dramatic scenes, and for grandiloquent eternal farewells.

In the political sphere, public meetings are less popular. There questions were asked and opinions expressed. The individual could at least assert himself by a show of hands, by responding warmly to a speaker, or by booing or clapping. Now people more rarely take the trouble to go and listen to local orators, for they can listen to, and look at, the blue-eyed boy of the whole nation in the comfort of their own home; but now they make no protests, they never applaud, but sit in a state of absolute receptivity.

But, we must not despair. Other means of expression are available. Do we really speak less than we used to? There are no precise statistics to answer this question, and it would be almost impossible to compile any. Then again, there is talking and talking. What is essential is the assertion of the personality. A few interminable meetings, where people talk to no effect and no conclusions are reached, where one has the impression that no one is prepared to listen to anyone else's point of view, are no substitute for the right to be heard in a meaningful dialogue between equals or for the involvement of someone listening to such a dialogue.

The problem must be considered as a single problem, detached from other problems, isolated from the protean and disquieting evils which permeate the whole social fabric. Here, as elsewhere, I do not claim to offer a perfect solution, only to attempt to clarify the situation, to seek out possible lines of enquiry of which I see three.

Firstly, and this is obvious, one of the main tasks of the modern state is to use radio and television as instruments of freedom and not as instruments for political propaganda or for brutalizing the masses. This not only implies the systematic refusal to indoctrinate the audience, the need for impartiality and serious news reporting; it goes even further. Radio, and even more so television, must help man to understand himself and to understand the world, i.e. to develop the faculties which promote understanding, namely a conscious awareness of the world and intelligence. Television might take as one of its natural objectives the kind of multidisciplined education of which I have been speaking. By the diversity and the very number of the informative broadcasts transmitted and the subjects touched upon, it tends to do precisely what I was talking about: to break down the partitions between separate branches of knowledge, to arouse man's curiosity in unfamiliar topics and to take him out of his social, economic and psychological rut. Of course it will be said that it is easy enough to talk about such a perspective, but that it is a very different matter to make television into the vehicle for knowledge and intellectual development that I am dreaming of.

However, it seems important to me that these aims should be specified, for I am forced to admit that many people do not accord this liberating function to television at all, either because they regard it as a despicable instrument of popular amusement to be tolerated, or because, consciously or unconsciously, they see it as a painless and, in the long run, effective means of getting the audience to accept the existing social set-up without question. The initial choice concerning the aims of broadcasting is a paramount one overshadowing all consequent decisions.

In any case, and this will be my second line of enquiry, it will always be necessary to pick and choose the programs we are subjected to. The temptation to tune in all the time to every program must be resisted. In order to make the best use of so many marvellous instruments at our disposal, we must use them sparingly. We must not surrender to them blindly. The personality and time which *is* the personality must be safeguarded. Let Marx's teaching be of some use to us: time not spent working must be spent in the education of man as his own capital. This protection is not a destructive, scornful rejection of what is offered: it is simply a question of choice and moderation.

166

This is one of the roles of training and education: to bring a wider range of knowledge within a man's grasp and make the personality self-sufficient, to eliminate the feeling of inferiority which leaves the unpretentious man paralyzed before the relentless onslaught of broadcasting. Man must be able, not just meekly to accept the programs broadcast, but to make a choice and to pass judgment on them.

Finally, and this is my third line of enquiry, man's role as a transmitter of communication must be reasserted in ordinary life. The new man must have his say, if not more frequently, then with greater authority and greater influence.

Here, the two essential and complementary concepts of education and participation, which I have already mentioned, join forces. Participation in education is a particularly useful example of this point. It is not just a question, as I well know, of allowing students to send their own delegates to sit on committees, although that is a great step forward. The students speak with their delegates, make their views known to them; the student delegates talk with the teachers and administrators; both sides transmit their opinions and hold a dialogue with those whom their opinions must affect and interest.

But it is also a question, and I have always maintained that the two experiments should go hand in hand, of giving all secondary school pupils a say in running the education system, no matter how young the students are (how old was Rimbaud when he wrote poetry? How old was Mozart when he composed music?). Parents, too, the teachers themselves, administrators, delegates from outside should all be called in to give their opinion.

Even more so the pupil—and not just the pupil at school or university, but adult pupils too—must participate in education which must cease to be purely receptive in character. Thus each individual would actively express his own views, consequently forming his whole personality and not simply one aspect of it, namely the characteristics of a culture consumer.

Finally, must I remind the reader of the great importance of team work and the dynamism of the group? Within the group each one expresses himself in his turn, realizes his potential as transmitter and receiver. The hierarchy within the group is supple and pivots around the various skills of the members of the group. Individual work, which our education system used to put at a premium, symbolized by the schoolboy's arm round his work to hide his 'answers'[1] from his neighbor, and the ban on 'communication' between pupils tend to make the child, and later the adolescent, and later still the man, into a passive being, for whom the expression of an

[1] The French has *composition* here. In France, a *composition* is a written test, success in such tests being essential for a pupil to pass into a higher grade. (Translator's note)

opinion is a rare event, an effort at odds with his true nature. Collective work allows each individual within the group to express himself effortlessly and fearlessly, to abandon the passive role of the perpetual receiver, a role, which he was first of all willing to put up with but which later became irksome, and to strengthen his personality through self-expression.

22

Creative man in logical society
(continued)
The synectic computer
Creativity and participation

'For the man of straw, a servant of steel'. Man has taken into his service a peerless assistant, the computer. I must now analyze the opportunities and dangers this represents in so far as they affect my essential preoccupations in this book.

One evening, Maurice Schumann and I were arguing amicably. Following Louis Couffignal's lead, I had spoken of 'thinking machines'. Schumann protested, saying that machines do not think. He was right, but it must be admitted that machines have taken over what used to be an important part of the thought process.

The role of cybernetics can be compared with that of the first machines to be used in industry. The non-thinking machines of earlier days relieved man of a great deal of purely physical work, but they did not eliminate the need for all physical effort.

Since the advent of the machine, fewer, less tiring, but infinitely more efficient, physical actions were sufficient to accomplish a comparable amount of work.

Similarly, the new intellectual machines absolve the thought processes of herculean efforts which, without the machine, would have to be undertaken with, moreover, very little chance of the same end result being achieved. The brain is freed from what might be compared to the setting in motion of a mechanical and mechanizable mental musculature. Just as the body, which formerly had to strain to lift fantastic burdens, can now limit its activity to the movement of the arm raising and lowering a handle or of the finger engaging and disengaging the switch of the black box, movements which are, however, indispensable, so too it is enough for the thinking being to be at hand ready to play its part at the beginning and end of an ever longer and more complicated process. But the thinking capacity of the brain must still be on call, in working order, for it must provide the premises for and draw the conclusions from the long involved middle process.

Just as 'executive' machines have not freed man from the rigors of physical activity, in the same way 'calculating' machines have not abolished mental effort in its so-called automatic and molecular forms. But when using either type of machine, man knows that he is replaceable, that the effort he accomplishes is not characteristic of his essential being nor indispensable to his effectiveness as an individual. The Pharaoh could stand in for one of his slaves, but not for all of them. Modern man can accomplish the task done by the machine, although only in small stages. Human dignity demands that there should be no task from which a man is excluded, but it is natural that this dignity should seek expression in the highest form possible, that is to say in those tasks which are still the prerogative of man, tasks for which he is indispensable, in which *he* is indispensable to *himself*.

Man's anxiety in the age of logical machines is tied up with the need to define, to delineate and, to some extent, to defend the above tasks as a domain apart. However, like the wild ass's skin[1], this domain seems to be shrinking every day.

What frenzy this causes! What disarray, bordering sometimes on despair!

Man would like to establish eternally viable, definite bounds to a citadel of the human, a citadel unassailable by all that, although the result of the work of man, is not human. He would like to draw a magic circle around its ramparts within which he feels besieged, beleaguered from without.

And then, gradually, we cease to think about what is happening. Just as Hérault de Séchelles's[2] *Journal* reveals how men, who lived through the intense days of revolution, still continued to lead their ordinary lives, just as Fabrice del Dongo[3] witnessed the battle of Waterloo without realizing it, this miracle too is cloaked in everyday happenings. The exhilaration it causes and our awareness of it are swallowed up in apathy. The only people who really get excited by discoveries are those who make them or who were waiting for them in order to exploit them; but they are protected by the routine of their jobs. Being accustomed to the unaccustomed becomes a habit.

And yet, how is it possible to assume that even the most ordinary, uninventive, indifferent individual is not affected in his innermost being, is not shocked or changed in some way by some great development, the inner workings of which are beyond his comprehension but whose consequences are all about him?

[1] This is a reference to the novel by Balzac called *La peau de chagrin*, in which the hero is given a wild ass's skin possessing the power to grant wishes. However, each time a wish is granted the skin shrinks a little, and when it finally disappears altogether, its owner dies.

[2] Hérault de Séchelles, president of the Convention, June–July 1793. He died on the scaffold with the Dantonists in 1794.

[3] Fabrice del Dongo, hero of Stendahl's *La Chartreuse de Parme*. (Translator's notes)

Any one of us can be Blaiberg. That is easy enough to admit. But we must go further. The rhythm of our lives is that of the heroes who are not of this world. We are all Armstrong.

There is only one solution, and that does not consist in refusing to look for a solution. There is only one wager open to us, and this is not the refusal to accept the wager. There is only one course of action to be adopted, and it is certainly not the refusal to adopt any course of action.

During the last century, the Luddites and the silkweavers of Lyons[1] thought that the first machines would take over the execution of their menial, badly paid jobs, thus depriving them of their reason for living. However, many machines went into operation, the results being more far-reaching than was supposed. The workers are still working and they enjoy a higher standard of living.

Although, as I am willing to admit, there would appear to be very slight grounds for comparing the two phenomena (yet both the manual and the intellectual workers might have had similar views on the ordeals they were going through), I must make use of this example. Computers have introduced us to another type of 'non-work'. They free us from one type of brain work, so that the thought processes can be concentrated on other tasks; they give us time to engage in a higher level of activity. Instead of believing that our domain is shrinking, we should believe that it is expanding. No more limits here below? No more limits above? Wherever obstacles are removed, frontiers are violated.

Once more, the ever-vital theme of the relationship between freedom and necessity puts in an appearance, though it has by now undergone considerable change. For a long time, Engel's assertion that freedom was born of necessity appeared surprising. Certain people still hesitate to accept it. However, it is a striking truism. Freedom is the product of the awareness of necessity. It is because we recognize necessity, the impossibility of making further progress in certain fields using certain methods, that we are able to make progress in other fields using other methods. As the field is narrowed, possibilities are opened up. The imposition of bounds in one area reveals areas that are boundless. Because astrology proved to be impossible, necessity ruled it out, and we applied ourselves to astronomy. Because Icarus's experiment met with adverse necessity, other ways were tried, and now aeroplanes fly because man was unable to fly himself. Because it was impossible to go to the moon by balloon, man made tremendous efforts to go there by rocket. Henceforth, advances in the electronic field allow us to eliminate the innumerable temptations to do the impossible; they impose a finite sphere of activity upon us, a sphere within which we become the masters of infinite possibilities. Because they deny us

[1] The *canuts*, the Lyons' silk-weavers were noted for their militant action to safeguard their economic interests and were consequently suspicious of all attempts to mechanize their industry. (Translator's note)

171

an astounding variety of impossible solutions, they reveal to us the possible solution or the limited range of possible solutions.

An awareness of the bounds imposed by necessity frees us from what have rightly been called the bounds of ignorance, which force us to hazard a choice involving a whole range of possibilities instead of being able to make a choice for each possibility as it arises.[1] According to Oppenheimer, scientific conscience is nothing other than an awareness of the errors which will not be made.

Freedom, generated by necessity, is itself creative of necessity. Our great advances have given us the freedom to impose bounds on nature. Our decisions, correctly arrived at and scientifically applied, imply necessity. And our freedom creates a necessity for ourselves. We can no longer go back. We must realize this. We must act upon its consequences. The mechanization of physical force has created, along with industrialized society, a different man in a different world. The mechanization of intellectual force, achieved in a much shorter length of time, cannot fail to produce even greater effects. They present us with new problems and, at the same time, they lead us to look at the old or permanent problems in a new way, if only because of the very considerable resources placed at our disposal to resolve them.

Now, the essential problems for man and for society present themselves within the framework of politics in the complete and authentic sense of the word.

How will it be possible, tomorrow, to consider politics in the same terms as we did yesterday? If each of us agreed to think about this problem from time to time it would be a very useful mental discipline.

But for now, let us admit that there is a certain distinction between mechanized thought and that which is not yet mechanizable.

Perception, memory, the capacity to utilize memory, application of rules, expression, machines can be endowed with all these ... and all these operations are considered to be operations of the intelligence, demanding some voluntary effort so much so that they constitute a classic test of the level of intellectual attainment[2].

While Aurel David writes,

Our clearest thoughts are the result of minor intellectual labor, but does this constitute true thought? It is not that machines think but rather that man does not think when he throws light upon a subject without adding anything new or specifically human to it[3].

[1] Kolm, O.
[2] Ruyer, R. *La cybernétique et l'origine de l'information.* Paris, Flammarion, 1954.
[3] David, A. *La cybernétique et l'humain.* Paris, Gallimard, 1965.

In reality, the domain set aside for effective human thought or, in more prudent terms, its own domain, is most clear at the two extremities of the circuit: the (initial) question and the (final) decision followed by a command.

The question itself presents several different stages: the initial choice of the question (other questions could be possible), the manner in which it is formulated, the combination of a certain number of questions. The decision itself is not a simple concept. Man may be called upon to choose between different 'decisions', which the machine shows to be feasible, to take a different decision from that indicated by the machine; he may decide upon a course of action which the machine considers impossible or catastrophic; finally, he may decide not to make a decision at all. He can, having reached a decision, choose not to carry it out or to modify it in some way.

And so we have at our disposition an *arbitral retreat*. It is perhaps more extensive than might be thought.

Human intervention, in the fullest sense, is characterized by the combination of three things which, etymologically speaking, are: the *cogito*, so dear to Descartes's heart, which involves the collection of data (and which is, therefore, mechanizable); the *intellego*, which involves a choice (and choice does not mean sorting through various possibilities); the *dialego*, which means to hold a dialogue and which is the source of the dialectic.

Man is distinguished from the machine by the initial or terminal choice, and choice is creative: it creates the question, it creates the decision, and it creates too the situation resulting from the decision.

Man is not only a rational being. He is a creative being. In the exercise of his creativity, he can take into account irrational phenomena which, by their very nature, escape logical mechanization, phenomena such as affectivity, moral considerations, or aesthetic appreciation[1].

Thus, it is creativity and not rationality that distinguishes man from his inanimate delegates; it is because he is creative that man cannot develop into a *cybernathropist*, a mere machine endowed with human form.

Ideas which I have already mentioned recur once again. Man, in creating, creates himself. The degree of creativity of which he is capable, his ability to be creative on his own account and of himself is a fundamental factor in his escape from alienation.

Creativity is a bulwark against alienation. It is on the rock of creativity that we must build the new man.

---

[1] Besides, as far as decision-making is concerned it would seem that man possesses, at least for the time being, a structural superiority over the machine. In fact, 'human thought processes can consider only a restricted number of variables at any one time, and cannot manipulate them very quickly'. However, man's response time is in the order of one-tenth of a second. Now the response time of computers is longer, although messages circulate within the computer several million times faster than in the brain. (J. Sauvau.)

I am going to try to continue this study along another line of approach. Without in any way neglecting its beneficial aspects, what dangers may we expect to be confronted with in 'the logical era'? I think they can be classed as follows:

(a) on the part of the manipulators, the temptation to gain power by the falsification of data; also on the part of the manipulators, the temptation to make a decision based on strictly rationalized, statistically measurable motives without taking into account purely 'human' affective, intuitive, psychological, etc., motivations;

(b) on the part of the public, a host of negative attitudes, such as a weary docility, the unquestioning acceptance of purely mechanizable decisions, a feeling of fear and panic which could give rise to uncontrollable movements of resistance and revolt;

(c) total indifference, the absence of '*consensus*' as well as of protest.

And so it is necessary to preserve, fortify, strengthen, and promote— both in those who control the machines and, consequently, the power they provide, and in those who are controlled through the medium of the decisions prompted by the machines—the human element, to reassert the value of the whole spectrum of human qualities, including both rational and irrational elements. Such a project demands first and foremost, a point which has already been made, that the level of education attained by every man is high enough to enable him to understand the development of the scientific world, which, then, need not be a source of terror, repulsion, or depression.

The views to which I find myself drawn find a considerable and enlightening confirmation in the studies carried out by the school which has given to its works the name of 'synecticism'. The researches of this school were carried out under the patronage of large industrial concerns. For this reason, it seems that they have not been widely distributed in political and university circles[1].

I believe that they are worth mentioning.

The word synectic comes from the Greek and means *the combination of apparently heterogeneous diverse elements*. It includes both a theoretical conception and an educational technique of creativity. Essentially the method used is to integrate, within one and the same group, a number of individuals, chosen from different educational backgrounds and with different temperaments, with a view to making *conscious* use of *subconscious* mechanisms and of arriving at new solutions.

I have retained the following conclusions as being of interest to my own work:

(a) In the first place, experience has shown that, contrary to a popular belief, it is possible to attempt to analyze inspiration without causing it

[1] Gordon, W. J. *Synectics: The development of creative capacity.* Macmillan, 1968.

to dry up or destroying it. The tape-recording of conversations of the working group has facilitated the comprehension of the various stages in the inventive process without destroying it. The almost magical aspect of intuition, of 'genius' (an aspect formerly symbolized by the belief in a revelation coming from without) is thus, if not disproved, at least made less important. The result is, and this is what I would like to emphasize here, that the activity of the inventive, innovating mind can not only be charted but actually encouraged.

(b) The same basic fundamental processes are used for creation in all fields, in the arts, in literature, in the scientific and technical sphere (the latter being the principal field of study for these researches). The decomposition, or rather the composition, from life of the process of technical invention is identical to that which precedes the conception of a fictional character, of a literary or an artistic topic.

This analysis confirms the opinions, already expressed by eminent specialists, denouncing the artificial character of the traditional distinction between minds of a scientific and those of a literary bent. It accentuates the necessity for multi-disciplined education, each separate discipline benefiting from discoveries in new forms of knowledge or method in another discipline.

(c) In the process of innovation, the emotional element is more important than the intellectual element, the irrational more important than the rational. The (final) solutions to problems are rational but the means of reaching them are not.

Invention is the result of unlikely associations, combining the unaccustomed and the familiar: 'one starts with a commonplace and aims at making a familiar idea unfamiliar'. Whence the role of the metaphor, and especially of the more outlandish ones. It is the *incongruous*, of which Lefebvre is so fond, which marks the launching point, '*the initial leap forward*'.

'Productive metaphors seem to have their origin in a "subliminary" activity, but they are necessarily thoughts taken from already acquired and available stock.'

Thus, experiments have proved, for example, that a knowledge of biology is advantageous in areas unconnected with this field, for it provides a great number of non-logical associations:

It is the best breeding ground for the potential metaphor ... The evocative power of the commonplaces of an animate world has no equivalent in the rules of abstract mechanics. To be original thought must return to the sources of organic life.'

This is the standard by which the truth of principles already exposed by thinkers who were unable to reach comparable observations are measured. Einstein has already said, 'The interplay between the different

175

disciplines seems to be the essential characteristic of creative thought'. And according to Ernest Mach: 'All that prompts us to make our ideas more precise and to develop them has its origins in the new, the unaccustomed and the unknown'.

(d) Finally, it is important to note that the creative process includes an agreeable element, a sensation of pleasure, which Gordon calls the 'hedonistic response'. It is not entirely due to the euphoria of discovery; it comes a little before, at the moment when the researcher feels he is somehow on the right track, that he will arrive at a solution.

These few reflections do not incline me towards pessimism. They corroborate my views that man must not place his hopes in the development of the superior machine.

Moreover, I believe that the conclusions derived from synecticism can be exploited in many other fields besides those of invention and innovation in the narrowest sense. Even in the century to come, not everyone will be an inventor.

But the observations that have been made as to the elaboration of a process or an original instrument have a more general value.

One can be creative, inventive or an innovator, in all circumstances of life, and all human activities demand a certain amount of creativity.

Active comprehension itself, the assimilation of knowledge elaborated by others involves an element of creativity. The vital element to retain is the productive, pleasing, and satisfying nature of the combination of the rational and the non-rational, the affirmation of the personality in all its complexity, memory and imagination, theory and technique, efficiency and morals, reason and feeling.

And so the theme of creativity is a natural ally of a theme mentioned earlier, that of participation. It indicates the object of participation.

Participation must not be, in Touraine's word, 'dependent'. It leads to a choice, a decision. Participation, at whatever level, does not play its part fully until it has some influence on the decision itself. Through this decision, man asserts himself, not as a mechanical being, but as the master of himself, a creator and a self-creator.

23

Participation and freedom

'Man is in a state of tension striving towards freedom, which reveals itself as an inner finality.'

L. Soubise

If it is neither reasonable, nor indeed possible, to reject the technological society, if it is both shameful and, indeed, stupid, to sink into a state of passive acceptance of the alienation of man which is a degradation of his destiny, the only course open to us is to assume the responsibilities laid on us by the technological society while refusing to accept alienation. Few politicians are willing to make this choice, some because their blind hostility to the technological society imprisons them, when confronted by it, in an illusory attitude of defiance, others because the alienation of man appears to them as a necessary evil, if not as a positive advantage then, at least, as something which facilitates government. Both sorts of politicians have in common the instinctive or conscious rejection of the only course of action which seems to me both objectively reasonable and morally acceptable: that is the refusal to regard the technological society and alienation as indissolubly linked or, if you prefer, the decision to retain the advantages and opportunities presented by technological society while refusing the annihilation of the human personality that it would seem to imply.

And so it is a question of 'dis-alienating', if alienation has already got a hold, of forestalling the risk of alienation, if it is only just threatening. Obviously, to dis-alienate man is to free him from his alienation. But even this definition demands two preliminary explanations.

Under the general heading of 'alienation', I include all that imposes a limit on man, considered either as an individual or as a part of a collective body, in the normal possibilities for the expression and development of his personality. Understood thus, alienation includes all those elements which restrict the human personality. Alienation must be judged, not just in the light of man's relationship to man at a given time, but in the light, though this is obviously more difficult to do, of what man could become if his opportunities for self-expression were preserved or increased. The corollary to a definition as elastic and comprehensive as this is that there can be no such thing as a unique, instant solution, which would do away with the evil once and for all. First, it must be admitted that certain forms of alienation can be eliminated only in stages; second, that dis-alienation is an open-ended project: even if, hypothetically, one alienation has been overcome, another will take its place. Calvez believes that humanity advances 'from alienation to alienation'. By changing his terminology a little, one could say 'from dis-alienation to dis-alienation'. The man guarded from all forms of alienation is perhaps just as mythical a character as the immortal man: but this does not stop us fighting illness and wresting victory from death for as long and as often as possible.

Then, the proposed formula implies a re-definition, a definition in depth, of freedom. The legal definition of freedom to which we are, or pretend to be, so committed can no longer satisfy us. Freedom is not only the right to move from place to place, to express an opinion, to look for work, to defend one's rights before a court of law, to choose one of several electoral candidates. These are necessary, valuable liberties, but they are often purely formal liberties, stripped of any real meaning by the social and economic environment. To be content with just these freedoms, to devote one's energies and attention simply to defending them, is to risk, and the French Left has not always avoided this risk, fighting over mere formal concepts.

The freedom to choose one's place of residence is severely limited by the housing shortage and, of course, by social inequality. The freedom to choose one's job is limited by unemployment and the inadequacy of education received. The freedom to defend one's rights before a court of law is limited by the slowness of the legal process and the cost of bringing a court action. It is even further limited by the defendants' inequality before the law, for attitudes differ depending on a man's social class—is he an aristocrat or does he come from a middle-class background?—and on his nationality. A man's freedom to vote is restricted by the practice of choosing candidates in advance from the ranks of those who have already risen to positions of eminence locally or from among those favored by the party machine. A further limitation is the inadequacy of education received by the citizen in politics and, even more strikingly, in economics.

Greater efforts must be made; these mere empty forms must be given some meaning, the links with the principles which originally inspired them must be reforged. It is not a new objective, though it is one which has often been lost from sight. A long time ago, Benjamin Constant exposed the dual nature of political freedom, sometimes considered as a guaranteed-freedom sometimes as a participation-freedom (participation in power). Lenin's famous formula goes even further: 'The people are not asking for freedom. They do not understand the meaning of the word. What they demand is power'. And yet even this distinction is today revealed as inadequate. Mere legal formulas cannot create participation-freedom any more than they could guaranteed-freedom. Benjamin Constant advocated the right to make an electoral choice, but today we know the limitations of this freedom. We find Lenin advocating the people's right to exercise power through a party dictatorship, but we now know what remains of this proposed objective.

I thought these explanatory comments were necessary to eliminate a few ambiguities. The dis-alienation of man does not consist in bringing to his notice or guaranteeing basic freedoms if they have no real meaning or if he is incapable of exercising them fully because he is prevented from so doing by his economic, cultural, and psychological situation. Neither does it consist in endowing him with the right to participate in the exercise of political power if this right, totally or even partly, rests on illusions. Or perhaps I should say these are but two necessary steps, which, without loss of any of their essential features, might be used as stepping stones to greater things. Participation-freedom represents a considerable though insufficient advance on guaranteed-freedom. Rather than participation-freedom, I think it is now necessary to talk of freedom-participation.

This is not a play on words, a mere game or a sophistry. It is rather a semantic reversal. In the first case (participation-freedom), the freedom to participate is affirmed; freedom institutes participation and, more often than not, destroys itself in the process. In the second case (freedom-participation), participation is the origin of freedom. It institutes freedom.

This definition of freedom, or more accurately of the freeing of man, is based on the inescapable postulate of man's alienation. Man is not free. He is not free when he disposes of essential freedoms of which he can make full use only with difficulty and which have no effect on many of the factors maintaining him in a state of slavery. He is not free in the periodic exercise of his sovereign political rights over which he has almost no control. The only point on which there must be agreement is that man's progress consists in attaining an ever greater degree of freedom or, if you prefer, in being freed, thereby acquiring the right to exercise his freedoms to the full.

This, for me, is the role of participation. Participation is the antithesis of alienation. It consists in giving man every opportunity and every means to participate in his own destiny, to understand it, to master it and to bend it to his will. It is totally opposed to alienation in that it tends to make man his own master once again. I am not so naive as to believe that a man living in society, limited by his own physical capabilities as well as by the demands of the social group in which he finds himself, can ever be completely his own master. But participation is not a state, a final end. It is a state of mind, a striving towards. In every aspect of a man's life, at every moment, it is a question of ensuring for him the greatest possible degree of understanding and control of his own behavior. This implies the tracking down and overcoming of everything which tends to transform him into a subject (in the positive sense of the word), into a 'reified' object.

In short, participation is rehumanization. And this is important and

179

necessary, not only in the work state where alienation is often more apparent than elsewhere or at least likely to attract closer attention, but also in the leisure state. Firstly, because the state of non-work plays a large part in determining the nature of the work state. Indeed, the training, which will enable the worker to choose his occupation, to assume its responsibilities and to transcend it, takes place during the preparatory stage of life, a period of time which varies in length according to the individual. Then, even during the period of productive activity the *man formed during non-working time* continues to exercise a great influence on his double. His family situation, his habitat, his interests and amusements ceaselessly form and transform man in his whole being. Secondly, because the active period of a man's life comes to an end while he still has a quarter, and often a third of his appointed span left. Thus, it will be seen that the duration and influence of the lesisure state has all too often been neglected in our preoccupation with the symbolic but incomplete image of the 'worker'.

Above all, participation must involve every aspect of a man's life right from the first moment of conscious awareness, for alienation marks all stages of life, A little later I will be dealing with worker participation in management, which I see as a fundamental remedy for the alienation of the worker in his job. But, as Lefebvre was astute enough to point out, the problem of 'everyday life' must be our constant concern. The risk of alienation is present at every moment of our daily lives; at every moment an opportunity for participation must be offered, in school, in university, in family life, in professional activity, and in the material life of the body. Cultural activity and artistic interests must present opportunities for participation, too. The problem of participation is a major preoccupation of Church people, of politicians, and of trade unionists. As Luigi Longo put it,

> The struggle against authoritarianism is a general problem; at the present time, in both capitalist and socialist countries, in Italy and in the whole world, the problem which presents itself is that of ensuring the greatest degree of participation for those who will be affected by the decisions, i.e. the masses, in the actual process of decision-making.

Participation in decision-making is only one vital part in the process of participation as a whole, a process which involves participation in knowledge of the basic facts, in the period of deliberation, in the decision-making and in the resulting action.

An authentic definition of equality is an integral part of this definition-in-depth of freedom. Obviously, equality can only be equality of opportunity. But its exact meaning must still be spelled out. It could never be a question of imposing from without equal opportunities for everyone to assume any responsibility whatsoever, to engage in any activity they like.

180

It is rather a question of bringing to the fore the existing potential of each individual, of arousing and adapting this potential according to the circumstances. I would like to point out that, in the field of education and professional training, and this is only one example, it is not enough, although this represents considerable progress, to throw open the doors of the same schools to all children of the same age, schools where they would all receive the same type of lessons: for such apparent equality, which is obviously preferable to inequalities based on social background or on wealth, would still give some children an unfair advantage and hold back others. This type of equality would benefit those, of whatever background, who could adapt easily to a uniform system, while others would be maintained in a state well below their real potential. True equality of opportunity goes further than this: it implies a type of education in which the detection of aptitudes is an integral part of the system, in which children are given a sense of motivation, in which vocational guidance is seen not as the movement of an irreversible lock but as a system of canals through which the original choice may be pursued or modified.

Finally, though the conventional and naive emotional response is to be feared, the presence of both freedom and equality as essential factors in counter-alienation irresistibly brings to mind the imagery, so dear to Frenchmen, of their national motto and leads naturally to the concept of fraternity. Why not, common decency apart, admit that this apparently commonplace and debased motto sums up a philosophy of man which is in no way old-fashioned or devalued? Freedom and equality, as I understand them here, are born of a fraternal conception of man, that of the generic conscience: the universal man of all humanity. If man's progress is to be manifested in an increasing concern for his own destiny, in fuller awareness of his position, in a greater degree of responsibility, if it is true that his participation in every aspect and moment of his destiny is the only means of guaranteeing both continuing freedom and authentic equality, care must be taken to ensure that no man is left out of the project, neither can any man accept that a fellow man be excluded from the project. The constant promotion of each individual's resources and opportunities constitute the basis for a *fraternity* which is neither a mere verbal concept nor a mere convention, a fraternity which is inspired not so much by love of one's fellow, though this of course is not excluded, but by an awareness of his dignity; a fraternity based less on the rather doubtful concept of solidarity between men than on the esteem and confidence which man shows towards man, an adult fraternity, which is neither sentimental nor provocative; a fraternity, finally, which maintains that it is in all honesty impossible to claim as equals and brothers any human beings neglected by us for so long, those faltering shadows at the wayside, the incurable victims of the march of progress.

Part 5

Suggestions for an overall strategy for political action

24

The controlling factors
General education

The general tenor of this book will have perhaps surprised the reader coming, as it does, from the pen of a politician. It may be that the reader will be disappointed. It was a risk I had to take. This book will be judged as a non-political work, and yet I maintain that it is essentially political in its nature.

It was never the intention of this work to catalog all the short- and medium-term problems which present themselves for consideration in the sector of governmental and legislative action and to compile a more or less coherent and realistic list of 'points', as is the custom in ministerial declarations and political programs.

The public has had enough of such programs. That is understandable. A program which one intends to put into operation is then called a plan. A plan can only be drawn up to any purpose if the feasibility of its execution is kept in view. Discussions about programs between parties or politicians can only result in the more or less original reformation of generalities and restatements of good intentions, in putting into operation, either to keep up appearances or because it is a matter of some urgency, a compromise solution for the most acute and immediate problem—or problems—demanding attention. Where no preliminary basic agreement as to objectives has been reached or where there is no common inspiration to stimulate activity, the search for a compromise generally results in the retention of everything that was least good in the proposals put forward, while only an inadequate number of the really good suggestions are retained.

On the other hand, I believe that the options which I have been able to bring out in the course of this book, not *in spite of* but *because of* its general, essential character—whether you qualify this character as philosophical or ideological—could, at any time, provide a way of tackling the task of drawing up a program or a plan, on condition that the only difficulties left to be resolved, those of an operational nature, are dealt with.

However, I have not reached this point yet. There is a preliminary step that must be taken, that of clearing the dross from what is conventionally called political life. By this I mean it is necessary to breathe new life into political thought, to make it raise its standards, to get it away from the banalities, repetitions and clichés in which it all too often wallows, right away from the *meta-language*, to bestow upon it much thought and conviction so that eventually it will of its own accord become a thought-provoking subject and will generate conviction. This would be a starting point for the evolution of distinct schools of thought, which would base their decisions, on whether to oppose one another or cooperate, on the authentic consideration of the real major problems and not, as they do now, on hoary, useless myths, to which they have become attached, or on the routine voting according to the party line or according to decisions reached at a congress, all of which produces the impression of a phenomenon in direct contrast to that described by Touraine (a-political politicization) and which could be called political-depoliticization.

Can the study which I propose lead to this result? I think so. At least it could be taken up again, made more complete, more effective. I present my analysis as a line of enquiry, as an approach, as a positive invitation to participate in a common study which might be undertaken by groups or by men who have been politically ostracized or even politically indifferent, up to now.

My concern was to make the concept of humanism a meaningful one, to define a type of man and a type of society, a task which is, in my opinion, the rightful preoccupation of the whole of politics, of the whole of political sociology—for the state is no longer distinguishable from the citizen body.

There have always been humanists, but they have not professed the same kind of humanism throughout all the ages. There are humanists today and they profess different brands of humanism (both different from each other and different from what true humanism should be). The great Greek philosophers were humanists who regarded slavery as the most natural thing in the world. Cicero was a humanist who, without taking the question of slavery into consideration, found it normal that enemy commanders should be butchered and prisoners thrown to wild animals. There have been great Muslim humanists, and they had no objection to women being shut up in harems. Turgot was one of the most complete humanists of the Enlightenment and, like his physiocrat friends, he believed that only property owners were fit to take a hand in public affairs. Jules Ferry was a humanist and the founder of state primary schools, but his prime concern was to found an empire for France by force.

Today the war in Vietnam is waged in the name of (liberal) humanism, while Czechoslavakia was occupied in the name of (socialist) humanism. In the name of an inflammatory super-humanism, which incites men to defy paper tigers, Mao's China undertakes irresponsible ventures and issues ominous threats.

The definition of humanism as the refusal to accept alienation implies the rejection, in foreign policy, of all forms of 'dependence', which might commit France, directly or indirectly, to an active or passive dominant role,

186

and which might force her to assume responsibility for a violent or oppressive act. Then again, I find myself in agreement with the Gaullist line on the importance of aid for the underdeveloped countries. I feel that I am committed in advance to supporting and, if possible, actually promoting every effort towards disarmament, conciliation, the settling of disputes by arbitration, international security, peace[1].

As for home affairs, my work leads me to see the necessity of going *beyond the new social contract,* though this naturally implies that I am committed to this contract, i.e. to the necessity of the equitable and corrective distribution of the increased national income (socialism of communal wealth) as a necessary first step. The principle of counter-alienation reinforces the aims of this type of political economy, for those sectors of the population who live in conditions of real economic hardship must be classed as alienated. May I point out that if, since 1963 when they were published, the main tenets of the social contract had been retained, and if the practical suggestions accompanying them, in particular the scientific investigation into social disparities, had been carried out, many things might have occurred differently, not least the May 1968 eruption[2]?

The new set-up, which I am presenting in this book, the new enlarged social contract, emphasizes education and participation in the light of human and social creativity. These views are not just theoretical ones. They are the views most calculated to reawaken the only kind of political thinking worthy of its name, to reanimate it, make it more exciting, to bring hidden motives out into the open, to get contentious points back on to a real platform where they can be debated by a revised and updated cast of real actors.

We have seen evidence of this, all this last year[3], in the open attacks and the behind-the-scenes manoeuvring going on in what used to be my area of responsibility: the galvanizing into action of the fuddy-duddies and anti-democrats in the University and elsewhere, the tirades of the self-styled Dijon CDR[4] and its rivals, the opening of a second front by the twenty-four anti-reformist deans and professors at the particularly well chosen time of the presidential election, plus many other episodes besides, show all too clearly that this time there was a real *issue* (in the French and

[1] Cf. my introduction and the proposals I submitted to the 1955 Geneva Conference.

[2] I must be fair and point out that progress has been achieved in this direction with the new concept of the minimum wage (SMC) which implies not only a sliding scale (for which I was so bitterly reproached some time ago) but also a minimum growth rate. The sliding scale, while being a novel enough measure to scandalize the conservatives, nevertheless was derived from the (expanded and updated) conception of a paternalistic welfare state. The minimum growth rate is a new development to meet a recent public demand, the result of a new awareness of the nature of the welfare state, a new conception which reveals itself in the commonly quoted reflection: 'What is the guaranteed minimum? A 3 per cent increase a year'.

[3] This would be 1969–1970 as the French edition was published in 1970. (Translator's note)

[4] CDR—Centre de Défense de la République. (Translator's note)

English sense of the word) at stake[1]. No longer was it a mere fencing-match or a combat which would end at the first sign of blood. It was obvious that a new, deeply democratic humanist conception of education, the veritable renovation of the whole pedagogical structure had entered the arena, and this accounts for the fury of the Malthusians and the élitists, of those fanatics who would ration culture through a process of pseudo-selection, of all those to whom the very mention of the common syllabus is as a red rag to a bull, of all those who felt their period of proud office as absolute rulers threatened, of those who felt threatened in their secure University positions which they had come to look upon as their birthright, of those who had revelled in the oligarchical exploitation of the power of knowledge, a power acquired by a process of cooption and which they expected to enjoy until they died, but who now felt threatened. While, on the other hand, around my team one could see forming a group of kindred spirits, inspired by a (often long-standing) conviction and by a (new) sense of hope, the conviction and the hope that, from its origins in educational circles, began to spread in concentric circles, till it reached the public at large. A current of opinion, at first with few sources of information at its disposal, often misinformed, easily nonplussed, clinging to old scholastic habits, tempted by the realistic, natural, 'genetic' aspects of selection, by the belief in *natural gifts*, in competition, in the quarter of a mark separating individuals, in tying for class positions, in the 'open sesame' of examinations successfully taken, hampered too by the violent and chaotic demands made by the young and by the 'absurdities' of revolution, gradually came to realize what the real problems were; they no longer confined themselves to the terms of reference dictated by the conservative conscience and they committed themselves to battle. A clear and growing majority declared itself for reform and against stagnation, for the open door and against the closed shop; a majority began to be interested, concerned, and committed in this fight against darkness, in the politics of the new man, of the new world, although its individual members still refused to believe that this was the very stuff of politics, for until then politics had been uninteresting, a matter of no concern, which did not encourage commitment.

How many letters I received from complete strangers when I left the ministry—I still receive some—letters whose value for me owes something to the approbation and regard they express but something, too, to the quality of joy which emerges, the hedonic response of truth. These testimonies make it possible for me to work as I do and to learn lessons from my writing for the future[2].

[1] The French word *issue* has the restricted meaning of a 'way out' an 'outcome'. Here, Faure wants to make the point that the new reforms did offer a way out but they were also 'an issue' a point of some controversy. (Translator's note)

[2] Let it be remembered that the different opinion polls put the degree of support for my policies at somewhere between 75 and 80 per cent.

Now we have reached a position of stalemate. The opposing camps are entrenched in their positions and their relative strengths appear equal. The partisans of reform, obviously disappointed at my departure, have been somewhat reassured by the understanding and lucidity of my successor. They fear that if they seek to speed up the forward movement, which is really a very moderate aim, it may be seen as excessive and may provoke attack from the obscurantists. As for the latter, their whole plan of campaign was concentrated on, first, getting rid of the reformer; they are savoring their success and regard the joy it has brought them as the first of many perks, for they are often vindictive men. They are too, at least in their own way, clever and far-seeing. No doubt they would have preferred the new minister not to be such a sincere and honest advocate of reform. But they know from experience that the departure of the initiator of a reform always checks that reform's progress, whatever the intentions of the successor. In any case, they felt that it would have been asking too much of their forces to have attempted to destroy what had already been achieved and to put back the clock. Besides, at first, the execrable reform brought them all the advantages of appeasement, an indispensable condition for their next moves. Finally, some sections of the new system were, so they thought, useful—even advantageous—to their plans, provided the spirit in which the changes were made underwent a subtle change. For example, they fully expect to exploit the autonomy of the universities to encourage not *specialization* (which is my objective and which would facilitate, either in the framework of the French system or, better still, within a European framework, the concentration of material resources and brainpower and which would allow French students to make up the leeway existing between them and the Americans in the more advanced branches of knowledge and research), but *competition* between universities, thus facilitating the emergence of superior universities by a form of limitation-selection and relegating the mounting tide of plebeian students, the products of mass culture, to the 'ignoble' (in the etymological sense of the word) universities. This plan really exists; it is not difficult to get proof of this from the occasional chance remark.

Thus, even the *ultras* have accepted the cessation of hostilities, for this gives them the opportunity to engage in minor skirmishes (such as the introduction of the compulsory medical and all the red tape connected with improving examination methods). The comparative peace gives them time to marshall their resources, to reinstate conservatism, to re-establish old routines. At the same time, the innovating spirit grows weary and the revolutionary finds himself in a dilemma: should he doze off in his turn or mount a violent demonstration, thereby alienating public opinion and turning it against the reform program, which is bound to be held responsible for all ills and which, because it has never really been applied, would have to confess itself incapable of remedying them.

The present situation, which might be compared with the phoney war, cannot be prolonged indefinitely, nor indeed for very much longer. The battle will be resumed. It will last for a long time. If there are really going to be far-reaching, authentic lines of demarcation in the new political struggle, the problems of education and teaching will form one of these lines, no doubt the main one, and if there is to be only one line of demarcation it will certainly be this one, as we have seen in the past.

But it is not a question which uniquely, or even chiefly, concerns the University. Its effects are felt throughout the whole field of education. The May 1968 crisis was only superficially a crisis within the University. Shaken to the core, the University bore the brunt of a double crisis. From below, there was the crisis of education in the schools, a crisis due to the failure to adapt curricula to the pupils' needs. From above, there was the crisis of adult education, a crisis caused by the non-existence of facilities in this area.

Although the matter has been discussed many times, both by me and by others, a brief recall of the facts is warranted.

If the May uprising served to reveal the discontent felt by the young, a crisis in spiritual values, a pathological hatred of the consumer society, etc., the question still remains as to *why* this crisis should have occurred in France, when deep-rooted crisis conditions exist elsewhere. It still remains to be shown *how* the uprising could have erupted in France, the very country in which it seemed the most unlikely since, on the one hand, there had before the crisis been fewer troubles in France than in many other countries (Latin America, USA, Germany, Italy) and, on the other, the two things being connected, the student revolution in France could not draw on the usual political stimuli: racial tension, anti-Vietnam war protests, resentment of NATO, etc. Gaullist policies, though often grossly misunderstood, the policies expressed in the program for decolonization, in the Pnom-Penh speech, in the inauguration of the Paris Conference, presented no targets for attack. The crisis occurred in Paris and in France for a reason directly connected with the University and the teaching system as a whole; it occurred because of what I call *the disequilibrium between the qualitative and the quantitative.*

During the immediately preceding ten years, successive administrations had given their consent to extraordinary measures, involving both money and materials, to welcome the growing numbers of students and schoolchildren. Boldly, they had decided to raise the school-leaving age. However, this extraordinary growth in numbers was not accompanied by the necessary qualitative adjustments: hence, the specifically French problem. There are countries where the students are more numerous than in France, but education is more advanced in these countries. There are countries where education is in as backward a state as in France, but here there are fewer students.

190

This disequilibrium led to a series of critical results:

(a) although the democratization of education represented a certain degree of progress it did not seem to have gone far enough. A preferential system of recruitment for jobs arouses less indignation when students are few in number than when they are many. Many students felt bad about their privileged position, hence the romantic reflex which drove them towards the factories.

(b) the inflexibility of over-specialized teaching programs became much more noticeable; the students became alarmed less by the possibility of there being too few job outlets (a possibility which had not then emerged and which is still not proved today; the army of out-of-work graduates is non-existent for the moment, except as a figment of the conservatives' imagination), but rather by the depressing prospect of not enjoying their professional careers.

(c) the excessive number of students, who had received an exclusively literary and classical education, filled the think-tanks, which is what universities are, with a host of critical minds, trained to perfection in the techniques of expression and criticism but completely ignorant of the technical world upon which they would be summoned to practice aimlessly their peerless and, in their case, sadly sterile qualities.

Then the detonator provided by the proposal that authoritarian measures be taken to introduce compulsory vocational guidance in secondary schools and would-be selection in higher education went off. The discontent of the parents and the teachers, which had already found expression in a twenty-four hour strike, acted as a sounding-board for the misgivings of the students, now faced with the prospect of being turned away from university yet who had received no proper training to equip them for their entry into the real world.

The remedies demanded by this situation were completely different from those dictated by a desire to close the ranks and retrench. The reader will be aware that I recommended and, as far as it was materially possible, put the necessary measures into operation without delay. On 25 July, the date of the first debate in the Assembly and ten days after assuming office, I announced to the House the institution of the common syllabus in secondary schools, the postponing of the introduction of the classical humanities to higher forms, the introduction of technology as a subject, the inclusion of technical training as an integral part of general education. Such a policy if carried out would constitute an education completely worthy of modern man, would allow students to choose their own careers more wisely, would effect a better distribution of manpower among the various disciplines (deriving an added advantage from the multiplicity of disciplines in the first year at university) and it would be of benefit too, to those who wish to go out and earn a living directly they leave school, for their schooling will not have discouraged them and cut them off from real life. This venture in the field of higher education was complemented by a symmetrical effort in lower echelons. It was imperative that adult education should no longer be a philanthropic exercise left to the good offices of paternalism and patronage; it should be progressively extended over a wide area, according to the carefully worked-out methods which it demands, to reach the whole population, thus assuring a second chance for those who ended their schooling at an early age, and giving everyone the chance to better himself.

Such a plan should have pleased—enchanted even—the proponents of so-called selection, if this word had really signified to them the best vocational guidance for each individual once his motivation had been aroused and his abilities stimulated. But they do not think like this. They do not choose to accept this line of reasoning. They place their melancholy faith in other precepts. Their selection is what has been called *the terrible act of treachery*. They found completely natural an educational policy which turned out annually, after the *baccalauréat*[1], 100 000 pupils qualified in just a few branches of the arts and which had cost France 12 000 maths graduates in two years! Perhaps in the depths of their smug, sadistic being they rejoiced over this. It was enough, was it not, to erect barrier after barrier, to cause failure after failure. Is this democratization? Yes, so they claim; but is there anyone so blind that he cannot see that among the latest batch of failed students the ones who come from well-off families (the advantages derived from a good cultural background apart) are precisely those who have the best chance of being able to present themselves for the re-sits. Humanism? No doubt yes, if by that you mean it is advisable to learn Latin at the age of eleven. But no, if humanism means that it is 'human' to throw into active life tens of thousands of pseudo-humanists deprived of all knowledge which might be put to practical use.

They have tried, they are still trying, to cajole and trick the public. I can prove that by playing on the word selection, a word graced with Darwinian scientific overtones, they often succeed. Sometimes I am asked, 'But is not selection a *natural* law'? Yes, but are natural laws *social laws*? Bertrand Russell wrote: 'We have become used to quoting natural law to support our actions; this, I believe, is a great error; the imitation of nature can only lead to enslavement'.

In fact, the *selectionists*' conception of selection is a genetic one incorporating man with the animal species. They believe children are either gifted or not gifted, workers or non-workers; they will even go so far as to say a child is gifted or not gifted for work. However, modern science and educational research have long shown how much care is needed in the use of the concept of 'the gift' and how many unexpected aptitudes can reveal

[1] *Baccalauréat*—school-leaving certificate essential for access to the University. (Translator's note)

themselves in children if the right methods of arousal and true vocational guidance are employed.

For its (more or less overt) advocates, the genetic conception of selection is coupled with an élitist conception of society. They experience a profound feeling of resentment at the suggestion that the knowledge they have acquired might be shared by so many, perhaps all, other people. They believe themselves to be democrats simply because they are perfectly willing to admit that a 'gifted' child of the people can aspire to high office (it may well be that this is the case of individuals among their number), but the thought would never cross their minds that an élite could be made up of a vast number of people. This attitude is easy to discern among many of the stalwarts teaching medicine. They try to regulate the number of students admitted according to the rules for administering doses of medicine; they are determined to erect a wall around the teaching of medicine, to protect and isolate it from other disciplines—though recent Nobel prize winners in France have indicated the opposite way is more fruitful; they secretly nurture a longing for the old miracle workers and apothecaries.

If the selectionists had been sincere, should not they have applauded the measures I introduced—and executed—to suppress the September re-sits for the *baccalauréat*? Not a word of congratulation did I receive; I did not expect any. Such a measure is too simple and in some ways too honest. Selection is acceptable to them only if it is also a rather painful process. Strange as it may seem, that is how their minds work. It is like the Jansenist conception of grace, only they are the ones who dispense it.

At the same time, they have a confused feeling that their only weapon is to employ delaying tactics, that they will have to be satisfied with ephemeral, symbolic successes, that the days are numbered when they will succeed in raising above the faithful masses the emblem of their soulless cult, the tight-fisted Christ of their parsimonious faculties.

25

The controlling factors (continued)
Participation

The example I have just given was chosen, first, because I experienced it personally and, second, because it is more conclusive as an example than that of the still-continuing quarrel over the role of the trade unions and worker participation in management. In this case, reactionary opinion made itself felt in a different and more insidious way. The context was not the same. No one had been forced to act in the heat of the moment. It is true that the May uprisings did reveal that the working classes had certain aspirations which were totally unconnected with mere material demands for higher wages and better working conditions. Some of the young trade-unionists involved are known to have expressed criticism of the whole structure of industry and to have demanded the establishment of a new system of consultation within industry (not necessarily following the Marxist line, at least not as practiced in the Soviet Union, but, as far as I understand this rather confused situation, based on the Yugoslavian system, of which, incidentally, these same trade-unionists had only slight knowledge). However, these rather vague aspirations were never expressed clearly and were soon swallowed up and lost among general demands for higher wages. Consequently—with the exception of the agreement reached on the role of the trade unions in industry—there has been no evidence of active interest among the workers in the formulation of a collective demand for a greater degree of participation and for the restructuring of industry; there is nothing, in fact, comparable to the demands made, and not only by professional people, for a greater say in university administration and for the reform of the education system. The big business men, who were afraid of certain projected reforms even before demands for reform had been clearly expressed, chose as the main target for their opposition the text submitted for referendum, although the forms of participation envisaged contained nothing they needed to fear. Thus—and we have proof of this—there was a further build-up of negative votes, which perhaps was decisive. The trade union movement did not come out in favor of the development of worker participation; far from it. Some trade-unionists were afraid of what this would involve; others, while wanting to bring the worker nearer to the center of power, declared themselves hostile to all the proposals actually made, and even to those which might be put to them in the future, because they believed in advance that they would get the worst of the bargain, and because they were unrelenting in their mistrust of management, whose thinking on this question, however, had for a long time been on exactly the same lines as those followed by the unions. A prime example of the paradoxical misunderstanding which bedevilled the whole Gaullist experiment! It should be pointed out that the situation was completely different in the field of educational reform, where I could always rely on the constructive if critical support of the FEN[1] and the SGEN[2]. We might usefully learn from these latter negotiations that opposing political views do not necessarily entail the adopting of irreconcilable attitudes. These same negotiations also gave me a chance to appreciate the value of firmly held beliefs. The enthusiasm they engender infects other people. It brings your opponents round to your way of thinking. It can supply something often lacking from a reform program. Those in favor of reform often waver in their support; those against, however, are ever resolute in their fight: from the outset the power struggle is weighted in their favor. Firmly held beliefs can create *credibility*. I must admit that I owe much of my success in these negotiations to the tenacity of my opponents, and I would like to take this opportunity of thanking them for it.

Eleven months' experience would seem to suggest that the double objective of making politics more lively and the redistribution of political power can be achieved with some measure of success as far as the problems of education are concerned. The problems of participation, which, given different circumstances, are not insoluble, present a greater challenge, as does the planning necessary for joint schemes with a new look.

The theme of *worker participation in business management* will only be used here as an example of the general principle of participation. Of all the forms of alienation, alienation in work has been the most thoroughly analyzed, because, throughout the nineteenth century, it represented the most oppressive form of alienation in industrial society. We have already seen what aspects of Marxist thought on alienation are still valid today and what aspects have to be rejected in the light of observations of contemporary society. But the problem of alienation in work still remains. First, because the exploitation of labor by capital is not yet a myth in a showcase in the museum of defunct doctrines; the French economy which is not, for the most part, one of those great techno-structures described by Galbraith, still provides some aberrant examples of exploitation. Second

[1] FEN—Fédération de l'Éducation Nationale, the principal federation of teachers' unions.
[2] SGEN—Syndicat Général de l'Éducation Nationale, a teachers' union and part of the CFDT (Confédération Française et Démocratique du Travail) the second most powerful union bloc after the CGT (Confédération Générale du Travail). (Translator's notes)

and more important, the problem of alienation in work has not disappeared. It has simply shifted its ground. If, contrary to the Marxist view, the worker were presumed to be well paid with good prospects of promotion, engaged in activities as interesting as his abilities allow him to undertake, would he then be dis-alienated? Experience indicates the contrary. The alienation of the worker in modern industrial society is caused less by the convention that the boss *owns* his workers than by the difficulties *in relating to the powers-that-be*. The great frustration prevalent in organized societies is the result of the bad relationships between those in authority and the people under them; the fact that the superior is unaware of his inferiors' problems, the mystifying nature of the social hierarchy, the exclusion of the majority of the working force from the collective decision, these are the true symptoms of alienation in work. I call this administrative or bureaucratic alienation, although both these adjectives have the disadvantage of covering only a few of the aspects involved. Mystification appears at all levels within the organization, and the intellectual workers, however elevated their position[1], are just as subject to it as are the manual workers. The bureaucratic pyramid tends to function like a hierarchical system where each individual sacrifices his individuality to his 'superior'. And in this waterfall of successive submissions, the reasons for, the stages in, and even the precise contributions of, individuals towards the decision are swallowed up without trace.

The antithesis of this form of alienation is participation: in the gathering of information, in the deliberation process, in the actual decision-making.

In this context, 'incentive schemes', which are either enthusiastically welcomed or else deplored, form but one limited aspect of participation. They provide no more than a variable, aleatory supplement to the wage-earner's income. They are originally inspired by a desire to improve the worker's financial situation in so far as the firm's growth prospects make this possible without upsetting the balance, for bonuses are related to increased productivity. An incentive scheme can have the disadvantage of weakening the profit margin available for plough-back into investments, but it is technically possible to incorporate an incentive scheme with an issue of non-voting shares or redeemable stock.

On the other hand, if the incentive scheme is to involve issuing the workers with equity shares, this particular reform takes on a completely different meaning.

In the latter case, it is no longer a question of simply improving the workers' financial position through an aleatory share in the profits. In the latest scheme, the worker is to be given a controlling voice in the management of the company on an equal footing with the other shareholders. Now, the incentive scheme becomes just one vehicle for participation.

[1] Cheverney V. J. *Les cadres. Essai sur de nouveaux prolétaires.* Paris, 1967.

Numerous justifications for this kind of incentive scheme have been put forward[1]. The question has been asked as to why one of the agents of production (capital) should be alone to benefit from one of the results of production, while the other (labor) is totally excluded. Is not the part played by labor in the common effort at least as important as that played by capital? Besides, would not the plough-back of profits have been on a decreased scale if the basic wage had been raised, which, as the results show, was a technical possibility? Thus, the workers' right to share in the increased capital accumulation achieved by the plough-back of the profits can be justified on the grounds of fairness.

Personally, I am not convinced that a consideration for what is fair provides an irresistible reason for worker participation in business management. It is doubtful whether the capitalist sphere is really ready for a truly 'fair' organization: besides, a desire to be fair would lead to far more upheavals than just the participation of the workers in the surplus-value of ploughed-back profit. Then again, how can an equitable solution be arranged between two production factors as dissimilar as labor and capital, between which one would be hard put to it to find a common denominator. Above all, how could a 'fair' balance be established between their respective rights and the might of the techno-structure? If confined to the question of fairness, the debate seems to me a largely sterile one, and I can understand why the trade unions more often than not refuse to take part in it.

Participation in business management finds its real support in a *political philosophy which runs alienation to earth wherever it may have taken hold.* The degrading or simply inhibiting bureaucratic alienation of the worker is an evil which cannot be tolerated. Participation in management implies that the worker is informed of all the problems confronting his company, not just those concerned with the only sector he knows in what is otherwise an incomprehensible puzzle; that he is informed of the reasons for essential choices; that, with all the facts at his disposal, he can influence the final decision upon which the fate of his firm, and consequently his own fate, depends. In short, what is needed is for the worker to understand the aims, the mechanisms and the reasons for the collective decision so that, in the last analysis, he may participate as far as possible in this decision in the reasonable certitude that he has some responsibility for, and influence upon, both the deliberation process and the action taken; then—and only then—can bureaucratic alienation be effectively defeated. Taking it one stage further, it might be said that worker participation in management constitutes a reasonable and viable remedy for the problems of 'reification'. If it is unthinkable that the worker should recall, rehumanize, the objects in which so many precious hours of his own life are materialized by a measure of direct control or enjoyment of them, a meaningful substitute

[1] In particular, see Thierry Maulnier's series of articles in *Le Figaro*.

for this impossible venture can be envisaged in the transfer of this control and enjoyment to the company he works for.

This kind of participation in management, for example in the topical form of employee investment in a firm's capital, a procedure which was the object of my first legislative initiative when I was elected member for the Jura, is both desirable and feasible. Sooner or later it will become general practice. Why not sooner rather than later? Recent events in the world of big business have demonstrated just how abnormal and shocking the lack of worker participation in management is. The Homeric struggle which brought Boussois and Saint-Gobain into the arena as opponents will be remembered. Saint-Gobain, or his publicists, had the happy idea of giving the shareholders a chance to look over the firm's 'open house'. They were taken on conducted tours, supplied with information, welcomed with open arms. The impression was given that, for once, the life and future of a great firm was being shared by the faceless army of the small-scale *shareholders* who were awestruck at being shown so much consideration, whose interest was aroused, who were suddenly touched because pains were being taken to supply them with information, to ask their opinion and to explain the present and future uses to which their capital would be put; they had taken over for a few weeks the exercise of their allocated sovereignty from the techno-structure. These shareholders thought they were participating in the management of the company, and they derived from this belief a feeling of dignity and importance. But what about the workers? In the general festivities, they seemed forgotten. And yet it was their livelihood that was at stake, for many of them their whole future and that of their families was in the balance. But no one thought it was any business of theirs. Rarely has the non-participation of the workers seemed so strange, so reprehensible. How can a rational organization entirely exclude men from problems which concern them, not just by chance, but in every aspect of their lives?

Thus, General de Gaulle acted wisely in attaching so much importance to worker participation in management, not just as something demanded by considerations of fairness but as a basis for political philosophy. Nevertheless, the value of the reservations expressed both in trade-union and employer circles must still be assessed. While not actively resisting it, the trade unions are doing nothing to promote the higher form of participation. Made wary by long years of adverse experiences, inured to offers of a helping hand, they fear for the masses a trap and for themselves a loss of power, for all the risk of the unknown. This must be taken into consideration. The victims of alienation are certainly not the first to be aware of it, even less are they the first to demand that a stop be put to it. It is one of the characteristics of alienation that those who suffer it are rarely aware of the phenomenon and it is not necessarily irksome. When it becomes so, action and reaction may be extreme. The hostility or the reservations of the trade unions, therefore, must not be an insurmountable obstacle; but neither must they be ignored. The spirit of participation implies that the unions receive precise information about the ends to be pursued and about the means available; that they are consulted about the drawing up of the most effective plan of campaign, that they see quite clearly that their participation in management is inspired by one overriding aim, that of freeing man, an aim which they may or may not share, but which does not play directly into the hands of the capitalists, which is not designed just to salve the bosses' consciences or to put off indefinitely the day of reckoning.

The uneasiness of the capitalists is less easy to justify; but money is as elusive as the squirrel and just as mobile. However, worker participation in management does not essentially interfere with the shareholders' degree of control, the last preogative left to them by the techno-structure, if indeed it leaves them any prerogative at all. In fact, the most bitter hostility is likely to come from the techno-structure itself. The bureaucrats fear the intrusion of worker capitalism into the company, or more precisely of capitalism practiced by their own workers, for this would give the latter a double function, a double power, while at the same time causing them to see matters differently. The shareholder keeps out of sight or just puts in an appearance at general meetings. Then again, more often than not, he signs away his rights and prerogatives to the techno-structure. He is an absentee, a trusting absentee. The worker, on the other hand, is within the factory gates. He sees how the business is run. He is on the spot, suspicious, sometimes hostile. Will he use his right to control affairs like a shareholder to guarantee profits, like a manager to see the business is run efficiently, or like a worker to promote his own interests? Such apprehension is not necessarily unfounded. And so certain schemes have been envisaged from time to time to guarantee the workers some degree of participation in other companies besides the one in which they work. But the effect of this is to transform the worker into a shareholder or an administrator, to make him participate, in a general way, in the economic system in which his own activity has its place; it does nothing to rectify the immediate alienation created by his working conditions. In being watered down, participation thus loses some of its usefulness.

The problem is not a simple one. It would be sheer charlatanism to pretend to have a ready-made solution. Care must be taken not to upset economic expansion; the overlapping of European economies must be taken into account. The only suggestion that can be rejected out of hand is that of worker control of industry, the results of which have always been disappointing and which are not really applicable to our present economic system.

This reservation having been made, attempts must be made without delay to establish the main lines of a participation compatible with our economic system but which does not, by its timidity or inappropriateness, rob the reform program instituted of its chances of success. In this attempt we must keep in mind, first and foremost, the fact that the fear of change is much more terrifying than the actual change itself. Then again, the workers' participation in business management will be all the more reasonable and beneficial if they have received a training in economics, a training which, because of the grave defects of an archaic educational system, is generally lacking in France, even among those who are called cultured. Participation in knowledge is thus inseparable from participation in management, which it must both justify and encourage. This is just one factor among many which demonstrates that participation cannot be an isolated enterprise introduced as an experiment in just one sector of human activity. The only justification for its existence, its only chance of success, is dependent on its being the inspiration for the whole of the political, economic, and social legislation of the State, and, beyond the State, of the whole society.

However, the research I have done and the conclusions I have drawn from it prompt me to adopt a completely new way of looking at things. From now on I must have the confidence to believe that education and participation are far more than just two factors in an overall problem. Their significance extends beyond a few legal texts and statutes among so many others, beyond a few paragraphs in an encyclopedic program. They are not just embarrassing topics to be avoided in interviews, the subject-matter of an eloquent speech, points to be conceded in a difficult argument.

I have defined these two phenomena as two aspects in a fundamental interpretation of a type of society, as the complementary keys to a type of man. They must become the dominant factors in a political program. That is not to say that other topics do not exist. What it does mean is that other matters must be dealt with in relation to the principal objectives and with direct reference to the solution unequivocally demanded by them. Now, if my calculations are correct, the problems of articulation this would involve should not, hypothetically speaking, present insurmountable difficulties. If all the problems requiring attention are arranged in a strict order of priority, the means and conditions cannot fail to be in accordance with the ends; there can be no revolt of matter against man.

Thus, it is obvious that a weak economy cannot easily support an ambitious educational program. But have resources expended on education ever imperilled an economy? The handicap of which France is now feeling the effects is precisely due to her failure to adapt her research program and to the great shortage of engineers, skilled scientific researchers, management specialists, etc., that is to say, to the archaic and undemocratic nature of her educational system.

However, let us not imagine that the great effort needed of us can be arithmetically limited to the direct requirements of a program to produce a thousand engineers, researchers, etc. That would certainly be a misleading assumption. But it is, for example, imperative that an urgent and massive program be instituted to make education a permanent process, though this would constitute a program whose returns are not immediately realizable and whose full beneficial effects can never be assessed accurately. A third television channel must be created without delay, a channel whose programs would be entirely given over to education and culture. All this will demand supplementary budget aid, which must be forthcoming, though without undue extravagance. But not all these measures demand great sacrifices. The creation of the Institute for Economic and Social Research, one of my chief sources of gratification, required only a few thousand old francs, although their allocation was bitterly contested and endlessly called into question. Often, initiatives requiring little or almost no extra expenditure meet with the most stubborn opposition. A fair compromise will have to be reached between the huge sums of money spent on relatively unambitious schemes and the often meagre sums allocated to really ambitious ventures.

Naturally, there are some exceptions. The putting into operation of an undeniably urgently needed overall plan for permanent education, the first stages of which I had earmarked for 1970, would require quite substantial budgetary assistance; but this need not be an intolerable burden and could be paid for quite easily, either by cutting back expenditure in other sectors (preferably the least productive ones) or by a special allocation of resources.

Taking now the other side of the coin, it is certainly possible to conceive of a thriving economy in which no efforts are made to prepare the more satisfactory forms of worker participation in the running of their companies. However, surely it is a good idea to move some way towards the transcendence of the present condition of the wage-earning classes. If concerted action could be taken to this end, would it not provide a guarantee of social harmony and, consequently, provide a more or less long-term method of avoiding major upsets? The study of the most recent economic phenomena reveals that the most volatile element, the one most difficult to control, that which can confound all predictions and cause reversals, is related to the problems of social equilibrium among the forces of production. If it is possible to control this element through a qualitative change in the relationships between labor, capital, and management, then indeed crises will no longer be inevitable; the society of expansion will have come of age, and it will also have found another justification for its existence besides the material advantages it brings.

France, a country proud of its traditions, in this case actually drawing strength from her weakness, from her extreme degree of sensibility to currents of unrest, from a sort of susceptibility to revolution which makes an early warning system vital, can play the role of pilot. After all, it is not pure chance that the capitalist type of economy, in spite of the evidence of its obvious successes, has not succeeded in imposing its structures on the whole world; it is no quirk of fate that socialism, in spite of its relatively unspectacular performance, hangs on to its strongholds and occasionally breaks new ground. Although it seems stupid to me to try to thwart man's aspirations towards increased consumption, I do know that the new man cannot see himself solely as a consumer, nor even as a producer-consumer, and that he is swept along by the march of progress and feels somehow obliged to achieve the fullest possible expression of his own personality, to become dis-alienated and to promote his own essential interests. This feeling is so strong that it is no rare occurrence to find the *idea* of progress preferred to the *reality* of consumption; this is perhaps true for the time being, but soon it will be too late.

These reflections, which lead me to define education and participation as the dominant themes, oblige me to look upon them as themes which affect every aspect of life. Just as our view of the education of the whole man must include far more than school and university training and must form part of an overall plan for permanent education, so too participation cannot be limited to the specific aspects of worker participation in business management (incentive schemes, worker control). Neither do the formulas put forward in the plan subjected for referendum (regionalization, representation of the professional categories in the various Assemblies), nor even a combination of all the proposed suggestions, provide a comprehensive answer. Participation is a complete political program which must strive to leave no area of life untouched.

A striking example is furnished by the problems of town-planning and the habitat.

The environment, the choice of a home, the whole idea of housing, is not this what really counts most for so many people? Often the choice of a job is dictated by a desire to live in a certain area, by the fact that a suitable home is available nearby, by the proximity of members of one's family, or by the friendliness of the neighbors. But a man might also choose a job because it was familiar, well liked and because no other job was as attractive or open to him; in that case, he has to set up a home where he can, according to the means at his disposal. Rarely does he have a free hand; rarely is a whole range of possibilities open to him. His choice of domicile is the first link in the chain that he will bear for so many hours in each day and for so many days in his life.

However, it is extremely rare for the chief interested party to have a say in the essential organization which, more often than not, will affect his whole life. Town councils draw up plans, the developers dream up schemes and build as they will with the valuable aid of the State and the commercial enterprises. Not only is the customer not called upon to express his opinion, but hardly any attempt is made to take advantage of the opportunities offered for consultation after the event or to use the information thus gleaned in planning consequent building programs for other customers.

The conception behind the production of goods and the conception the users have of the goods have no bearing on each other. Administrative offices draw up directives, ministers launch new fashions. Debates are concentrated upon quantitive factors, on the number of building sites in operation and housing units completed, on the extent of budgetary credits and financial possibilities. Modern research techniques for sounding out opinion which are used on a large scale in private enterprise, the methods, sometimes used in attempts to encourage worker participation, of drawing lots for consultants according to their category and on a rotary basis, in short any method, which might be perfected once the existence of the problem was recognized, should permit some progress towards customer participation. It should be possible to make the host of present and potential users understand that their experience is not discounted, that their requirements are not systematically ignored and despised. That could be a very important point in bolstering up their morale; it could have some bearing on the 'alienation of town life'—at least in so far as it is reflected in the prevalence of a sense of disillusionment.

No doubt participation in this area can be exercised through political participation, by voting in municipal or national elections. However, with the exception of certain local affairs which can, at any given moment, polarize the opinion of a neighborhood or of a whole township and, as we say, create a swing at the polls, questions relating to housing and the environment do not have an importance in politics in any way comparable to that which they have in family life. Can anyone recall important parliamentary debates on architecture or ecology? Do the political parties clash over their ideas on the nature of urban complexes, on individual homes, on how to infuse life into the new towns? The general practice is to be satisfied with trying to outdo each other in the allocation of budgetary resources and in making statements of the type: 'By economizing on an atom bomb, how many houses could be built if the money were to be allocated as a building subsidy'?

My remarks on town-planning and the building industry could equally well be applied to television, an entirely different phenomenon. Although there are viewer associations, a specialized press, and some sounding of opinion, can it be said that the great mass of viewers benefit from an audience in this Church? Where can one see the major political parties making any attempt to formulate their respective policies on the most suitable measures, not only to guarantee the impartiality of the information broadcast (which is only a limited aspect of the problem) or even their quality (a rather imprecise term), but to deal with problems in depth, to try to compensate for the disparity between transmission and reception, to combat the danger of passivity? How are the necessary enquiries to determine the intellectual, psychological, or disturbing effects of this or that program carried out; what is being done to draw inferences from those opinions expressed or from the suggestions put forward by 'the grass roots'; finally, where can one see a political policy for the mass media being elaborated, a policy which would have a real influence on the choice of political candidates and programs?

This reticence, this disinclination on the part of politics to deal seriously with serious problems is really due to the absence of a humanist definition. A political program's chances of escaping the influence of antiquated mythologies and of gaining a foothold among the problems of real life as in a domain which belongs to it by right are in direct proportion to its involvement with some sort of philosophical and therefore abstract doctrine.

The most important considerations in life, those which affect man in his everyday existence, seem to fall outside the scope of political thought. They are allowed to be the exclusive concern of philosophers out of touch with reality, to provide fuel for revolution, to be administered in a purely down-to-earth, functional manner by technicians who proceed according to the methods dictated by rationality and who ignore the really important, human aspects—technicians who latch on to a problem once it has arisen, but who are incapable of *setting* themselves the problem in advance, incapable of *imagining* it.

Now we live in an age where reality has to be *imagined* to be *grasped*. Once again, there recurs a theme which I have indicated in various parts of this book, both when talking of the governmental *techno-structure* and of creativity in modern life. The ordinary man, the man in the street, even if he never stops talking, has difficulty in putting his true preoccupations into words, no doubt because of an inadequate education or because of the dearth of opportunities for participation, or because of an incomplete awareness and acceptance of his responsibilities. It is up to *us*, therefore, all of us, the State, Society, men in the public eye, elected representatives, to understand him before he has spoken a word so that, knowing he is understood in advance, he will be able to express himself.

Machines cannot understand, that is not their function. Robots cannot feel, they are not made for that. Neither can the technocrats or the men who make up the techno-structure apprehend the whole human reality, for their role, an important and necessary one, was not designed to this end and demands qualities and experience of another order. It is up to politics, to those who elaborate policies, to those who put them into operation, to accept responsibility for man, to listen to him, to take into account the part played in every man by feeling and instinct, by the irrational and the creative, for without these qualities the technical skills and the technocracy, upon which the politicians' arrogant rejection of man is now based, would never have appeared.

True political participation must become a reality—in a double direction. The participation by politics in the problems confronting man and the participation by man in the problems confronting politics. Politicians, those who make politics their business, must see themselves as men, see other men as they really are and not take refuge, claiming increased efficiency as an excuse, in an artificial, calculated, financially accountable view of man. Man who presents the world with an algorithm must not be an algorithm to himself. Conversely, and henceforth this will be easier, the man who is not a politician must not behave towards politics as though it were, by definition, something which does not concern him and which is not concerned with him. There are several attitudes to be avoided, all equally harmful. The first: 'What do I think, sir? Oh, I've never been interested in politics'. The second: to see politics as a kind of sporting fixture. The only important question is who will win, because the fellow wants to back the winner. The third: to begin by raising the main challenger's hopes then, at the last moment, to change one's mind and say: 'Let's steer clear of change after all. We know where we are with the old guy'. Yet another example of man's eternal tendency to dredge up from the past memories of a happy age, or one which seemed so at the time, or which seems happy in his memory . . . which naturally tends to forget certain aspects. Just as it is stupid to vote 'for the sake of change' without knowing how the new system will work or where it will lead, so it would be ridiculous to expect a new government team to adopt the same ideas and methods as those employed by yesterday's men.

Is it not amazing that technology's most spectacular triumph—for example computers and television—should be at the beck and call of a pre-technological ideology, of a pre-expansionist economy and of an educational system worthy of the Stone Age. Is it not remarkable that the major confrontation of ideas with which French viewers are regaled on millions of miraculous pieces of apparatus, those same viewers who have just parked their cars in front of their house and who will take their dinner out of the refrigerator—the car and the refrigerator being just as miraculous —does not attain a higher standard than that achieved during electoral campaigns at the end of the last century, campaigns which the candidates waged on foot, stick in hand? Is it not incredible that, in what are essentially the same debates, there should still be some speakers who will trot out Guizot's maxims, that advocates for the teaching of Latin to eleven-year-olds should still be found? Is it not unbelievable that the only remedies proposed to the French people to get them out of an economic crisis, a venial sin after all, involve the cutting back of domestic consumption (which was not excessive in the first place), of blocking of already inadequate budgetary aid (especially for scientific research), and the postponement of essential construction programs (especially in the provinces) which will be carried out at a later date anyway and will then cost more?

Unlike younger disciplines, psychology has long been a subject of study. How can politicians so completely disregard its basic principles that they propose to a modern man working with advanced industrial techniques that he should accept *material* cutbacks in his *individual standard of living* without offering as compensation the satisfaction of moral and collective demands; in fact all the voter is presented with is the prospect of cumulative deprivation in every sphere. How can the politicians then be surprised when their policies are not greeted with heartfelt cries of satisfaction?

The reanimation of political thought, its rehabilitation (often for its own sake, for it is amazing to see to what degree highly educated men can strive after or resign themselves to the worst kind of mediocrity—voluntary mediocrity—when addressing the 'average' Frenchman), the reassessment of the rival political tendencies by means of an analysis of the differences between their real positions on fundamental problems and of the genuineness of their attitudes on man's essential concerns, all this constitutes a program, which to me seems useful in itself, as a means of dissipating, or at least minimizing, the phenomenon of alienation caused by political theorizing and of leading the electors to a real participation in their civic duties. But it is also an indispensable condition for the success of a truly humanist political system. The policy redefining politics and encouraging political participation demands the enthusiastic support of the public. The same is true of the most important themes of international politics. The powerful support of national feeling can help a government to present its views more convincingly to the outside world, make other governments understand and accept its own views on independence; with its people behind it, a government can obtain a better hearing for its not academic but realistic, urgent proposals concerning development aid, disarmament, and peace. If public opinion were to be mobilized in one single country to express its belief in, and enthusiasm for, a world-wide 'humanism', this would serve as a wonderful example which might spark off, in the industrial societies of both the Eastern and Western bloc, a powerful and beneficial *politicization* to promote the causes of life.

26

The entropy of political democracy

However, it would seem that we have in electoral democracy an admirable and still irreplaceable instrument to ensure two-way contact between the citizen body and the central authority, between man in society and the government of that society. And yet, I am forced to admit that this two-way contact does not work very well.

Generally speaking, the Western democracies are suffering the effects of the so-called law of entropy: a slow degradation, a creeping paralysis. What evidence is there that public life is a source of perpetual excitement? What personal interest in public affairs does the citizen reveal from day to day? Where is that *identification*, in cinematic terms the involvement of the public with their chosen protagonist? Eagerly awaited for so long, the reward, sometimes, of a bitter struggle, the right to vote, though still an adequate means of expressing a choice, is no longer an effective instrument to stimulate interest.

Of course, I am well aware with what jealous eyes we are looked upon by those peoples who have lost the right to vote or who have not yet been granted it. If they were to obtain it, what relief, what euphoria! Emotions which would persist well beyond the time it takes for an election. But we must not allow ourselves to be deluded by this kind of reasoning. The fact that those deprived of the vote would be happy to get it is no reason for those who have it (at least for the time being) to think their cup runneth over. For anyone who cares to think about it, the feeling that the democratic process is incomplete and that, if some progress is not made, there is a risk that the people will become disenchanted with it is a very real one. In short, there is a feeling that democracy is not pulling its weight.

Everywhere I detect the three factors which I have retained as significant: inadequacy of the significance, substance, and power to excite support of the guiding principles; difficulty in ascertaining and clearly distinguishing the demarcation lines between the principal conflicting tendencies; finally, and most obvious of all, the need to establish channels for the expression of opinion, for intervention and participation, outside and complementary to the precise recording of a vote.

Traditional liberal democracy has remained at the stage described by Montesquieu and which he saw as highly desirable. The people find themselves relegated to the role of chosing qualified representatives and of appointing, directly or indirectly, administrators to act on their behalf instead of being allowed to settle great issues for themselves and to bring to the fore the problems which concern them most.

> The people's only contribution to government must be the choice of representatives, a task well within its capabilities. . . . This same people, which would be incapable of dealing with affairs on its own account, is admirably qualified to chose those to whom it must entrust some part of its authority[1].

More recently, J. Schumpeter has expressed similar views[2].

Now, the new man, especially if he has received a suitable education and has grasped his creative responsibility for his own behavior, demands a more real form of participation. Even if he does not formulate an express demand for participation, he experiences a more or less confused awareness of its lack.

If we consider a more specific problem, that of the relative composition of the parties—a key problem, for it is through the parties that, at first sight, an increased degree of participation should come—what do we see in the world around us?

In Europe, excluding Spain and Portugal who do not enjoy a parliamentary democracy, I note that Italy finds herself in a position rather similar to that of France under the Fourth Republic: plurality of parties, diversification of objectives among the parties, difficulty in obtaining a monolithic, stable majority, ceaseless intrigues, both between rival parties and within each individual party, in short, governmental instability. In Belgium and the Netherlands, the position is similar though not identical. As these countries, unlike the Fourth Republic, have not as yet had to resolve weighty problems or surmount major crises, they get along quite well. Instability, that bogey-man, is not guilty of all the shortcomings attributed to it, nor is it worth sacrificing anything and everything to get rid of it. The type of uneventful ministerial reshuffling which can accompany instability just serves to demonstrate the extent to which the different approaches to various problems resemble each other and overlap and just how artificial the divisions, hallowed by routine, have become. At the same time it allows, by the mechanism which I have described as 'government in fits and starts'[3], a certain number of inevitable and unpopular decisions to be taken to deal with a crisis. The point should also be made that, even in a régime as institutionally stable as that of France, an analogous procedure was adopted to push through the policy of devaluation: the change in

---

[1] Montesquieu. *The spirit of the laws*. Chapter 6.

[2] Schumpeter, J. *Capitalism, socialism and democracy*. London, George Allen & Unwin, 1943.

[3] Cf. my article 'La crise de la démocratie', *Le Monde*. 27 March 1953.

ministerial team, by dividing responsibility for the action taken, made the public more willing to 'swallow' the need for drastic measures.

However, care must be taken not to trust to mere appearances. This kind of régime is dangerous. It is lucky for us in France that we have left it behind. It jeopardizes the execution of an overall plan and it leads to decisions being postponed until they can no longer be avoided, by which time their effectiveness is diminished because they come too late. It is not conducive to the spirit of reform, it is more effective than anything else in discouraging involvement, and it lets loose a danger which threatens the very principles of democracy. The partisans of democracy grow disillusioned, while its opponents draw from this danger reasons to justify their own position and they grow bold. Thus, during the last Italian 'cliffhanger', rightly or wrongly, certain threatening features were remarked upon. The most recent events in a sort of 'social war' also serve to demonstrate the setting-up of a sort of extra-parliamentary opposition which could, as could the feeling of irritation inspired by the parties' inability to make decisions, inspire an authoritarian backlash.

The German Federal Republic has two main parties, thus achieving the type of parliamentary democracy generally held up as an example because it facilitates the confrontation of dominant trends and eventually the substitution of the opposition for the majority. However, at an earlier point in time, these two same parties had found it expedient to form an alliance to govern; later, during the electoral campaign, they became bitter enemies once more, until an extraordinary *coup de théâtre* made the emergence of a very slender majority depend upon the unexpected decision of an insignificant, residual party at the very time when the credibility of that party was wearing thinner. This drama serves to confirm that democracy is incapable of providing sufficiently authoritative guiding principles or of presenting the conflicting issues in a clear enough way for popular majority feeling to emerge and make itself felt; though if the problems were to be presented coherently, this feeling could not fail to materialize.

In England, the two great parties have not yet resorted to coalition government. It would not be impossible for them to adapt to it. With the exception of a few characteristically Labour measures—of, however, very limited impact—in the main Wilson did what a Conservative government might have done; and if a Conservative government were to follow him[1], it is unlikely that any changes made would be dictated by anything other than differences in style, technique and opportunity. In fact, the balance is determined by the opinion certain members of the electorate have of the personal qualities of the two leaders, irrespective of their political beliefs and ideas. The weak hold that ideological democracy has is further illustrated by the existence of 'rebels' within each of the two main parties.

[1] The French text appeared before the June 1970 election when Heath did in fact succeed Wilson. (Translator's note)

The situation is not all that different in America. It might be expected that the exceptional advances made in that country by industrial society, the higher standard of living enjoyed by so many people, the modernity of its traditions, would have been conducive to the emergence of the new man with the high standards expected of him. In a country justly proud of its national achievements, conscious of the possibility offered to it of settling the world's affairs, it might have been expected that public opinion would formulate—or at least accept and support—a plan for a truly modern humanism, a grandiose plan and yet a realistic one too, because of the immensity of the resources available. Something of the kind might have been anticipated from Adlai Stevenson, who never made it, from Kennedy who—alas!—did not survive long enough. It fell to a man of a very different type, Barry Goldwater, to put forward a systematic and exaggerated conception of reactionism. More often than not, American politicians are administrators, and doctrinal questions do not arouse great excitement and controversy. Those intellectuals who are interested in politics are rarely militant and they avoid the electoral race; they have their place as advisors and top civil servants in the administration of the President of their choice (if he is elected), or they form an extra-institutional and extra-parliamentary opposition among students and the Blacks, even among the hippies. This is what is termed the New Left. Among those who have influence are poets like Allen Ginsberg. This tendency is by no means negligible. It must not be measured in terms of electoral success. It has chalked up some real triumphs using methods totally alien to the normal mechanisms of representative democracy. Thus, the New Left has succeeded in persuading several of the more important universities not to place contracts with public services and industries which manufacture biological and chemical products for use in warfare[1]. If it shuns parliamentary action, it takes advantage of election periods to develop a special form of propaganda: doorbell-ringing campaign[2], chiefly in the slum areas and concentrated on the more receptive housewife. It draws support from a 'new working class', whom it roots out from among the lower-grade technicians, engineers, and specialists employed in the manufacturing industries. It helps the Blacks to get themselves put on the electoral register. Many students abandon their studies altogether to devote themselves to direct action. The New Left is aware of the limitations of its action: thus it was admitted that, while it would be easy to collect a considerable sum of money to send medicines to the Vietcong, it would be a very different matter if it were a question of buying arms with the money. It does not entertain many illusions as to its chances for real success in the near future, but it continues untiringly, thoroughly, and painstakingly with its task. On the whole, it is neither

[1] Marcuse, H. *Five Lectures.* pp. 107–108.
[2] See Marcuse, H. *Five Lectures.* p. 91. (Translator's note)

Marxist nor Socialist. 'Its chief characteristic', remarks Marcuse who knows it well, 'is a deep-seated mistrust of all ideologies, even of the socialist ideology because of vague feelings of betrayal and disappointment'.

This phenomenon is certainly not of a nature to overthrow the American political system, and yet it does provide food for thought. The falling-off of the effectiveness of the values of traditional democracy as intellectual, spiritual, and moral values provokes, by a sort of external reaction, a polarization of the search for these values in pressure groups who play no part in general political life, who consider themselves excluded from political life or prefer to feel that they are outcasts from it. For this reason, instead of injecting into political life new ideas and new sources of energy from which it would benefit, they choose to shut themselves away behind a locked door and will admit the validity of no other way out, of no other calling than revolutionary extremism, the 'unreasonable reform of unreason'. This is all the more remarkable for taking place in a country where political or philosophical Marxism has had only a very limited impact.

Thus, it would seem that although exclusive bipartism (or at least something approaching it) represents a slight improvement on a plural party system from the point of view of the technicalities of government and provides, in any case, a more effective means of ensuring more convenient working conditions for the politicians, it is still not entirely satisfactory. The search for a solution must not be confined mainly to the substitution of one system for another, especially as such a substitution can only be brought about by authoritarian methods.

A more far-sighted view is needed. It must be recognized that the traditional party is no more effective than the democratic voting-paper in guaranteeing the adequate and satisfactory working of a modern democracy.

Why should this be so?

Once again, the fault lies with the divorce of the problems of democracy from those of modernity.

On the whole, the parties cling to the traditional idea of what constitutes democracy: freedom of the individual, protection against despotic government action, genuine electoral fights, some degree of social progress—all phenomena which depend on effective legislation and which are part and parcel of the world of carefully drawn up laws.

All this is perfectly honorable and they should be given credit for it.

But, when it comes to something outside the scope of these limits, something concerned with the real movement of life within institutions, the parties, hampered by their lack of technical expertise, by the incompetence of their most ardent militants, and by the inadequate education of the electoral body, show signs of timidity. Believing they will be safe if they cast around for those of their own persuasion, they put their trust in certain technocrats; but, although these technocrats may share the party's convictions, they still find it difficult to shake off their systematic habits.

To take a stand against technocracy, it is not enough merely to want to combat it: a certain technical competence is also necessary.

Then again, the technocracies and techno-structures seize upon all the positions which the parties, according to the traditions of the infantry, do not care to occupy. In a situation where, as it might happen, the parties call for simple but inadequate or impracticable measures, for example an increase in all forms of budgetary aid or a lowering of all taxes, the techno-structure takes advantage of their ignorance, draws up its own schemes, and imposes its own balanced solutions. It brooks no challenge to its calculations, no prying eyes are allowed to see details of what is included in the overall budgetary allocation; no breakdown is given of the kind of housing program to be adopted, of which road-building programs are to be given priority, of where industries are to be sited, of what is to be done about the death of the villages, about the conservation of beauty spots, about the exodus of whole families to the towns, about vocational guidance for school-children, about radio programs, or about making old age more comfortable[1]. Nowhere better than in the field of education is the dissociation between a democratic conception out of touch with modernity and a modernist conception out of touch with democracy more clearly illustrated.

There is a tendency too for technocratic administrations taking advantage of the a-politicization of so many topics which are rightly the prerogative of politics, to establish a system as far removed from democracy as it is from modernity with consequences which recent events have made all too clear.

It would be unjust to reproach the technicians with not seeing the human content of problems, with not taking spiritual values into account. And it would be unjust to reproach the parties with a generous idealism which causes sincere convictions to be expressed under the guise of self-evident truths or in now meaningless formulas, in demands which are sometimes too vague, sometimes too specific and limited in their scope.

---

[1] Obviously, the problem of old age deserves much more than this passing reference. But I cannot tackle it in all its complexity here. All I want to do is to underline its great importance. The rise in the average life expectation, combined with the lowering of the retirement age, creates a *non-active population* of a size comparable to that of the whole of the *active working population* during the last century. As far as this huge sector is concerned the problem is not just to guarantee an absolute minimum income to cover their material needs, nor even to improve, quantitatively and *qualitatively*, their material existence, but rather to give them a genuine feeling that their life is socially useful, to make sure they can *participate* in life in so far as they are able and in spite of the obvious difficulties of the undertaking. Political minds will have to devote a great deal of effort to solving this immense problem. The last years of existence must not be a negation of existence. Old people vote; they have a part to play in the government of the city: they must not be relegated to the status of morons.

Similar anomalies lie in wait for us as, following the logical development of my study, I come next to the problem of the mandate.

The new demands for participation raise the problem of the mandate in its two chief forms, the union mandate and the political mandate. There has already been a significant development in the union mandate[1]. Since the May uprisings, the union leaders have agreed to a kind of direct democracy. They wait for an upsurge of feeling from the 'base', take careful soundings of opinion, consult their members, follow the lead suggested by the base, and try to organize and carry through the movements thus unleashed to the best possible effect. Their own role has not been abolished, far from it; this manner of conducting affairs by no means indicates a renunciation of power or a sign of weakness. It marks the end of a fiduciary, delegatory conception of the mandate according to which the mandator offloaded on to his elected representative the task of taking decisions in his place and relied on his proxy to act for him. It marks the birth of a new type of relationship: the leader becomes an expert, a technician who provides the necessary documentation, engages in difficult negotiations and, finally, formulates advisory documents which he tries, by using his powers of persuasion, to get accepted and which are always put to the vote. Certain observers have expressed surprise at this timidity, which to them seems all the more illogical since the union leaders have usually managed to acquire a solid grounding and genuine competence in economics, whereas the masses remain generally ignorant of the basic technicalities (yet another example of the great lack of economic teaching within the contemporary educational system, a lack so often emphasized in this book). This seeming paradox is in fact not a paradox. The aim of participation is not to raise the level of individual competence in a single discipline but to promote the general interests of society as a whole; besides, those who have personally achieved a certain level of competence experience less difficulty in ensuring for themselves, in one way or another, opportunities for participation. As they acquire experience and technical expertise, the professional trade-unionists become divorced from the ordinary members and it becomes more difficult for them to put themselves in their members' shoes. In extreme cases, they can fall prey to the temptation to become technocrats themselves, but if they do so, the penalty is immediate, for the wage-earners can decide to stop or to resume work regardless of orders and directives. The transformation of the role of the leaders is therefore easily explained. It is, in fact, nothing more than an expression of the increased degree of 'participation' enjoyed by the workers[2].

[1] The situation in France with respect to the unions is quite unique. Owing to their plurality the union confederations are driven to fierce competition, each one trying to outbid the other.

[2] Recent events have revealed the (new) role which can be played in this sphere by an external element: the reaction of the (buying) public.

The position of the elected representatives is quite different and does not allow the same facilities for adaption. Unlike the trade-unionists, they do not run the risk of suddenly finding themselves repudiated by direct action against, or the deliberate ignoring of, their initiatives. They can claim to be representing public opinion throughout the duration of their mandate. It is possible for their interpretation of public opinion to be an erroneous one; they may decide to ignore it in the hope that their action will be understood and justified later. They are accountable for the general interest and not for the short-term interest of this or that sector or professional class. For them, the most normal instrument of dialogue with the 'grass roots' is the party of which I have already pointed out the inadequacy.

Of course, it is true that the parliamentarians are finding themselves in increasingly close contact with the professional groups, but this is not enough to establish a satisfactory framework for consultation because:

(a) certain groups make it a point of honor to have no contact with politicians, or at least to keep contact on a purely formal basis. Alternatively, they may confine their friendships to parliamentarians belonging to one certain party to the exclusion of the others;

(b) certain professional activities are not really represented by their apparent spokesmen—there have recently been some shattering examples of this. The case of the factory workers in this respect stands out from all the others because, thanks to their being herded together in a single work place and their deployment of the right to strike, the factory workers can easily give concrete expression to their discontent;

(c) certain professions have no organized representative body;

(d) the demands made by the different sectors of the economy may be incompatible or cannot be dealt with by a single man and no deputy wants to reduce his role to that of a mere transmitter of grievances;

(e) finally, there are other things in life beside professional activities. If the professional man is already experiencing some hesitation before giving his problems a political form, more often than not the non-professional man believes his most crucial interests lie outside the domain proper of politics.

And so the deputy, and I do not just mean the mediocre but all deputies, has but an imperfect knowledge and awareness of the motivating problems, the deep-rooted dynamism and the dominating psychological traits of the electorate. He is not much more successful than the technocrat in discerning exactly when the limit of what is tolerable is about to be passed, in seeing the passage from the quantitative to the qualitative in grasping the moment when an apparently unconnected chain of circumstances will give rise to a sudden movement, though this, with minor differences depending on the situation, is the hallmark of revolution. 'A revolution takes everyone by surprise and astonishes no one'[1]. The flashpoint is all the more difficult to isolate because it is not just one episode in the unfurling of a particular conflict or of some specific demand—even though such a demand or conflict may be quoted as the apparent cause of the crisis or be used in an attempt to absolve the government of the day of any responsibility for the disaster. The final toppling over the brink is the result of the crisis situation built up by the refusal to encourage an adequate degree of participation and is, therefore, an emotional phenomenon. In the Stendhalian analysis of love, who can put his finger on the exact moment of crystallization? This kind of jamming of the system has revealed itself twice quite spectacularly in the course of the last two years. [1968–1970]. It is remarkable that it did not arouse greater curiosity and comment from the politicians and political experts. The opposition, engaged in the task of drawing up a motion of censure with the express aim of embarrassing 'the powers that be', were desperately striving—at least I imagine so—to observe, detect, sniff out, even to provoke and invent trouble. And yet, in both cases, they managed to overlook completely the most sensitive sector on the very eve of the explosion! The first time it was agriculture that caused the trouble; the second time it was national education. In both cases, the explosions occurred in the time elapsing between the date of the putting down of the censure motion and the not-distant day appointed for the debate. Thus, the opposition found itself forced to go to the ridiculous lengths of hastily adding a new paragraph to the existing text in order to challenge the government on the only point on which it was vulnerable, a point which they had miraculously overlooked. The failure of the parliamentary mandate to reflect adequately the feelings of the electorate and the inability of the political parties to attract the electorate's support are equally deserving of censure.

It is quite obvious that the mandate as an instrument for participation, which should logically abolish alienation, is no longer functioning as it was designed to do. It is even possible for the mandate to play a completely contrary role to the one intended and for it actually to become, as Sebag has demonstrated, a form of alienation. A doubly typical example of this was the law passed concerning social insurance for the self-employed workers and shopkeepers. The law was passed unanimously by Parliament and received the full agreement of the professional representatives of the categories in question. No less unanimous was the rejection of the law by the interested parties, by the very people whom the law was supposedly designed to satisfy and who were no doubt believed to be satisfied. And yet, a moment's serious reflection would have made it obvious that the less successful self-employed man was not going to be overjoyed at having to pay, first, his direct insurance contribution, a burden he already bore, and on top of that a large contribution to a common fund, unless he was going

[1] Faure, E. *La disgrâce de Turgot*. Paris, Gallimard, 1961.

to derive some personal advantage from this added burden. Yet again, the non-technicians had relied on the technocrats, and the technocrats could not be bothered with the human element, with specific, individual cases.

Varying solutions have been put forward with a view to infusing new vitality and validity into the mandate, but it is unlikely that any one of them, or indeed the sum of all the proposals, can achieve this result. It is felt that the members should work in better material and intellectual conditions; that they should be provided with offices, secretaries, good sources of documentation; longing eyes are cast on the paradise of the American legislators. No doubt this is a good thing, but it is not a very direct way of tackling the problem. There have been times when the idea of the *mandat impératif*[1] was toyed with, but such a mandate is only conceivable in the context of the relationship existing between the party and the elected member. The RPF[2], the Socialist Party and the Poujade Movement[3] (the last group even making the facetious proposal that hanging should be used as a sanction against those who stepped out of line . . . though it proved infinitely more unruly as a movement than did the orthodox parties) all flirted with the idea of the *mandat impératif*. However, such a mandate could only ensure an increased degree of participation for militants and tended, therefore, to 'alienate' the average elector. Then there is the revocable mandate, which the extreme Left keeps in its armory. This is, however, impossible to operate democratically for, to do so, life would have to become one long voting session. This type of solution is contrary to the trend which prefers to effect the dis-alienation of the parliamentarian through making the deputy independent of the party: this was the decisive argument in favor of the constituency poll.

The consequences of the defective working of the channels of communication in the Third and Fourth Republics are well known: the disenchantment of the citizens with their political institutions and a latent antiparliamentarianism—in which, rather curiously, two currents of discontent were seen to mingle. On the one hand, there was the discontent of the new men searching for a real participation and, on the other, the discontent of the old guard prolonging, as far as democracy was concerned, the age-old hostility of the émigrés and the papal condemnations of pre-*Ralliement*[4]

1 *Mandat impératif*—the French term has been retained because there is no direct equivalent in either the American or British political system. This type of mandate involves the election of a member of Parliament on the condition that he will vote on all issues exactly as directed to do so by his electors.

2 RPF—the Rassemblement du Peuple Français, 'the party to end all parties' founded on 30 January 1947 by General de Gaulle.

3 Mouvement Poujade—a political movement led by Pierre Poujade whose support came chiefly from the small shopkeepers. The party enjoyed moderate electoral success in January 1956. Its close alinement with the 'pieds noirs' and the OAS was the effective cause of its eclipse when Algeria was granted independence in 1962.

4 *Ralliement*—a movement instituted by Pope Leo XIII in February 1892 to encourage French Catholics to 'rally' to the Republic in an attempt to put an end to what the Pope saw as a dangerous rift between Church and State. (Translator's notes)

days. Extra-parliamentary activity provided the high-spot of the pre-war years, 6 February[1] and the sticker in the subway: 'I am not a deputy'.

To come nearer home, we have the example of the troubles leading to the 13 May 1958[2] and the laying siege to the Assembly by those members of the security forces who were on strike. Reactions such as these would seem old-fashioned today. Perhaps because of the attenuation of its role under the Fifth Republic, Parliament is now treated with indifference rather than hostility. It has often been pointed out that, during the May 1968 uprising with its street demonstrations emanating in all directions, the citadel of popular representation was ignored.

For many worried democrats, the contempt manifested in indifference is more serious than that manifested in active hatred. For more than ten years now, the peasants (either because of their deep-rooted republicanism or because of their conservative turn of mind) have been alone in demanding that the national representative body should play its part, should participate on their behalf, should dis-alienate them. Such naivety seemed derisory to the technocrats, the product of contact with the 'sinister slowness of cattle'. Although he did not share this point of view, General de Gaulle made the mistake of rejecting demands for the re-call of Parliament put forward by the agricultural producers' federations and approved by the parliamentary majority. He saw this move as an attempt to challenge his authority and the then existing Chamber did not inspire in him a feeling of great confidence.

No doubt he underestimated—I shall return to this point—the disadvantages of closing the communication channels, even though this may have been done for the sake of guaranteeing a stability and an authority which had been felt to be missing before.

The complicated issue of the vote on the censure motion, the dissolution and the May-June 1968 elections provide ample food for thought and are a constant source of perplexity. There seems to be a mass of inconsistencies. The government punished, by dissolution, an Assembly which had been faithful to it. The electors punished, by not re-electing them, members of Parliament who had been true to their obligations for, elected as opposition members, they had voted in favor of the censure motion. The election of a new Chamber looked like, in fact proved to be, the means of solving a crisis rather than the recruitment of a series of new representatives. All the decisions taken since then could have been taken just as well by the old Assembly as by the new one. That the old majority had been a slender rather than the now overwhelming one changed nothing. As Clemenceau

[1] 6 February 1934, the date on which the extreme Right-wing Leagues demonstrated against the government of the day. The uprising was suppressed by force.

[2] 13 May 1958—the day on which the extremists who wanted to keep Algeria French demonstrated violently in the streets and when it seemed that, if the Army would support the rebels, the government might be overthrown. This was the immediate cause of the institution of the Fifth Republic. (Translator's notes)

used to say, 'one vote is enough'. (A majority of one had been enough to vote in the Republic[1]—it had been enough for Combes and for Waldeck-Rousseau). In fact, the elections functioned like a referendum while, a year later, the referendum was to function like an election. The idea of the choice of representatives and the mandate itself practically disappeared, the elector's chief concern being to register his dominant wish for stability and his disapproval of anarchy. Even if one sees this as a cause for congratulation, it must be recognized as a form of entropy, a misuse of political institutions, a jamming of the mechanism.

I have put forward my arguments on the position of members of Parliament. The Senate too must be discussed, since it still exists. Here, things are simpler. The senatorial mandate really does function as a mandate, though with a very limited sphere of application. The senator is indeed the fiduciary of the mayors who have elected him; but the system only really works in the rural areas and the senator is an instrument of participation only in so far as those who elected him are; that is to say his effectiveness is limited to local problems, principally road-building programs and the improvement of local facilities. The various economic categories do not consider themselves 'represented' by the town-councils or local councillors as far as professional problems are concerned. There exists a sort of tacit division of responsibility between the trade-union organizations and the elected representatives. Thus, neither the mayors nor the senators could effectively take over the role of the incompetent spokesmen in the social insurance affair. Be that as it may, in the senate's case, counter-participation and 'alienation' of the mandate by the elected representative is unheard of. But the institution's declining importance has reached a point where a new conception of its role must be found by whatever methods are necessary; and General de Gaulle's aspirations to this effect were on the right lines as far as essentials are concerned.

In the preceding analysis I insisted upon the most important aspects which might lead to a somewhat schematic view of the problem. For, if the functioning of the party system and the machinery of the mandate create only very limited possibilities for participation, they have nevertheless a few positive virtues and the disillusionment with parliamentary life is neither permanent nor universal. A very encouraging example was provided last year by the debates on the law to institute vocational guidance which were broadcast on television. A large section of the public followed the events with interest and often with enthusiasm. I was able to see it for

[1] In 1875, the *amendement Wallon*, which officially established the Third Republic and effectively quashed the royalist aspirations was passed by 353 votes to 352. (Translator's note)

myself. The subject excited interest, the main outlines of the law and the spirit animating it lived up to general expectations, whether consciously expressed or not. The removal of the party whip led to an almost unanimous vote of support and rehabilitated politics in the eyes of the French people, who had felt that formerly politics had been too wrapped up in its own procedures. There was a feeling that contact was once more being established between the population and its representatives, between the users and managers of the public services and education; there occurred for a time (I have no personal axe to grind here) a long moment of dis-alienation. Why should the experience not be repeated? Why should similar *consensus*, justification, and ratification not be sought, and gained another time?

Of course, this particular subject lent itself to participation, but is it not all the same an excellent omen for the kind of society we need to create, one in which education and participation will be of paramount importance? Discussion about participation creates participation. Once participation has been achieved all topics will appear interesting.

27

The entropy of political democracy
A few tentative ideas and proposals

Some tentative proposals

A dynamic democracy, an authentic representation of the wishes of the electorate as expressed in the re-opened dialogue between elector and elected, the dis-alienation of institutions, can be achieved only within the context of a new political society, whose general inspiration I am attempting to define here. However, I can, here and now, put forward a few technical proposals on the functioning of institutions calculated to promote the attaining of these ends.

It is not my intention to propose yet another major shake-up of the constitution, for the country has had enough of these upheavals. What I propose are a few slight but significant institutional changes. Moreover, I offer them as subjects for detailed research and discussion and reserve the right both to adopt as valid, should I so desire, any objections which might be put forward and to continue my search for better methods of putting the changes I propose into operation.

(a) *The election of the President of the Republic*
The practice of direct popular election must certainly be maintained, for it is a vehicle for personal participation. In my opinion, just one amendment is required. This concerns the seven-year term of office, a hangover from the Third Republic and inexplicable for other than the historical reasons which brought about its institution as a compromise solution acceptable to both the Republicans and the Royalists. The seven-year presidential term persisted under the Fourth Republic, where it was no stumbling-block to progress, and was finally adopted by the Fifth Republic in the days before direct universal suffrage had been put on the statute books. Today, the accepted practice is no longer viable, not just because of the unusual length of the term of office, but because it is out of step with the legislative mandate. This situation gives rise to several sorts of disadvantages.

(i) *The risk of serious conflict* between a President and an Assembly *elected at different times*. If in fact the President and the Assembly are elected at about the same time, the ever-present likelihood that the President will be of a different political persuasion from the majority of elected representatives would be the result of a deliberate choice on the part of the electorate; each side would therefore have to accept it without question and try to make the best of it. On the other hand, with the present system, the most recently elected authority will always try to discredit the body elected earlier, though the latter will assert the validity of its mandate, and it is no easy matter to prove the contrary. Such a crisis situation was in everybody's mind in June 1969 when there was a theoretical possibility that the candidate supported by the parliamentary majority would be beaten.

There is plenty of evidence to show that it is possible for an American President to coexist with a House of Representatives of an opposing political tendency, which may have been elected only a short while before the President himself. Doubtless it is dangerous to generalize for, unlike the mixed French régime, the American system of government is a true presidential system. However, in my opinion a presidential system is not an indispensable condition for this type of coexistence. Can it be presumed that a French President who, unlike his American counterpart, has at his disposal the weapon of dissolution would be tempted to use it against an Assembly with which he was in disagreement? He would certainly resist this temptation at the beginning of his term of office; will he succumb to it after, say, eighteen months or two years? He cannot fail, even after this lapse of time, to see the risks for he knows *from experience* that public opinion can demonstrate its support for him as a president while at the same time being satisfied with a majority in the legislature of a different political persuasion. Conversely, the Assembly will be well aware of the President's personal popularity with the people and will, no doubt, not be so foolish as to multiply or exacerbate those issues which might result in a trial of strength. Besides, the referendum, as I will recommend it in a later section, should provide an alternative to dissolution as a means of gauging national feeling on this or that major problem. Fights to the death over minor problems are unlikely.

Between 1958 and 1962, President de Gaulle governed with an Assembly of whose support he was not absolutely sure. However, everything went smoothly until the day when he put forward proposals for the reform of the Constitution. A similar situation is hardly likely to recur. On the other hand, the Assembly elected in 1967 included a slender though unshakable majority in his favor: a series of censure motions gave ample proof of this. And yet, it was with this Assembly that peaceful coexistence came to an end.

The (according to my hypothesis more or less concomitant) election of a President and an Assembly of different political persuasions can normally be explained by two (related) circumstances:

Firstly, the President will have obtained the support of the electorate on the strength of his personal qualities (whence an authority which, receiving confirmation from the vote but existing prior to it, will facilitate relationships with the parliamentary majority);

Secondly, the elector will have accepted the delegation to the President of the responsibility for major decisions in the field of international affairs.

Finally, up to this point my arguments had been based on the presumption that the political 'tendencies' and 'allegiances' of the President and the majority would be at odds with each other. But is there any foundation for such a presumption? In the present situation, the idea of such hostility seems less and less of a reality; it would seem to be a question of an antagonism more nominal than real. If, on the other hand, we are witnessing a 'return to sincerity' in political ideas, if political life is striving towards authenticity, it is hardly likely that the people confronted with a simple choice about specific problems would adopt contradictory positions.

(ii) *Stability*. Curiously enough, the proposal I am putting forward here (and which has been submitted by other politicians) has met with the objection that it presents a threat . . . to stability, as understood by General de Gaulle. This is once more to ignore the fact that when the General adopted the convention of the seven-year presidential term, the President was elected by a restricted suffrage, which meant that his authority rested on a much shakier foundation than it does now. This point having been made, in so far as stability could be threatened by the coexistence of a President and an Assembly of conflicting political tendencies (the question examined above), it is quite obvious that the risk would be minimized by holding concomitant rather than well spaced elections. Finally, the decisive argument on this particular problem is to be found in actual government routine.

A stable régime normally requires a legislative government. (If the Assembly overthrows the government before the expiry of its mandate, the Assembly is normally dissolved and the electorate is called upon to make its wishes known.) Now, if the presidential and parliamentary elections are held at wide intervals, the result is the inevitable divorcing of the government from the legislature since, according to tradition, the election of a President calls for the appointment of a new government team. Even if the newly elected President finds himself confronted with a favorable parliamentary majority and even if, as a corollary to this, he finds no reason to disapprove of the existing government, it is difficult to deprive him (even morally) of the essential prerogative of choosing the Prime Minister and other ministers who suit him best: the bicephalous system of the French executive demands a special relationship between the President of the Republic and the Prime Minister.

In the system which I recommend, the newly elected President would choose a Prime Minister, and would form a government. This Prime

Minister and government would find themselves confronted with an Assembly, itself recently elected; normally the government would be called upon to exercise its powers for the duration of that legislature until new elections reveal the composition of the new cast who will fill the major political offices.

No doubt it is possible, even without the intervention of a crisis, for the initial composition of a government to change during the life-span of a legislature. This raises the thorny problem of the (usually recognized though not constitutionally established) right of the President of the Republic to change his Prime Minister, if he believes he has reasonable cause to do so. It is unlikely that the exercise of this right, in spite of its unofficial nature, would be the cause of a conflict resulting in the dismissal of the minister. More often than not, the decision of the President of the Republic will be well founded and, in most cases, the Prime Minister (who was appointed by the President) will agree to stand down. If this is not the case, the President, according to usual practice, has the right to enforce the change. But this is no cause for alarm, for this authoritarian act is subject to some form of control and is in no way comparable to the excesses of Imperial Rome. If Parliament can work with the new government, there is no cause for unrest. If it cannot, it is perfectly free to overthrow it: then the electorate will be called upon to pronounce its decision, against which there is no appeal. If the President is repudiated by the new election, obviously he cannot remain at his post, and he will be morally (if not constitutionally, there is a loop-hole in the law on this point) forced to resign.

The sort of situation which I made a point of examining in the preceding paragraphs has no detrimental effects whatsoever on the advantages to stability which I see resulting from the concurrence of the mandates for, by definition, the practice of holding concurrent parliamentary and presidential elections enhances a government's chance of remaining in office for the duration of a parliament. That some governments might be overthrown before the expiry of a parliament is of course possible: but this will be less likely to happen; the fall of a government will cease to be the quasi-automatic occurrence it was when the respective mandates overlapped.

(iii) *The position of the departing government.* To these reflections on stability I would like to add a few corresponding and complementary remarks about the position of a goverment which 'resigns' during a new parliament, following the election of a new President: 1969 is a case in point. The Prime Minister and certain other ministers find themselves obliged to resign with no possibility of explaining their actions to the Assembly or to the country; no opportunity is provided for them to account for themselves, to present their government record. This is an abnormal situation.

No doubt it might be tempting to observe that the situation would be similar if the *same* President forced the resignation, during the life of a parliament, of a government he himself had formed; but this is not a valid objection. In effect, the head of State, the leader of the executive, presiding, as he does under the present constitution, over all the Councils of Ministers covers, even if he does not share, the premier's responsibilities. The departure of the latter, in whatever circumstances, can never take on the significance of a repudiation (there may be a last-minute clash of opinion to explain the rupture, but the administration as a whole is not called into question). The new government chosen by the same President would, theoretically, continue to be oriented along the same general lines decided upon at the top.

The position of a Prime Minister whose departure is caused by a new presidential election is completely different. In his case—even if his successor quite sincerely bears him no ill-will—there will be no holds barred in the game which consists of laying any errors made at the door of the preceding government until the day arrives when the succeeding government can be blamed for failure to pursue policies. The large diagram, which must be made immediately decipherable if the citizen is to be interested in politics, if he is not to feel alienated in the political game, is covered with crossings out and overlaid with added scribbles; it is in a mess. That is quite obvious today. Everyone *talks* of putting their house in order, of presenting a balance-sheet. But who has done so? Who will do so? If the end of the Couve de Murville government had been accompanied by a vote of the Assembly or of the electors, then the whole situation would have been put into the melting-pot of controversy, the public would have made its voice heard, history could make its voice heard by some means or other.

This question is connected with the ticklish problem of proxies, which I intend to tackle shortly, and to which my proposals for a unified system provide an answer (or at least limit the most worrying aspects of the present system).

(iv) *The electorate's freedom of choice.* Finally, the seven-year presidential term presents another very serious disadvantage, of which we were given a hint during the last elections. To a certain degree, it limits the electors' freedom of choice: it is alienating. The elector tends to fear that if he chooses a President of an opposite political tendency to that of the Assembly or vice versa he may be responsible for creating a crisis situation, for prolonging the uncertainty inherent in the election of either the President or the Assembly by eventually triggering off a second election, either because the new President dissolves the old Assembly, or because the old Assembly engineers, by force or by some other method—take the case of Millerand[1] (a clear example of 'President, get out!')—the resigna-

---

[1] After the May 1924 elections, the victorious Cartel des Gauches forced the resignation of Millerand, President since September 1920, by a strike of the majority and the refusal to form a government until he had resigned. (Translator's note)

tion of the President. Now, periods of electoral 'suspension' of government present, as we all know, certain disadvantages. Is the elector who has seen the life of the country slow up for a number of weeks likely to experience great joy at the thought of the aimless period of waiting beginning all over again?

If democracy is to work fully, if its image is to remain untarnished by the passage of time, the citizen must feel completely free; he must feel that the only considerations he has to take into account when making his choice are the character of the man, the underlying philosophy, and the program put forward for his approval. He must always feel that change is possible, even if, in his opinion, the time is not then ripe for change. The impression that it was impossible to influence the course of events, however much one might have wished to do so, was one of the most significant reasons for the repudiation of the Fourth Republic which, because of its system of proportional representation, electoral alliances and the plurality of its parties, instilled in the elector the feeling of being trapped in a dead end and made him want to shout: 'Enough of this endless series of out-going governments' . . . but the outcome was always the same. There have been some indications of the existence of a similar state of affairs under the Fifth Republic. I am not convinced that it has entirely disappeared or that it could not reappear.

Naturally, any change in the duration of a mandate presents certain practical problems and would demand the acceptance of different methods of operation. The main factor to be borne in mind is that, in itself, a shortening of the presidential term is not enough to guarantee an absolute correlation between the President's term of office and the mandate of the concurrent Assembly.

For one thing, the President may not see out his five-year term: in view of this possibility, it would seem logical to take steps to institute a Vice-Presidency. But the Vice-President would not normally accede to the succession in the case of the voluntary resignation of the President. Then again, the Assembly, which cannot die and where few instances of collective resignation have been recorded, may be dissolved. In both cases, the concurrence of the duration of the respective mandates will be broken.

The simplest procedure would be to appoint the new President or the new Assembly for the period the interrupted mandate has left to run. However, more supple procedures could be imagined to re-establish the concurrence of the two mandates, depending on the actual circumstances. This is a mere technicality, and once the principle of the reform had been adopted, these minor difficulties would not prove insurmountable.

(b) *The referendum*

From the point of view of participation, it is essential to retain the referendum, which is an effective instrument of participation on a par with the direct presidential election. It was the referendum which allowed the French people to make its views heard on decolonization and peace in Algeria, at a time when its wishes might have been misrepresented by the political and press agencies. Now there is a risk that the most recent example of recourse to the referendum[1] will cause people to condemn it, whereas really this experience provides a justification for the procedure, since it demonstrates the possibility of a rejection, the freedom of choice of the elector, and the dis-alienating character of this type of poll.

I can see only one effective means of dissipating the prejudice against the referendum resulting from the last unfortunate experience: that is to see to it that the referendum is never allowed to function as a vote of confidence. As in Switzerland, it will be an opportunity for untrammelled consultation, a super public opinion poll, whose aim is to inform the central authority of the true feelings of the citizens. This proposal in no way implies on my part a retrospective criticism of the decisions taken by General de Gaulle and of the methods he personally adopted. But times have changed, and lessons must be learned from the facts. Far from abandoning the referendum, we should, after incorporating the safeguard I have just mentioned, reaffirm our faith in it, get it into working order, but without having too frequent recourse to it. During great crises of national consciousness, the referendum can be the least controversial means of ascertaining opinion. The best solution would be to make the referendum coincide, as far as possible, with the legislative election itself, as I had occasion to propose some time ago.

(c) *Proxies*

The problem of proxies is a fashionable one; the proxy system is a bizarre institution; there is talk of suppressing or modifying it, but each proposal put forward, however uncontroversial at first glance, has met with an avalanche of objections.

What is disturbing is not that a minister, on leaving the government, could, if indeed his proxy did not feel obliged to step down, find himself without a job for the duration of that parliament. That is just one of many risks which have to be taken on acceptance of an office which does, however, have its compensations.

What is disturbing is an entirely different aspect of the system. A minister or a head of government who is eliminated in abnormal circumstances finds himself in a position where he cannot explain his actions and justify

---

[1] This would be the referendum held on 27 April 1969 on the proposals for reforming the Senate and for giving the old provinces, under the name of regions, a greater degree of autonomy. The negative votes outnumbered the positive ones, and so General de Gaulle resigned his presidency the following day. (Translator's note)

his conduct to the nation or to Parliament. Thus, it was unpardonable for Maurice Couve de Murville to be reduced to silence, at the very time when it was being said that his administration was responsible for all France's misfortunes. No more was it admissible that I should have been reduced to silence at the time when, conversely, my handling of affairs was thought positive, even though it was believed expedient to terminate my period of office (perhaps because of its very positiveness). If a minister is to be incriminated or praised, if his decisions are to be reversed, or if he is to be forced to resign, especially when this is all done clandestinely, at the very least such a politician who has discharged great and heavy responsibilities should not be condemned to years of silence or to the status of a trouble-maker.

But, in fact, this abnormal situation is linked to the annoying lack of concurrence between the presidential and parliamentary mandate, which I spoke of earlier. If good sense carries the day, there will be no need to modify the proxy system, for I still think that this system is preferable to a return to the earlier system (which still, however, persists in most countries) whereby each minister is obliged to play an active part in parliamentary activity and to vote personally in all the divisions. Apart from the obvious inconvenience, there is the risk that pockets of support for individual members of the government will appear in the Lower House.

Besides, in a country where governmental stability is but a recent phenomenon, the practice of renouncing this or that convention which forms an integral part of that new found stability is not without danger. If the ministers are sure of automatically regaining their seats, they are more likely to succumb to the temptation to resign at the first hint of opposition to their views; similarly there would be less hesitation over ministerial reshuffles.

(d) *Ministerial and legislative functions*

Having thus broached the subject of the relationship between ministerial office and the legislative mandate, I would finally like to put forward, as a subject for reflection, some proposals designed to put a brake on the expansion of the techno-structure and to clear up some of the confusion existing between the various types of parliamentary office. My proposals will be simple. On the one hand it seems reasonable to me that a newly elected representative should not be called upon immediately to assume ministerial office (especially under the present conditions where a proxy is immediately appointed). The new member must learn his trade, he must get the feel of the new role he has been called upon to play, he must assume the character of an elected representative, he must remain in close contact with his electors and must observe both local problems (which are often instructive) and the reflection of general problems in the mirror of everyday reality. I believe that a period of two years to be spent in the

227

Lower House should be made obligatory to achieve this end. Then, it will be a true member of Parliament and not some play-actor who will enter the government.

The same rule would apply *ipso facto* in the case of a non-parliamentary minister who decides to present himself for election, a step which presents less of a problem for him than for any other person. He must be fully prepared to accept this interruption to his career, this two-year period of training. He cannot have it both ways. He cannot demand the right to both cut and deal the cards. I believe that it is desirable to retain the possibility of choosing ministers from within Parliament as well as from without, but we must be sure that the public is sure, indeed that the minister himself is sure, whether or not he is a parliamentarian.

(e) *Parliamentary secretaries*

In connection with the last point, and this time there is no need for the drafting of a constitutional amendment, we should adopt the institution of parliamentary secretaries along the lines of the British system. The ministers, or some of their number, could choose as collaborators members of Parliament who would provide a link with the Lower House and would work as personal aides to the minister. They would not be Secretaries of State, and would retain their seats. Thus, at one and the same time, future government personnel could be trained, elected representatives could be made familiar with the workings of the administration and with the government's way of looking at problems, while the techno-structure's stranglehold on the ministers would be weakened. At the same time, the tendency to excessively large governmental teams would be avoided; the inconvenience of too many armchairs crammed around the Council table would disappear as would the other extreme, namely the present practice of dividing the Secretaries of State into two classes, those who participate and those who rarely, if ever, participate, thus creating the ridiculous situation of a man barred from taking a seat, both in the hemicycle of the Assembly, to which he has been elected, and in the government councils, to which he has been called.

(f) *The elected representative in the House and in his constituency*

Generally speaking, in spite of a few inspired changes, the logical conclusions have not been drawn from the new situation in which the Assembly and its members find themselves, that is to say from the situation of the Assembly within a régime based on the concept of stability. From the time when political intrigue and the engineering of crises ceases to be the chief activity of Parliament, when the member, however green or experienced, must renounce his vision of himself as principally a candidate for ministerial office, the overall picture has to be reconsidered; new reasons for existence, new ambitions must find their expression in the daily life of the Chamber.

The part played by Parliament in a stable régime can still be an important one, provided all concerned share the same views on its importance and that the practical means for the exercise of its function are there. Its role is not limited to legislative and budgetary technicalities; normally its role is a political one; Parliament is a forum for the expression of views and for consultation. If the government considers the Assembly's contribution as a mere formality, simply a matter of protocol, a sort of ritual which poses no problems, provided a certain number of placatory gestures are made, the members will themselves be inclined to conform to the idea the government has of their role and methods. The first few months of the life of the present Chamber are a perfect illustration of this idea of Parliament's role, an idea based on the government's good-natured paternalism and its desire to spirit away troublesome problems which might worry the Assembly, a desire all the more easily explained by the fact that in this particular Assembly a clear majority has failed to emerge. Even taking old habits and allegiances into account, it is no doubt inevitable that the feelings of the public should reveal themselves now and again in movements of opinion within the national representative body, in fact, to be more precise, within the majority which is the only body of opinion to have any effective power. That is quite natural; it is also desirable and necessary if stagnation and major explosions are to be avoided. On the other hand, a government's refusal to yield to a panic reaction at the first sign of trouble or the first hint of opposition to its policy is also understandable. It is natural for the government to have every intention of following the line it has chosen for itself; it may have good reason for finding this line admirable, even if it comes under attack. However, the government would be wrong to ignore demonstrations of dissatisfaction and unrest, for they provide valuable information about the feelings of the electorate and may contain a warning of troubles to come. It would be wrong, too, to attempt to dispel anxiety by the systematic use of mere placebos: the special meeting of the various groups in the Salle Colbert with the ministers and, if the tone of the criticism expressed has been harsh enough, even the Prime Minister himself in attendance; a meeting in which it has been agreed in advance that every effort will be made to appease without really listening to the other side, a meeting to be brought into line though without the use of force.

When members of Parliament become agitated, efforts are always made to reason with them; rarely is any effort made to see whether, by chance, their criticisms might be valid. Taking into consideration French politics over the last seven or eight years, one cannot but be struck by the contrast between the (considerable, often catastrophic) concessions made to wild-cat pressures and the deaf ear turned to claims transmitted through the normal channels of parliamentary democracy. It is a serious cause for concern for, on the one hand, the institutions are not playing their part properly, while, on the other, the opinion is widespread among members of the public that only violence will get results. Are the same errors to be perpetuated indefinitely?

Can it be said that parliamentary 'opposition' lacks punch? Is not this all too understandable? The majority-party members, whose continuing success depends on that watchword 'stability', are not going to get the government into difficulties. They have become accustomed to being courteously, even affectionately, shown the door. Compliance gets you nowhere and resistance is not allowed. 'Hearts grow weary with planning a crime the execution of which will be a pleasure always denied them.'

It is true that the practice has been introduced of from time to time conceding to a pressure group or to 'the majority', usually after protracted chin-wags with a friendly informer or with slightly inebriated colleagues, an amendment which goes a little way (very timidly, naturally) towards meeting the desires of the general public or towards satisfying the demands of one sector of that public. Even in these cases, it is more a question of the parliamentary engineering of a concession which the executive had already decided to make of its own accord but which it seems expedient to present to the public as an initiative of the Lower House; for this enables the government to appear gracious while, at the same time, it makes it easier for it to bring pressure to bear all the more ruthlessly later. A true collaboration between the powers would necessitate the use of other methods and, above all, the existence of a different state of mind. On major problems, a far-ranging debate, free from all preconceived ideas, between the executive and the members of Parliament themselves, the reasonable and reasoning interpreters of public opinion, the non-bureaucratic observers of everyday life, should produce, not just a few minor concessions over details, but a general line for the orientation of government policy towards the working out of a solution. Thus, the public would be assured that its wishes were understood, listened to, if not followed, and the government could, by using the normal, efficient channels provided by parliamentary debates, far-reaching debates whose repercussions would be felt in every constituency, present its own case, make known its objections and the facts at its disposal. This would be a means of avoiding many polarizations and prolonged misunderstandings which result, as we have seen, unexpectedly but inevitably, in confrontations and clashes 'which surprise no one except by their power to surprise'.

Within the framework of the general role thus allocated to it, Parliament normally enacts laws and budgetary measures and at the same time keeps a watchful eye on the actions of the executive (which leads to conflict only in exceptional circumstances). The complexity of the problems presented by the modern world, the resources at the Administration's disposal, the competence of the techno-structure and indeed its arrogance, which grows even more rapidly than its competence, makes the task of government even more difficult and necessitates improved methods. We are not starting from scratch. Committee work is already well organized and often bears results, in spite of the executive's high-handedness. However, much remains to be done. The existence of too few committees means that each individual committee has too many members sitting on it, although this does not prevent some sessions taking place with very few members in attendance. The creation of a few supplementary committees would allow a better distribution of the members (thus, to quote only one example, the committee now working jointly on cultural, professional, and social matters should be sub-divided) and, at the same time, would limit the number of committee members to a reasonable figure, somewhere between forty and fifty (as far as possible, fewer than forty-five). Efforts must be made not only to allow, but actively to encourage, the setting up of sub-committees and working groups. These diverse groups must be allowed untrammelled contact with central administration and, taking due care not to abuse their privileges and encroach on other people's rights, should be allowed to invite the directors of the public services to express their views in committee, a right sometimes denied them today. The committee presided over by Alain Peyrefitte set an interesting precedent during discussion on the law for vocational guidance by summoning various people to appear, especially deans and schoolteachers. I can see no reason why there should be greater difficulty in admitting a director of a public service than a dean, for both hold public office.

Finally, I would be in favor of the creation of work units outside the framework of the committee system. These units would bring together, not just members of Parliament attached to the same group, but members from different groups who would concentrate their efforts on a given problem. Opportunities for such meetings already exist, but their usual object is the defense of certain existing institutions rather than serious efforts to elaborate new policies. There is nothing to prevent, on the contrary there is everything to recommend, the organization of working parties and think-tanks made up of parliamentarians (of various groups) and non-parliamentarians (of differing political tendencies). An initiative of this kind was taken to deal with the problems of regionalization and I envisage the use of similar procedures for discussion of the ideas put forward in this book.

It is important for each of the nation's elected representatives to become a specialist, to be trained in the use of techniques which may often be foreign to him, to go back to school if need be, and to be conscious of the need to concentrate every effort on the job in hand. He must be aware that the ceaseless striving after the accolade of ministerial office to the exclusion of all else is not the only way to obtain promotion and advancement in the generally accepted meaning of these terms. To be the chairman of a committee, to lead a sub-committee in carrying out its tasks, to draw up and present a report are activities both interesting in themselves and conferring deserved prestige on the man who performs them. Years of uninspired government count for less (at least in the positive balance) than a single well-thought-out amendment.

The public must cease to consider—and for this to happen the deputies themselves must stop considering—that the position of legislator and elected representative of the nation is nothing more than a prelude to governmental promotion.

The other side of the coin is the role of the deputy in his constituency. I can claim to do no more than open the chapter on this subject, I cannot claim to write it. In this sphere too, the essential aim is to invest the office of a national representative with a new dignity, to secure for the deputy the worth and esteem which provide the initial justification for his position, to make him a vector of participation both against the alienation of the citizens and against the ravages of the combined forces of the bureaucrats and technocrats. There is hardly need to make constitutional amendments to achieve this[1]. This is a task for those elected to carry out themselves; but naturally it is a difficult business in which they must be helped by their colleagues, for the initiative can hardly come from the outside world. I am reckoning on devoting myself personally to this effort in the near future, by drawing on the experience I have been able to acquire during the different stages of my career. A plan must be drawn up; public opinion must be sounded; non-militant, non-parliamentarian, non-biased correspondents must be found to help in organizing a far-ranging network of information. (In the midst of all this activity, individual, personal contacts of a political nature must not be neglected.) The representative must take up a position at the centre of real problems; he must be there when they are studied and discussed. Regional television can be an invaluable aid. Regular transmissions should allow the representatives and the spokesmen for the interested parties to be seen and heard; but the listeners, the men and women with no mandate, no office, but people placed by life at the heart of the problem should also have a chance to express their views during these programs. Finally, television could provide a forum for the confrontation between the deputy and representatives of opposite political tendencies, debates in which new men, 'unqualified' people, would be given ample opportunity to speak. I do not claim that this constitutes a program for action. It is just a few ideas jotted down on paper, an appeal to all

[1] Let me mention, however, a minor, but necessary reform, namely the need to ensure that the electoral ward corresponds to the administrative district. The powers of the sub-prefect must correspond to those of the deputy. It is ridiculous to force a deputy to deal with two or three different sub-prefects, depending on the district to which the villages and *communes* [see p. 4, footnote 1] in his catchment area belong.

those forces present, those impatient, unexpressed—often inexpressible—forces. Let every member of Parliament, who is so often so desperately keen to become a minister (and I can understand this ambition), first be a minister of participation within his own sphere of action. Let him be an example of living democracy, on hand and willing to listen to the views of all his constituents.

(g) *The Senate, the Economic Council, the Regions*

The reader would no doubt be astonished if I made no mention here of the problem which gave rise to the last referendum and which opened up the presidential and governmental succession[1]. My comments on this matter will be brief. I agree with General de Gaulle's overall view and with his principles, though not with the means employed, the timing, and the methods. But when it comes to participation, the only way of being in the right is to suspend judgment. Disagreement on the part of the participator over the way to participate is neither revocable nor evocable. And, in any case, the damage has been done; the affair cannot be reopened.

Many difficulties arise; I shall not trouble myself with resolving them here and now on paper, for they are connected less with the building of ideal structures than with obtaining multiple and transitory agreements.

The average Frenchman is for regionalism and against the regions; no one plan for the redrawing of boundaries can satisfy everyone, no one plan can overcome opposition to it, for there is no plan which has a solid foundation. It could hardly be otherwise in a country so strongly centralized for such a long time. If attempts are made to satisfy all demands, this only leads once more to departmentalization; besides, is it not true that the policy of creating the regions without abolishing the departments has been accepted in advance, a compromise which could only be justified by a rapid, tactical success? As for recreating the old provinces, this would have needed an act of faith, which has not materialized and which can hardly be hoped for now. It is possible not to accept all the criticisms made, not to satisfy every demand, but how can their relative merits be assessed and a choice be made?

Everyone, even the senators themselves, agrees on the need to reform the Senate, but when one gets down to brass tacks only a few minor changes have been made. As for the Economic Council, the candidates for office on it are so numerous that one has qualms at the thought of even reducing its numbers let alone suppressing it. That the senators are not keen on being assimilated with the councillors is easily explained; that the councillors see the senatorial function as distasteful is also a fact but one for which I can see no rational explanation.

If regional organizations are created without recourse to an election, understandably their authority will be somewhat shaky; but would not the

[1] See footnote on page 226. (Translator's note)

holding of elections for every category of office be an over-politicization in the worst sense of the word; would not the position of the nationally elected representatives be threatened by the regional and local delegates, etc? The holding of a plurality of mandates leads to overwork and in-efficiency, the individual distribution of mandates separates spheres of influence to an exaggerated degree and weakens the position of each delegate by reciprocal competition. To appoint members directly to regional bodies without an election would be to create fewer representative assemblies with too many members; to exclude the deputies from what would be an essential part of the life of their constituency, is that even thinkable? To force them to call their own election into question by another is one way of achieving the revocability of the mandate.

All these difficulties can be resolved, but only by preliminary discussions, by the exercise, not just of good will, but of the will to succeed. The chief difficulty, the only one which may eventually prove to be insurmountable, is the obtaining of the agreement of the professional organizations, and more especially, of the trade unions. The latter will have to overcome their long-held prejudices and allow, not the politicization of syndicalism, but rather the syndicalization of politics, that is to say they must put an end to the misconception which isolates politics from world movements, which sees politics as a game for specialists, the fief of the bourgeoisie. The main effort to convert, the main concentration of forces must be directed at trade-unionism. Such an undertaking demands conditions which appear to be lacking at the moment. This problem is very closely connected with the fundamental problems I shall touch upon in my last chapter.

The logical development of my study should now lead me to tackle two great series of problems. Firstly, the outline of a plan for the demo-cratization of European institutions (where, to be more precise, the Senate and the Economic Council might find further fields of activity). It is pos-sible, too, that such an extrapolation of internal democracy might well be conducive to its rejuvenation. Secondly, in marked contrast, the organiza-tion of a true local democracy.

But, as I indicated at the beginning of this section, my aim is not to present a list of proposals but simply to suggest lines of inquiry. If I have made a few precise suggestions about government and Parliament, it is because these problems are familiar to me; I have travelled this particular road for many years and am used to thinking about these problems. But I have reserved the right, and I emphasize this point once more, to re-examine, with other people engaged in the same task, all the proposals put forward. As far as the regions, Europe, and local democracy are concerned, I thought it better to undertake directly the kind of discussion I have in mind, and to place these topics high on the list of priorities for the kind of joint consultation I propose to institute.

28

A review of the past

No campaign against the 'entropy' threatening political democracy could have been waged more vigorously or more spectacularly than that to which General de Gaulle gave his name during his last ten years in power. It almost succeeded. Who can say today that it has failed?

If General de Gaulle could be classed as a politician, he would give the lie to Louis Althusser's categorical statement, 'A Hegelian politician is an unknown phenomenon'. In many respects, de Gaulle is the perfect illustration of the ideas so dear to the doyen of Iena. He is the epitome of the great man seen, not as the inventor, but as the incarnation of history. He possesses 'heroic judgement', of which the best definition is in my opinion that of the Cardinal de Retz: 'The ability to distinguish the extraordinary from the impossible'. In action, de Gaulle applied the dialectical method to a high degree (thus his attitude to the Allies after 18 June, his handling of the *ultras* after 13 May[1], etc.), and from this point of view he can be compared to the great revolutionaries of the twentieth century. Even the Marxists could appreciate in him their own highly prized rule for conduct: the concrete analysis of a concrete situation. Finally, there is one recurrent theme which gives a profound unity and continuity (though these qualities are not always immediately apparent) to General de Gaulle's actions and work; this is the theme of alienation, that is to say his resistance and hostility to all types of alienation. This main preoccupation was to reveal itself in different forms: positive, neutral or negative, in refusal, resignation or project.

Thus, his refusal of the defeat of 1940 (I have already demonstrated how the refusal of the defeat was also and more importantly the refusal of the *acceptance* of the defeat by the non-representative executants of the popular will—the vice of consent—the misuse of constitutional power). This is no doubt the most striking example of the distinction between the extraordinary and the impossible being made with great aplomb and of the consequences of the idealistic, concrete, logical analysis being carried to their furthest point, which is precisely the condition for success.

After 1958: the far-sighted acceptance of decolonization, for attempts to

[1] See p. 217, footnote 2. (Translator's note)

secure the dis-alienation of the colonies and their peoples by other more acceptable means, by the institution of a Commonwealth, had failed. But any remedy for alienation, which is not the product of the perfectly free will of the people concerned, is itself alienating. This seems obvious, and yet eminent men have always refused to understand this truism, taking refuge in impossible statements of the type: 'Algeria will work out her own destiny, but she will remain French'.

In foreign affairs, the refusal cannot take an offensive form, it is essentially a clear statement of position. The Pnom-Penh speech, the situation of Russia's satellite countries, the concurrence of a policy consistently favorable to closer links with the Eastern bloc and a repeated denunciation of Soviet hegemony was to appear illogical to all those who believed de Gaulle was a Machiavellian and who did not understand the dominant role played by alienation in the evolution of his political judgment. Other chapter headings, Quebec, Biafra, Palestine, China, the underdeveloped countries.

In internal affairs, in the institutional and economic sectors, the concept of alienation no longer involves a mere refusal or a statement of position; it takes on the positive and creative aspect of participation.

General de Gaulle's awareness of the double phenomenon of entropy and alienation was of long standing; he could sense a certain intellectual and emotional disillusionment on the part of the populace with institutions, administrative bodies, artificial conventions, and meaningless procedure, a disillusionment accompanied by, and this is the more crucial phenomenon (the one occurrence explaining and, by the unbroken chain of causality, bringing the other in its wake) the distortion of the national will by those responsible for its expression and transmission resulting in the substitution of a pseudo-will for the authentic will, which either the politicians pretended to have no knowledge of—perhaps this really was the case—or to which they were indifferent. Ignorance and negation of 'the other', who thus becomes alienated from his own life, for it is in the hands of the politicians, and from his own way of thinking, for the politicians assume he thinks otherwise and substitute their own system of thought for his; (if the process were taken one stage further, the politicians could even inculcate their own way of thinking into the elector; he could be conditioned; but this point was not reached in the Third and Fourth Republics which provide the basic structure for my political theories and for those of General de Gaulle).

The type of alienation prevalent in internal affairs is more acute than that found in foreign affairs, for in the former case alienation is the work of the very people who should be preventing it. The man (the group) is alienated by his elected representatives, by those who claim to be his delegates or who impose themselves as such. Either they are imposters or traitors, perhaps both. Here L. Sebag's analysis is particularly apt.

Alienation is born and takes on concrete form when the processes through which the historical energies of individuals and social groups are exteriorized become destructive of the energy which created them[1].

The experience of 1940 and the occasion of his renunciation of power in 1946, when he interpreted the party leaders' proposals that he should withdraw as meaning that his retirement from the fray was to be a break, a breathing space to be used to prepare for a new and not-too-distant resumption of power, the breaking of what he had seen as a contract, served to confirm General de Gaulle's belief that political parties were incapable of interpreting the nation's true wishes and merely served to alienate the general will. The 1946 Constitution, which he rejected, the organization of the Assembly, of which he disapproved, were simply instruments in the service of the dominant alienation of the parties. This vision was the inspiration behind General de Gaulle's actions during the so-called 'years in the wilderness' and, more particularly, behind the launching of the RPF[2], a movement which he saw as a super-party, a party which would really pull its weight, which would establish contact between the base and the top and which would promote a sincere relationship between the deputy and his constituency. This represents something similar to the role played by the party in a single-party state where the political education of the electorate is not very advanced. The party is not necessarily designed to bolster up authority over—and perhaps against—the people, for the army, the police, and the security forces are adequate instruments for this. The principal task of the party, at least in theory, is the training of political cadres. The aim is to promote the emergence of a political class from the ranks of the people to coincide with the embryonic élite in all walks of life, in short to provide possible outlets for participation other than the rather restricted one offered by the vote, especially when the voting-slip carries a pictorial representation of a party's emblem or the picture of an animal. In the same way, but this time in an advanced country, it is possible to envisage a party, not a single party (General de Gaulle's liberalism prevented him from ever imagining such a thing) but a free, dominant party; dominant because it expressed the wishes of the majority, which would provide a freely available outlet for participation, which would provide, at one and the same time, training for, exercise in, and control of participation. This concept could be valid in a pluri-party or at least a bi-partite system, in which no one party could ever be qualified as perpetually dominant. It could even be the party's most significant role if it were possible to lessen the importance of the 'machine', to put the accent, within each individual party, on the intellectual and concrete facts of political life, to institute a completely open forum for discussion, to adopt a very liberal view towards recruitment from which were excluded

[1] Sebag, L. *Marxisme et Structuralisme*. p. 76.
[2] See p. 216, footnote 2. (Translator's note)

237

all forms of sanction, expulsion, etc[1]. I had entertained great hopes in this respect of the possibility of the emergence of a party drawing its adherents from people of differing political tendencies. Moreover, this had been General de Gaulle's hope for the RPF, a party in which militants of every political persuasion could have found a home.

Be that as it may, the RPF experiment was not followed up and, even more remarkably, was never taken up again, which it might well have been in the years following 1958. General de Gaulle never abandoned his distrust and reservations where the traditional parties were concerned, though he never really attempted to animate a new party, for neither the Union for the New Republic[2] nor the Democratic Union for the Fifth Republic[3] deserve the title of new party. They were political formations formed chiefly for the purposes of electoral alliances and parliamentary cooperation. Having renounced the idea of the super-party, the General no doubt feared that a new majority party would suffer the same involution, which he had condemned in other parties. However, certain hints about his attitude indicated a subtle shift in position during the last two years. For example, remarks were passed about his favorable allusions at the Congress of Lille[4] where the presence of Jacques Foccart on the platform was thought to be significant. However, this change in attitude did not lead anywhere, and during the decisive crisis of 30 May 1968 it was noted that an appeal was made, not to the UNR group—which had, however, that very same day taken it upon themselves to demonstrate their support by marching from the Place de la Concorde to the Place de l'Étoile—but to the Committees for the Defense of the Republic.

These and similar organizations (bearing in mind their purely tactical superiority) no doubt appeared to de Gaulle the symbols of a more characteristic, more authentic 'participation' and commitment than that inspired by a half-hearted and often provisional allegiance to a political grouping oriented chiefly towards electoral success[5].

General de Gaulle's views on traditional political parties—I am not going to exonerate them from their responsibility for certain misunder-

[1] This was written before the expulsion of Louis Vallon had been made public, which only goes to show just how topical the subject is.

[2] UNR—Union pour la Nouvelle République—a Gaullist party formed in 1958. It was the majority party in the Assembly after the November 1958 elections, the first elections to be held under the new Fifth Republic. It was eclipsed in 1967 by the UD-Ve.

[3] UD-Ve—Union Démocratique pour la Cinquième République, yet another Gaullist party formed in 1967 in an attempt to give Gaullism a new image to appeal to the younger voter. The name of this party was changed to the Union pour la Défense de la République (UDR) in time for the June 1968 elections.

[4] The Fourth Party Congress of the UNR held at Lille in November 1967. (Translator's notes)

[5] I am not for one moment imputing to General de Gaulle any responsibility for the later misconduct of certain of these groups: in their case, the distortion of intention is blatant, the entropy truly shattering.

standings—were no doubt mistaken ones. It is now possible to see that these views constituted one of the causes which prevented him from taking his ideas to their logical conclusion. The situation is a complicated one; the stagnation and failure to adapt, which I have pointed out in the traditional parties, does not mean that their credibility has been completely eroded (in which case there would be no problem of adaptation) nor that the parties have been reduced to a laughable state of impotence. Organizations whose structures have aged and which are said to have no future become for that very reason all the more formidable, for their activity tends to produce only negative results.

In fact, General de Gaulle underestimated the resistance and, more important, the residual ability of the political parties to represent the electorate, this latter remark only applying, moreover, to so-called Left-wing parties. Left-wing parties have always had a more robust structure than those parties or rather 'formulations' said to be Right-wing or Centrist. They possess hard-working, devoted militant organizations. Their party machinery, because of its authority and stability, no doubt does have the disadvantage of not reflecting accurately the opinion of the non-militant voters (who far outnumber the militants). We all know this from experience, recent opinion polls provide undisputable proof of the fact. But, on the other hand, the party machinery is an accurate reflection of the opinion of the militants, a force to be reckoned with, for they form the élite of their particular society; they are its propagandists. Left-wing party militants, like militant trade-unionists with whom they share certain affinities, with whom they are often closely connected, extend their influence daily into areas far beyond that of the party. They are active in the world of their professional activity and in the life of the neighborhood; they comment upon events, they give voice to their criticisms more violently than do the uncommitted, often with documentary evidence to support their case. Their influence can never be decisive in persuading people *with definite views* to change their minds; it can sway someone who has not yet made up his mind. Finally, this influence can have a galvanic and rapidly spreading effect if the general public's reaction is an, initially, rather vague and tentative inclination to favor the unions. Then, the active minority causes the dough to rise.

The tactics of so-called Left-wing parties and of many of the trade-union leaders have persuaded the public to believe something which they were pre-disposed to believe anyway, namely that Gaullism was a Right-wing doctrine, and have thus deprived the Gaullist movement of many of the adherents which it should logically lay claim to.

It was believed that the restoration of political democracy and the dis-alienation of the popular will could be achieved through new constitutional procedures: the referendum instituted in 1958, the popular election of the President introduced in 1962. It cannot be disputed that these provided important vehicles for participation. But here again, one part of public opinion was induced not to recognize the true character of these reforms. The innovations were attributed, not to the desire to stimulate the citizens' interest in democracy, but to the 'central authority's' intention to maintain itself in power by trickery. It was seen not as the resurrection, the promotion of the popular will but, on the contrary, as an expedient dreamed up to cheat and channel that will into a certain direction. The Frenchman is a historian and a legal expert. Mention was made of the *plebiscite*, which originally represented a triumph and an affirmation for the will of the people but which, after the use to which it was put under the Second Empire as described in the history books, took on rather unfortunate connotations. Today, no one would seriously think of disputing the validity of the election of the President of the Republic by universal suffrage, which only goes to prove that the 1962 referendum, no doubt the most violently contested one, has in retrospect been invested with the crimson cloak of legitimacy and now appears as a remarkably accurate vehicle for the popular will, though this was not apparent at the time. It is a remarkable fact that the appointment of Georges Pompidou has nowhere been denounced as irregular. No allegations have been made to the effect that his election was an example of the cardinal sin of the violation of constitutional procedure. On the contrary, the new President has been recognized by all (his adversaries included) as having been constitutionally elected. But the referendum procedure has not, for all that, received the ultimate consecration.

The same criticisms, which petered out when directed against the 1962 reform and which had been forgotten, were trotted out again against the 1969 proposals for a referendum, and this time they led to a negative result, thereby justifying, in the very act of condemning it, the concept of a referendum, for it was demonstrated that the referendum need not necessarily lead to the extortion of a rubber-stamp for presidential policy.

General de Gaulle genuinely believed that the institution of the Fifth Republic would guarantee more effective consultation within the democratic system, while at the same time increasing stability. I think he was right. He did not, however, think that the use of the voting-slip, even with the additional opportunities for expression and the more effective use of the vote provided by the referendum and the popular presidential election, was enough to ensure that the new man in modern society would increase his potential and would develop the decision-making ability and creativity demanded by the great changes taking place in the world, changes of which General de Gaulle had a clearer vision than many of his younger contemporaries with a less conventional educational background. This was the inspiration for his three-fold attack: in the educational field, the autonomy of the universities, participation at every level, the pedagogic revolution; in the institutional field, new views on the regions, on the administration, a new look for the Senate; in the economic field, worker participation. The first campaign succeeded, the second failed, the third was never really put into operation.

The decisive failure can be laid at the door of Gaullism's failure to attract support from the general public and especially from precisely those categories and groups which should have been its enthusiastic supporters. There was, however, one compensating factor. General de Gaulle could always rely on the support, though it did vary in volume and tended to fall off as the years passed, of a certain number of voters, who would not normally have been attracted to his brand of politics, but who went along with it, either because of their hero worship for the General or because of blind faith or because they feared change. It could therefore be supposed that an authentic reassessment of values and political trends would not have much bearing on the course of events.

Perhaps, but we cannot be sure. And anyway that is not the real problem. A confrontation on more clearly delineated themes, between two camps separated by sincerely held convictions, would have had the merit of being a real fight over real issues. If, after this reassessment, victory was not certain, defeat could never be final.

General de Gaulle's failure is—and is not—the failure of the first experiment in a conceptual political system based on a modern, coherent, and comprehensive humanism, a humanism embracing the world problems facing the diplomats, the problems of the reanimation of democracy and the problems of the place of the producers in the production cycle; a humanism which has in its sights many, if not all, the facets man presents to the world; man seen not as object but subject, not as the means but the end, not as matter but as being.

Fighting alienation on all fronts, in all its forms. In some cases, Biafra for example, it is quite simply the supreme alienation, death. In others, for the host of underdeveloped countries, it is backwardness. For Quebec, it is language, social status, employment. For China, it is national existence, her identity refused in the year-books of the world's legations. For Vietnam, it is war. For Europe, it is the risk of dependence. For the worker, it is something along the lines of the Marxist analysis but not going so far as the Marxist myth of the proletariat, the restriction of his life by work, the deprivation of all (financial and psychological) interest outside the meagre pickings represented by his wages, the earning of which deprives him of what was once part of himself.

This is the political philosophy which *failed*, for it was all of these things and should have attracted all those who feel deeply the need for humanism and the horrors of alienation; (I am speaking here from the point of view of principles and tendencies, but not from that of the methods for putting them into practice, for the choice of means and the style of operation may cast doubt upon the essential aims). And yet, the political philosophy itself *did not fail*; it was the rally of troops which failed to materialize, the masses did not flock to the colors, because the issues in the confrontation were not clearly defined.

Looking at the past, it is hard to understand how General de Gaulle failed to attract or retain a larger number of, to use the accepted term, Left-wing votes (he still had quite a considerable volume of Left-wing support, but not enough to guarantee success and certainly not enough to be explained logically), even though, had he attracted greater Left-wing support, he would have risked losing some Right-wing votes. But he had already lost a good few of the latter and, in any case, many Right-wingers would have remained with him, for there are not many true reactionaries among those generally reckoned to be, or who class themselves, on the Right.

What General de Gaulle and his policy of modern humanism lacked, above all, was credibility, an essential quality as I have already pointed out.

There were several reasons for this.

(i) a certain prejudice (however absurd it may seem) against his title of General, his education, which was considered too conservative, the *hauteur* of his bearing, his preoccupation with form;

(ii) the hostility of the administrative bodies, which the General believed were all too likely to present a biased view of affairs, of officials, of local representatives (who were worried, though without just cause, about regional reforms and changes in the Senate), and, above all, of the parties and the trade unions;

(iii) finally, it must be said, certain gaps in his handling of affairs, especially in economic and financial matters.

Totally involved in 1963 in the painful and difficult clearing-up after the Algerian War, intensely occupied during the years immediately following by foreign affairs, the head of State who was, into the bargain, not an expert in the financial field, where initiative and idealism will open no doors as if by magic, was naturally drawn to rely on the formulas put forward by the more eminent technicians and by those ministers convinced of the validity of stereotyped economic theory. The orthodox system, lightly overlaid with a thin Keynesian coat, with its sights firmly fixed on financially accountable, numerical indexes, admirably suited the General's liking for order and balance in all things; it fitted in with his belief in the respectable values of saving and security. Moreover, his discerning eye showed him that the traditional psychological motivations were still very much in evidence; the housewife's chief concern was still price stability; gold was still the French nation's favorite form of financial security.

However, all this would not have been enough to quell his ever-acute

242

anxiety over social problems without his concurrent and bold plans for giving the workers greater incentives and for participation. His firm belief that he could open up perspectives of a post-capitalist era for the working class allowed him to accept with equanimity capitalism's well-tried recipes for the short-term bolstering up of an economy, which would soon have to withstand the shock of structural innovations.

General de Gaulle was not alone in believing the 1959 devaluation to be a great success. Technically speaking, it was an efficient operation, calculated to allow the return of a new inflow of capital and to put an end to uncertainty in financial circles. It seems that it is fairly rare for devaluation to have such a result. It could be said that this was just one isolated technical operation and not part of a consistent political program. Unless resolute, far-reaching, and thorough measures were taken to deal with essential economic factors—since the same causes would continue to produce the same results—France was cruising along towards a situation which would sooner or later demand similar drastic action.

It was easy to foresee that, when promises of an immediate guaranteed rise of 17 per cent in government subsidies were made, the increase would, in normal conditions, be achieved at a more modest rate of 2 to 3 per cent a year[1].

The first signs of trouble were prompt to appear. The latent crisis, which began in the autumn of 1963, inspired two very capable ministers who succeeded each other at the Rue de Rivoli to adopt very different policies, yet these policies both rather curiously revealed the same defects: on the one hand, an exaggerated emphasis on the need to retrench coupled with a failure to understand the social realities behind the financial indexes; on the other, a lack of urgency.

Giscard d'Estaing's plan for stabilizing the economy, a very well-concocted plan using technically sound means, a well balanced, well thought out plan, inched along at the speed of a horse-drawn cart and finally failed at the very moment it had seemed it might succeed. Michel Debré decided upon a policy of reflation, employing no less suitable measures, but he hesitated, applied the brake, took if off again, and the May events cut short his progress, just when light could be seen at the end of the tunnel.

This parallelism worthy of Plutarch can be explained by nothing other than the desire for political stability, which incites politicians to place greater emphasis on caution than boldness and to take their time. For men who have sailed through stormy seas, a period of careful navigation is a pleasure and a comfort. But experience has shown that the passage of time cannot be regulated by constitutional means and that the risks threatening a government are not only, not even chiefly, parliamentary ones.

[1] Cf. Faure, E. 'Chances et risques du Plan Rueff'. *La Nef*. February 1959. p. 7 and foll.

The most dangerous reefs had been avoided and things were proceeding quite nicely, provided everyone was prepared to be patient. However, financial measures present a double disadvantage: technically, the slow-moving pace and the uncertainty of financial matters create certain contractual difficulties; and, often more damaging than total unemployment, which was never very widespread, was a more extended, partial unemployment created by the suspension of overtime, which is paid at a higher rate and upon which the wage-earner's wife depends to pay off outstanding debts. At the same time, the lack of progress made by the lower social orders became intolerable and gave rise to currents of unrest. The importance of these separate elements in a deteriorating, though not a critical, situation was greatly magnified by the coefficient of fear (the slightest movement in the economy brought with it fears of growing unemployment and increased prices before these actually became a reality) and by the interpretation that was put on events. It was all the more easy to accuse the government of pursuing anti-social policies because neither it nor the majority were supported by the political and trade-union elements, considered the most typical representatives of the working class and who do, in fact, represent the interests of the workers, though not as fully as they claim. This kind of attitude was particularly noticeable at the 1967 elections and during the following months until the May explosion.

The fatal blow was provided by the monumental error of issuing decrees to carry through the reform of the social security system; (I personally underestimated the gravity of this mistake and can see now that Edgard Pisani's warnings were not all that exaggerated). This measure struck a death-blow to participation; to parliamentary participation first of all, then to political participation. Participation is a whole. How can one promise participation to workers, who do not yet enjoy this privilege, who have hardly begun to make demands for it, while denying it to members of Parliament, for whom it constitutes the very reason for existence? From the moment this decision was taken, any far-reaching social policy was stamped, not just with low credibility, but with the seal of absolute incredibility for (the real abuses having been relegated to a place of secondary importance by the unfortunate choice of method) instead of moving forward in triumphant manner, the reform program began its career at a lower point than that reached by earlier social measures.

The style of Maurice Couve de Murville's administration was in direct contrast to that of earlier governments, an apparently logical development. Earlier governments had been slow-moving; he moved at a rapid pace. They had avoided reforms, he instituted, or at least proposed, them. He practiced a policy of expansion; earlier governments had retrenched and put the brake on expansion. I thought at the time and I still think that he was right, though with one reservation: at the beginning, inflation was running at rather too high a level. This was the result, not just, as it was

244

said, of the student troubles and the wage increases, but of a combination of circumstances: the two factors already mentioned coupled with the complete erosion of the advantages gained by the 1959 devaluation which, as I have pointed out, had not been consolidated within the economic structure. From the outset, the administration was jeopardized by a few minor blunders, whose importance was minimal, and by a more serious run of ill luck. Then, on top of this there was the chaotic world monetary situation and the under-valuation of the German mark.

In November 1968 it seemed that there was a chance of reaching some kind of social consensus and of giving credibility a new lease of life. General de Gaulle was careful not to let this chance slip by; his genius told him to make the best of the opportunity offered by refusing to institute panic financial measures, which was what the speculators were waiting for.

The result was not that which his quickness to act and his courage deserved. It proved impossible to gain the confidence of the financiers, who know all the ins and outs of the money business and who read the financial pages of foreign newspapers; nor was it possible, short of spectacular measures against the speculators (measures which are dangerous to execute and have but little effect but which do have a token, symbolic value) to galvanize popular support.

Thus, the referendum on participation took place in the worst possible conditions; it had no chance of restoring credibility, being marked from the outset by an air of unreality; it was incapable of creating a new atmosphere of confidence, for it was obvious that its initiators had only a limited confidence in the measure themselves. The arrangements made were, for the most part, sensible and were designed to meet a serious and long-felt need. But since such an important issue was placed in such a light and had been so vociferously welcomed, it would have been better to present it in a wider context. But that was not a practical proposition. It would be impossible even to begin to tackle the problem of worker participation, which is the most important and decisive factor in any political program claiming participation as an essential aim, without the support and sympathy of at least one section of the Left and of the trade-union movement. Not just because of the power which these groups represent, but because the capitalists, who, moreover, are not now really all that capitalist in outlook, can take part in this game—and their hostility to it is not as bitter as is generally thought—only if they are sure that within the new-style framework they will be able to organize effective cooperation with the workers' leaders. Such cooperation would engender a new sense of security, a new and hitherto unknown climate of opinion, the advantages of which could be immense and which would compensate the capitalists for the lower profits (though the drop in profit would not be all that great) and for the risks (and this is the crux of the matter) they would have to take in agreeing to allow the workers to take part in the decision-making process.

Given the state of hostility existing between the two sides, it was impossible to launch, impossible even to think about, an initiative on this scale, though such an initiative was so obviously at the heart of Gaullism. The events that followed are common knowledge.

It would be tempting to say in the devitalized language of dead republics, 'It only goes to prove that a government cannot go on indefinitely pandering to the Left while relying on the support of the Right'. In this pointed epigram, André Malraux has shown that the concepts of Right, Left, and Center no longer have any real meaning. They have come adrift from their moorings: entities out of control.

Political society, which is rethinking its basic concepts, must, for this very reason, rethink its traditional divisions.

The new humanism implies the adoption of a new set of objectives and, consequently, a new drawing of boundaries.

29

Humanism and modernity

The present French political set-up is a fairly good modern example of that 'enlightened despotism' so dear to the *Encyclopédistes*[1], it being understood that in this expression the word despotism has no pejorative meaning at all, quite the contrary in fact. According to Rousseau, the ideal government is an elective monarchy. Under the French constitution the President of the Republic is an elected monarch, and commentators have been pleased to point out that the powers of the French President are more extensive than those of any other executive ruler in the world (dictators excepted, naturally). Thus, he has the advantage over his American colleague—the only possible point of comparison—in the duration of his mandate—seven years instead of four—in the the added power represented by the right of dissolution, not to mention a few minor differences which all tend to make the French President constitutionally more powerful than his American counterpart. The spectrum of presidential candidates being wider in France, the appointment of the French President indicates a firmer preference. Each elector is called upon to hand in a voting-slip marked with the name of the candidate, which creates a personalized relationship between elector and elected, a distinct improvement on the appointment of intermediaries who will not themselves take office, etc.

For the duration of his seven year term, Georges Pompidou is a *constitutional* monarch, and he will certainly be scrupulously careful to behave as such. At the moment, he has in his favor an exceptionally large majority, a majority more likely to increase than decrease. He is assured of this majority for the duration of the present legislature and, as matters stand at the moment, the renewal of this legislature's mandate seems quite probable.

For many years now, no administration has enjoyed such a firm power basis nor a situation of such stability.

Now, the men who govern France are highly competent and the sincerity of their intentions is beyond doubt. They are bent on putting into operation a modern political program which is both liberal and social in its inspiration. They have received a legacy from General de Gaulle. There is nothing to indicate that they will betray this trust. Obviously, some changes and

[1] See p. 18, footnote 1.

innovations in operation and method are to be expected. How could it be otherwise? General de Gaulle's style of government was inseparable from his person; imitation would be neither a guarantee of success nor a proof of loyalty. Circumstances change; General de Gaulle himself might, given a different situation, have reconsidered his attitude and even, for no one is infallible and he never claimed to be, admitted his mistakes. The essential is to conserve the message, that is to say:

In the international sphere, independence—not as its denigrators believe or claim to believe, an independence based on jingoistic nationalism, but independence as the indispensable condition for initiatives which would escape the super-powers' clutches; initiatives which, for that very reason, would favor friendly relationships between countries and which would promote world peace, initiatives designed to orientate international cooperation towards the prevailing problem of world-wide under-development: in short, an open-door policy.

On the national plane, what Gaullism has to offer is a social (not in the popular, debased meaning of the word) political program which includes participation as one of its objectives. It is not simply a question of trying to improve material conditions, but of attempting to transcend the condition of the wage-earner. This is a very difficult undertaking and no one could be blamed for approaching it with great caution and after a great deal of preliminary thought. We are assured that the politicians are thinking about this problem; we have no reason to be sceptical at this juncture.

There are no signs of the emergence of what might prove to be a genuine cause for discord within the majority, neither is any issue likely to cause a serious upheaval in the relationship between the majority and the opposition.

As a consequence of its extensiveness and of the coexistence within its framework of such a wide range of opinions, the majority does not present one identical whole. Some of its members are enthusiastic Europeans, others less so. Some place greater emphasis on the Atlantic Pact, others on improved relationships with the Eastern bloc. But these are mere details and controversy arises over methods rather than policy. No one wants to destroy the structure of Europe, nor is it proposed to allow it to stagnate. The advocates of a single, unified European state are not powerful enough to demand the abolition of national sovereignties. Their interest is to promote their designs while continuing to work alongside their other colleagues. The question of British entry has lost its urgency if not its topicality. Since France objected on principle to British entry on the grounds of her precarious monetary situation, a situation which has now caught up with France herself, objections to British entry could now be waived without betraying any basic principle. Besides, this problem has never created a real division among the French people, though some may be bored by its recurrence. Within the majority, there are varying attitudes to nuclear armament. But there is no one who seriously suggests that we should retrace our steps, and the budgetary difficulties involved will bring everyone round to the same way of thinking. To sum up, there will be more European cooperation and fewer bombs. Neither the red-hot Gaullists nor those whose support for the General was less than luke-warm could do otherwise. Then there is economic and financial policy; but since everyone has the same objective, quarrels will be concentrated on technical aspects, a province in which those in the know, those at the levers of command, have an unassailable superiority, for the critic grows discouraged because by the time his criticism is broadcast, it is already out of date.

The comments I have made on the internal structure of the majority could be applied with no appreciable changes to the relationship between the majority and the opposition. The opposition is incapable of presenting a united front to challenge the majority on a major issue involving a clash of doctrines. The opposition is in no position to demand a more European or a less European policy, to propose the breaking of the Atlantic alliance or the reintegration of the French Army in NATO. As far as economic and financial policy is concerned, the opposition will agree to attack governmental policy on the grounds that its social measures are inadequate; it will be a more difficult task, however, for the opposition to propose effective and practical measures; but, if it can manage to avoid the pitfall of demagogy, it is possible that its views will be given a hearing. In all events, the only real difference between the opposition and the majority is that the latter group is better disciplined. The area in which the opposition can have a field day is that of national education. It will demand the allocation of more budgetary aid, and I believe it will be right to do so, though this is only one aspect of the problem. All confrontations will principally be concerned with means, possibilities, methods of execution. The opposition has no really serious designs to overthrow nor indeed to change to any great extent, the present mixed French economy to which the epithet capitalist is rather inaccurately applied. Opposition members cherish a few projects for nationalization, but these have a symbolic rather than a real value. They have been loth to come out in favor of participation which is, in my estimation, a grave mistake on their part.

If, for the sake of argument, the present administration were to be suddenly supplanted by a Socialist administration, the example of Britain and the Federal Republic show that the differences would be minimal.

When the mandate of the present legislature expires, it is theoretically possible that the mistakes the government may have committed or the setbacks it may have suffered will give the opposition a chance to assume office. But what opposition? This poses the eternal problem of the existence of the Communist Party, both a welcome and a dreaded ally. Welcome, because of the extent of its support in the country, which makes it indispensable as an ally. Dreaded, for the same reason, for its allies are afraid of being engulfed by it; then again, there is the fear of never being sure of the extent of the Communist Party's allegiance to Moscow.

Should this brief review lead us to conclude that everything is for the best, at least for the best possible, as near to perfection as we can get? Should we conclude that it is advisable to think along these lines because this situation is likely to persist for a long time? Many of the government's opponents are perfectly resigned to this point of view, at least in their heart of hearts. Should the government's supporters, among whom I number myself, be pleased with this situation?

I think a more far-sighted vision is required.

The already quite advanced evolution of the political system is leading towards a cut and dried division into two camps, a division coinciding, moreover, with the orthodox conception of parliamentary democracy: a majority and an opposition. In the one camp, the groupings reputed to be of the Right, the Center, even the Center Left. In the other, the groupings inspired by the various brands of Socialism: Marxist, post-Marxist, para-Marxist, even extra-Marxist, and a few ill-defined hangers-on.

This inevitable tendency to simplify the political scene tends to guarantee continuity, though a certain evolution is not excluded. The fact that the second camp is less homogeneous and more difficult to discipline than the first makes it difficult for it to recruit large numbers of supporters and to overthrow the government. This can only work to the advantage of the majority camp, give governmental action greater assurance and allow it to take the long-term view, which would seem to promote greater efficiency and, therefore, the public interest.

However, there is a negative side to this situation, which to me seems loaded with possible dangers.

(a) In the first place, if the discontented elements within the nation are to seek to redress the situation by parliamentary means, there is only one side to which they can offer their support. If as a result the balance of power is reversed, there is a risk that power will be in the hands of Socialism, but not in the form that is generally agreed to be harmless, but under the virtual or very real control of the dreaded Communist Party.

(b) There is, too, the very serious possibility of an extra-parliamentary build-up of frustration. We have already seen examples of this. Many citizens may resent the limitation imposed upon them by the voting card offering only two alternatives; they may be irritated at having to choose between a 'liberal' administration which infuriates them and a Socialist administration which fills them with the gloomiest forebodings. The memory of the first Poujade Movement[1] is giving rise to a certain uneasiness over the present unrest among the so-called middle classes. The

[1] See p. 216, footnote 3. (Translator's note)

unanimous and uncontested vote, which brought in the new social insurance scheme for the self-employed workers, unleashed a fury which was not without foundation. It only goes to prove that there is insufficient contact within the democratic political system between the elector and the elected; participation is non-existent, the law of entropy still applies.

(c) I would like to go one stage further, to go beyond the observations I have just made, observations inspired by what one might call the current state of affairs.

The government has understood and reaffirmed the necessity of modernizing the economy, of bringing it up to date in order to gear it to the cut and thrust of international competition where the French national economy is suffering from grave handicaps which, in spite of the advances made, are getting worse. When a rapidly moving vehicle and a slow-moving vehicle increase their respective speeds by the same coefficient, even if the second one is given a head-start, the distance between their respective positions as they move along simply continues to increase.

Defined thus, the task is a difficult one; if it were not so it would have been accomplished earlier. Many setbacks, upheavals, irritations—even actual sufferings—will be unavoidable. To accomplish such an ambitious scheme, the government must be able to count on the concerted will of the people and, most important of all, on the goodwill of all the workers. Now, rightly or wrongly, when it comes to having confidence in a reputedly Right-wing government, in a government suspected, however erroneously, of favoring big business, at best the workers are likely to treat the government's overtures with scepticism, their confidence in the government will, to say the least, be rather shaky.

(d) If we want to transcend the aims we now have in view, aims which are in themselves highly honorable, if we want France, following the general lines of Gaullist thought, to adopt more comprehensive political objectives than those of many other countries, if we want to institute a vast political program for education and participation, the kind of program I have tried to outline in this work, massive, popular support for the government is indispensable.

(e) Foreign affairs are no easy matter either, and here too dynamism is needed. There can be no question of relying on the automatic pilot system. Along with the expansion of her economy, France must expand her vision. The restructuring of Europe must be worked for; but there is no question of this being achieved at the expense of France's national independence. That is quite understood. But it is no more a question of simply conserving national independence; this independence must be exported. France cannot remain apart from the rest of Europe, but an independent France in an integrated Europe which would itself be dependent is unthinkable. For us to be able, indeed not to impose our views, but to take a stand, our faith must be contagious, our example must carry weight. Whether the new

Europe is a Europe of independent nation states[1] or not, it must be a Europe of 'peoples'. Let it not be a mere customs-union, a consortium of economic interests integrated into a larger whole with the status of a political fief. Social Europe, the Europe of the peoples, must be 'popular', and for that reason it must begin by being so in France. How can this result be achieved without first seeking the assent of the whole nation, without seeking the assent of those who ask for nothing better than to be Europeans, but who fear the 'cunning of history' and the machinations of capitalism.

(f) In the present situation, many intellectuals, many brilliant men, many idealists, many young people opt for a sort of voluntary segregation. Either they decide to militate rather half-heartedly within the opposition parties, bickering incessantly over the same old problems and waiting for a highly unlikely successful conclusion to their efforts, or they retreat from the world behind the ideology of the impossible revolution; they are perpetually packing their bags for a voyage into Absurdia which will never take place. What wasted energy, both for them and for us; what potential enthusiasm reduced to impotence! They could make a valuable contribution to society. And society could give them something, too. It could give them, if not the actual experience of running affairs, at least an insight into how things are done. They would have some contact with the real world where, although dreams are never realized fully, it is possible to go some way towards their fulfilment. Firmly convinced of theory-action unity, they find an outlet for their convictions in dreams of guerrilla activity and are unable to see that effective action, which does not involve violence, is well within their power.

A recurring theme of this study, a theme which will provide its unity if not its merit, has been that the time has come to surmount those barriers which have now become artificial. The frontier between liberalism and socialism is now nothing more than an ideal[2] line, as Giraudoux's customs officer[3] would have said, but an ideal line from which idealism has withdrawn. The demarcation, which has existed for so long between so-called Marxist philosophy and other philosophies, should have disappeared for all but the most superficial of observers. To be more precise, this demarcation never was the dividing line between two antinomic and irreconcilable philosophical systems but between two different conceptions of the same basic economic problems, between two different systems for assessing the

---

[1] The French uses the word *patries* here, which I have translated as 'independent nation states'. There is no one English word to convey the emotional overtones of *patrie* which, as well as implying independent national sovereignty, also includes the idea of the pride engendered by the feeling of belonging to a particular nation.

[2] Ideal in the sense of existing only in the imagination.

[3] See Jean Giraudoux, *Siegfried, a play in four acts*, Act IV, scene i. (Translator's notes)

progress of history. It was these mere details which were the occasion for a confrontation between thinkers inspired by basic philosophies which, at rock-bottom, were not only compatible but even rather similar.

The situation has moved on since then.

No one seriously believes any longer in the inevitability of imperialist wars, in (even relative) pauperization, in the eschatological role of the industrial proletariat, in the inevitable and redeeming advent of the revolution.

The Communists of Western Europe are adapting to the pluri-party system and are in the process of reinstating 'parliamentary cretinism'.

All the enlightened Socialists know full well that capital no longer holds the principal key to economic power. Now it is knowledge and technical skills which generate economic power and these are qualities which, once acquired, cannot be taken back, qualities which can be socialized without fear of expropriation.

The administrative structure of the centers of production is now simply a matter of secondary importance, just a question of practical organization. Nationalization is no longer a point of doctrine, but of opportunity, of efficiency, of returns on capital outlay.

Since Marxism is casting off its own myths, why should non-Marxists be so keen to invest it with myths? Marxism's contribution to the world has been a very great system of thought, an irreplaceable methodology, unquestionable advances in our knowledge of social phenomena, a powerful light focused on the human condition, the affirmation of the dignity and the progress of the whole of humanity in each of its constituent parts—in short, a humanism.

But there are other humanisms.

And yet perhaps, taking everything into account, there is only one humanism. What insurmountable barriers are revealed in the written works, the conversation, the personalities of true humanists, I mean the three families of modern humanists: Marxists (orthodox, dissident, marginal and fellow-travellers), Christians, and agnostics? What una-tonable crimes have been committed? What impossible problems arise?

If the three families of humanists succeeded in reaching agreement, in taking counsel together, in forming a unified whole, who would then have to be cast into outer darkness? Who indeed? But why should anyone be forcibly ejected? Those who felt they could not fit in with the new community would retire of their own accord; let them, it is their prerogative. Where would this leave the majority and the opposition? But does there have to be a majority and an opposition? 'So it is to be unanimity then?' My answer to this question is, 'Probably not; but then again, why not?' If unanimity between people of totally different beliefs is impossible, why not start by trying to create unanimity between all those who are animated by convictions which are, at root, identical?

Besides, it is a serious mistake to adopt a systematic approach to the problem of reaching agreement, but one which is so easy to commit if one is confined to the purely practical plane. But if, as I recommend, one is working on the philosophical plane, it is the search for points of contention rather than agreement which is often the most effective method. For even if disagreements do come to light, they clarify the issue, they remove ambiguities, they dissipate the mists. No doubt, if disagreement arises over fundamental ideas it will serve to reveal, not just simple differences between schools of thought, but a false humanism on the part of some participants in the debate; the hollow sham of their attitudinizing will be stripped of its trappings. On the other hand, it is quite understandable that minds loyally attached to the objective of promoting the human in the modern world may adopt different positions on the vast question of methods to be employed. But here, too, the advantage will be gained of knowing how far and along what lines common cause can be made—and the very rooting out of contentious points will often lead to their becoming less important or to a way being found to get round them.

Frequently, conferences are announced in which are brought together all those thinking people who are striving towards an understanding of the world in which we live. To this end, in the course of these conferences, the systems and tendencies to which the participants feel themselves drawn, either because of their upbringing or a sense of tradition, but which they can no longer accept as the final, definitive, satisfactory solution, are compared and contrasted. Some are not afraid to call themselves Marxists; Christianity or non-Marxism is not distasteful to others. But these are just experiments, intellectual exercises of the intelligentsia and the angry young men; they stop short at the boundary of politics as if for fear of trespassing on hallowed ground.

Within the political world I see a flurry of activity. Secret meetings, confabulations, conventions abound; new splinter groups make frantic efforts to get things done; older groupings amalgamate; congresses delegate their responsibilities; delegates present their reports but there are some inexplicable taboos; only 'Left-wingers' are invited to meetings, though no one really knows where 'Left-wing' politics begin and end or by what distinguishing features they are to be recognized. . . . This hair-splitting, these completely sterile exercises, the result of a refusal to adopt a more open view coupled with a preoccupation with political procedure when dealing with problems, result in the problems themselves being stripped of their real significance; their relationship with the essential is forgotten.

I envisage wider confrontations in which intellectuals would have an opportunity to inject their knowledge, the force of their carefully worked out thought, the keenness of their faith into politics. In return, they would receive an opportunity to assess a concrete situation, to evaluate obstacles; they would be encouraged to present their researches, which they are quite willing to focus on everyday life and on concrete reality, in a less abstract, a less transcendental manner. Humanists of differing political tendencies, from one or other of the main schools of thought, brought together to discuss as their prime object, not practical political manoeuvres dictated by the necessity to evolve a plan for urgent action but the search for a common language. Surely, this is not an impossible task; neither is it a venture to be dismissed as trivial.

There is one last obstacle to be surmounted if this dream is to become reality: the barrier presented by the Communist Party. Can one sup with the devil? Can one talk with a Communist? Can one draw up joint schemes for action with the Communists? I am well aware of the dangers inherent in such a venture; I know that some of my readers may be scandalized at the mere mention of such cooperation. However, the facts are there. The peculiar status of the Communist Party, its sometimes overweening sometimes contrite isolation have been a stumbling block for a quarter of a century to the normal mechanism of political life in France. A strange development in modern mathematics, a geometrical phenomenon unknown to both Euclid and Lobachetsky: a force which can move in only one direction, a force with a two-fold power of destruction—for both its opposition and its support are lethal to a government—but which cannot make any constructive contribution to the creation of a government. A figure recognizable from only one side. A guest to whom one pays court on condition that he stays away from the feast.

That the Communists are Marxists, well relatively speaking, is, as we have seen, no obstacle to cooperation. The fact that they owe allegiance to the big brother of the Party and to the Soviet Union, now there's the rub. Communists are French nationals: is it possible to believe that five million French voters are traitors and potential deserters? All those whom I have known personally were very sincere democrats. That is the paradox. These democrats support, sometimes blindly, another country's undemocratic political system, undemocratic even according to their own rather peculiar definition of democracy. The reasons for this are legion; often it is a question of something totally beyond the scope of rational reasoning. There is the distant memory of the social struggles of the preceding century, of strikes and repressions. The risk and the fraternity of militant action create a bond. They have the impression of living in a world apart. All this is stored in the collective memory, kept alive by family reminiscences, passed on from parent to child, perpetuated by habit and feeling. Such long-held beliefs cannot be rejected out of hand; it is impossible to fall out of love with a constant object of desire, in this case pride in oneself now projected into something barely resembling the original concept, the desperately sought-for reflection seen darkly through a glass.

However, there is nothing here to justify the hallucinatory insularity of the Communist Party. Why should we not make overtures to help the

Communists feel closer to their real homeland than to their adopted one? Closer to the democracy whose image is imprinted in their hearts than to the other democracy which is already no more than an illusion?

On our side, the problem is never discussed with them unless there is some immediate end in view: an electoral advantage, an agreement to withdraw a candidature at the second poll. On their side, there is a reluctance to make overtures to any parties but those to which they feel closest, to its sometime allies, who are also its perpetual enemies, and even then they are afraid of striking a bad bargain. Could not an exchange of views with parties not quite so close, debates where tactical manoeuvres do not enter into it but which are confined solely to the plane of philosophical, social and historical analysis, discussions on the 'project' of society, on man's future, give the Communist Party a reason for emerging from behind their barriers and for believing that we no longer want to shut them off from society?

My proposals may appear both tentative and unexpected. It has not yet been proved that they will serve no useful purpose. As the thread of my argument unraveled, the conviction was brought home to me that there exists a common basis for a modern humanism, and that this humanism will only be effective in the hurly burly of life if there is a great movement of the concerted popular will. A burst of creative energy is needed, an energy which will dissipate the unreal problems, which will show up the old hoary prejudices for what they are, which will redefine the authentic and the essential.

Was not this the kind of awakening that General de Gaulle was envisaging on a national scale?

We are not living in normal times when every problem can be solved by the technocrats' know-how, when it is enough to balance the accounts. Well regulated charity and noble sentiments will just not do.

Great world movements cast giant shadows of impending doom over the peoples of the world. If the consumer society were the only problem, would it not be imperative to ward off its evils before its benefits can be enjoyed and shared among all peoples. But there are some societies where consumption is at too low a level; the fate of these countries is in our hands. War is not yet a word in a dead language, a word to make out with difficulty from some tattered manuscript.

Attention must be focused on the new man, the man of the twenty-first century, on our society which is preparing the way for the generation to come, on our own efforts to make it welcome.

It is at least worth a passing thought.

MADE AND PRINTED IN GREAT BRITAIN BY
WILLIAM CLOWES & SONS, LIMITED, LONDON, BECCLES AND COLCHESTER